MW01146605

ALSO BY MELISSA FEBOS

Body Work
Girlhood
Abandon Me
Whip Smart

The Dry Season

The Dry Season

A Memoir of Pleasure in a Year Without Sex

MELISSA FEBOS

ALFRED A. KNOPF · NEW YORK · 2025

A BORZOI BOOK
FIRST HARDCOVER EDITION PUBLISHED BY ALFRED A. KNOPF 2025

Copyright © 2025 Melissa Febos

Penguin Random House values and supports copyright. Copyright fuels
creativity, encourages diverse voices, promotes free speech, and creates a
vibrant culture. Thank you for buying an authorized edition of this book
and for complying with copyright laws by not reproducing, scanning,
or distributing any part of it in any form without permission. You are
supporting writers and allowing Penguin Random House to continue to
publish books for every reader. Please note that no part of this book may
be used or reproduced in any manner for the purpose of training artificial
intelligence technologies or systems.

Published by Alfred A. Knopf, a division of
Penguin Random House LLC, 1745 Broadway, New York, NY 10019.

Knopf, Borzoi Books, and the colophon are registered trademarks
of Penguin Random House LLC.

"You who want / . . . ." (Hadewijch) from *Women in Praise of the Sacred*
by Jane Hirshfield. Copyright © 1994 by Jane Hirshfield.
Used by permission of HarperCollins Publishers.

Library of Congress Cataloging-in-Publication Data
Name: Febos, Melissa, author.
Title: The dry season : a memoir / by Melissa Febos.
Description: First edition. | New York : Alfred A. Knopf, 2025. |
Includes bibliographical references.
Identifiers: LCCN 2024028661 (print) | LCCN 2024028662 (ebook) |
ISBN 9780593537237 (hardcover) | ISBN 9780593537244 (ebook)
Subjects: LCSH: Febos, Melissa—Psychology. | Authors, American—
21st century—Biography. | Celibacy—Biography. | Solitude—Biography. |
Women—Identity.
Classification: LCC PS3606. E26 Z46 2025 (print) | LCC PS3606. E26 (ebook) |
DDC 814/.6B—dc23
LC record available at https://lccn.loc.gov/2024028661
LC ebook record available at https://lccn.loc.gov/2024028662

penguinrandomhouse.com | aaknopf.com

Printed in the United States of America
10 9 8 7 6 5 4 3 2 1

The authorized representative in the EU for product safety
and compliance is Penguin Random House Ireland,
Morrison Chambers, 32 Nassau Street, Dublin D02 YH68, Ireland,
https://eu-contact.penguin.ie.

for Donika

The Dry Season

I T IS RAINING. Drops spatter against the plane's windows as we descend through the clouds and prepare for landing. The woman is seated four rows behind me, but I spotted her before we boarded: tousled hair in a wool beanie, leather boots belonging to the category worn only by lesbians and Dickensian orphans, giant backpack. I felt myself begin to glow with a chemistry visible only to the object of my attention. I do not understand the biological protocol that enacts once it is triggered, but I do know that more often than not, the end result is sex, and if my past is any indication, some sort of romantic entanglement.

Just a few months earlier, I would have lurched at the call. But I am six months celibate and have made a promise to myself. In those first months, I was more vulnerable to the familiar siren song of a cute dyke, and while a few nearly pulled me back in, I'd managed to stay the course. The woman at the fancy book party. The sculptor. All the loose ends with whom I'd cut off contact months ago. But here I am, turning my profile to the angle mathematically most likely for her to see me, rolling my shirt cuffs up to bare a few inches of forearm tattoos, dangling my hand with its short unvarnished nails into the aisle.

Like most femmes, I am an expert at signaling my queerness through physical clues legible only to other queers. I can communicate my sexual identity through the set of my shoulders, if need be. I sit in the cramped airplane seat with my legs comfortably spread, my elbows on both armrests, exuding a physical entitlement to the space I occupy. So much of heterosexual attraction is contingent on the minimization and infantilization of the female body: crossed legs, tilted heads, widened eyes, slackened mouths. A disregard for this affect suggests that a woman's desires lie elsewhere.

This is why it's easy to mistake some women who have gone through menopause for lesbians: they have both stopped giving a fuck what men think of them. This secret language, in all its permutations, drove and defined over two decades of my life. I've largely abstained from it over the last six months. But now I think: we are on a flight to London and unlikely to come any closer to one another than we are now. There is little danger of a full relapse. There is no harm in indulging the pleasure of the dance.

We land at London Gatwick and the attractive stranger gathers her belongings, runs a hand through her messy hair, and, yes, glances in my direction, before she rises to her feet and steps into the aisle. *Goodbye, stranger,* I think with some relief.

To my great surprise, these recent months have been the happiest of my life. It wasn't happiness, exactly, that I sought when I decided to spend this time celibate. I had just gotten so tired. I met my first girlfriend when I was fifteen years old, and spent the next twenty years in relationships. I was a serial monogamist, the ends of many of my affairs overlapping slightly with the beginnings of the ones that followed, forming a daisy chain of romances. There were a few brief periods of singleness, but I was never *alone,* really. There was always a cohort of flirtations. A string of dates. A lover from my past ready to step into the present. After a few weeks or months, I'd found my next forever.

Our culture tells us that such abundance is a privilege, and in many ways it is. Sometimes, I felt proud, though I knew it was artificial. Whatever our accepted story about attraction, I understood that the magnet in me drew its charge from dubious qualities. Once I reached my thirties, I started having moments of unease when I contemplated my pattern. I was just a *relationship person,* I consoled myself. I had spent my happiest times partnered, I thought, without considering the givenness of that, having spent most of my life partnered. I was reassured by the fact that I never *felt* afraid to be alone. I did not consider how one might not ever feel the thing she had successfully outrun.

Then I spent two years in a ravaging vortex of a relationship. When I finally emerged, I thought, *I should take a break.* After this revelation I promptly got into five brief entanglements. Each had a frantic tinge, like the last handful of popcorn you cram into your mouth after you decide to stop eating it. I realized that my resolution would have to be more intentional. I drew more specific boundaries: no sex, no dates, no nothing. At the age of thirty-five it was time to meet myself unmediated by romantic and erotic obsession.

In only six months, my life has opened up like a mansion, half of whose rooms had been locked. There is so much more space in which to live. From the long mornings at my desk to evenings of reading myself to sleep, or nights spent dancing—the summer heat luscious and exhausting, each morning marked by my aching feet, the pleasurable wince as I brew coffee in the morning. I have luxuriated in the solitude and the companionship of true friends.

I am sometimes lonely, but that, too, is novel, a weather system that moves through me and, after a day, or sometimes just an hour in the late afternoon as the light shifts toward evening, it moves on. I anticipated that I would miss the thrill of seduction, the rituals of pursuit catalyzed by attraction, but that urge has also come and gone, never surging strong or long enough to compel me from observation to animation. Until today, that is.

The customs line is interminable, the booths woefully understaffed for the number of incoming passengers, but I'm distracted by the inching undulation of the line as it snakes forward, delivering my crush and me past each other by mere feet at regular intervals. Both of us studiously rotate between staring at our phones, squinting ahead at the front of the line, and posing in such subtle affectations that no casual observer would discern anything other than boredom and frustration in either of our comportments.

It must seem arrogant of me to assume that my airplane crush reciprocates my attention, but trust me that when you've been performing this choreography for more than twenty years, you know when your partner feels the music and when she doesn't. The first decade was spent being humiliatingly mistaken a good portion of the time, while I cultivated this precise radar, but in the years since it hasn't led me astray. The thrill, of course, resides in the slender possibility that this time, *this time,* I might be wrong.

She reaches the booth ten or fifteen people ahead of me and despite devoting a valorous twelve minutes to backpack reorganization and another three to shoelace tightening, she is left no other option but to continue on her journey. My disappointment as she disappears into the airport is matched by the return of relief. The spell is broken. I have not violated my abstinence. I dig my passport out of my jacket's interior pocket and shuffle forward, happily bored, mistaken once more in my certainty that temptation has passed.

Soon after I got clean and sober at twenty-three, my sponsor told me I couldn't steal anymore. She probably would have told me this sooner, if she'd known that I was still stealing things—mostly books from the Barnes & Noble in Union Square and bags of food from the self-serve bins at the overpriced health food store on University Avenue, but I'd never mentioned it, until I happened to be on the phone with her as I walked to my building's laundry room and found that someone had left a stack of quarters on the table by the change machine. *I can take them, right?* I asked her. *Absolutely not!* she said. *We don't steal.*

At the time, I wondered why I had even mentioned it, but now I understand. I wanted to stop. When she told me that I must, I felt awash in relief. I used to get a terrible wave of dread right before I stole, as if someone else was making me do it. Once I saw an opportunity, I felt compelled to do it, but the act was stressful to a degree never matched by the benefits of my loot. I wasn't addicted to stealing; it was a habit I had gotten into as an addict who wanted to spend every cent that crossed my palm on drugs. Necessity had been replaced by the inertia of habit. It hadn't occurred to me that I could give myself permission to stop.

Incredibly, after I have navigated the swarmed airport, retrieved my suitcase from baggage claim, ridden the shuttle to the adjacent train station, deciphered the cryptic train tables and British accents, purchased my ticket from a reluctant kiosk, and arrived at the correct platform, there she is, the woman from the plane. She glances up, probably sensing my stunned stare, sees me, looks momentarily stunned herself, then looks away.

We don't make eye contact again, but stand a few yards apart on the platform, waiting for our train. I hold very still, as if it will quell the tumult inside me. I have fleeting, stupid thoughts, like maybe it is *fate* and who am I to defy the Fates? Or maybe in a foreign country it doesn't count as violating my abstinence. I think of Saint Augustine, though I find him simpering, and the pears he stole as a teen with his ne'er-do-well friends. "Doing this pleased us all the more because it was forbidden," he wrote in his *Confessions*. "Such was my heart, O God, such was my heart—which thou didst pity even in that bottomless pit." I think of how when I was a child, my appetites were so great that my parents used to sometimes refer to me as a bottomless pit. "I loved my own undoing," wrote Augustine, and I know what he meant, the ecstasy of yielding to the forbidden.

The train finally pulls up to the platform, whipping my hair around my face. We board the same car from different doors. Again,

I settle four or five rows ahead of her. My body feels rubbery with exhaustion—I hardly slept on the plane—but buzzy, animated by the prospect that something is going to *happen*. The only question is whether what happens will be what has happened before, or if I have the power to change it. To do something different.

I

Six months earlier

ONE OF THE LAST people I had sex with before I stopped having sex was a museum curator. She was going through a divorce and had the manic eyes of someone desperate to escape their current situation.

In the Brooklyn lesbian tradition, we did not call our first date a date but simply dinner, therefore maintaining the possibility that it was not a date, just a meal between potential friends, until we decided whether or not we wanted it to be a date. We met at a wobbly table in a nice-ish restaurant in Williamsburg. She was beautiful in the candlelight, with high cheekbones and a shapely mouth, though our senses of humor seemed incompatible; she barely laughed at my jokes and didn't make many herself.

As I sawed into my cauliflower steak—the biggest scam of all vegetarian entrées, though I kept optimistically ordering it in all the little restaurants of New York City that had discovered they could charge meat prices for a slab of fibrous water sprinkled with capers—she squinted at me.

"Is this a date?" she asked.

I shrugged. "I don't know, is it?"

I didn't mean for it to sound like a riddle, but it did. Things deteriorated from there. She spoke about her ex-wife in a bereft, castigating tone, and I nodded noncommittally.

Still, she texted me the next day and I did not hesitate to respond. We flirted all day, which was exponentially more fun over text than it had been in person, though our jokes kept failing to land. I texted her while I ran on the treadmill at the gym, while my students wrote in class, at red stoplights on the drive home, and while I brushed my teeth, spattering my sleep T-shirt with toothpaste as I smiled at my phone like a baby. I ignored the bored feeling I'd had in her presence, which seemed reciprocal, and the way her grief had repelled me, an alarm that I chose not to heed. Instead, I thought about her beautiful face and the way my body vibrated when my phone did with her messages. *I* found my jokes funny, and maybe that was enough.

We kept this up and a week later, I flew out of state for a reading. During the trip, our texts accelerated in a sexual direction. Tucked in the stiff white sheets of the hotel bed, I called her and we masturbated together without speaking, just our breath in each other's ears.

After I returned, we met up again, but skipped dinner this time, as if dinner had been the problem. Instead, I put on some Nina Simone and we perched on my gray sofa drinking seltzer. Two weeks of sexy text messages had not improved our rapport. We went to bed abruptly, as if that were the only way to end the conversation.

Though I had stubbornly tried to prove otherwise, for me, sex without chemistry or love was a horror, and I felt quietly horrified as we lay together in my bed. None of the excitement of our text correspondences translated. We were strangers, and though I liked to fantasize about fucking strangers, in reality it felt outrageous to touch a stranger's genitals or let a stranger touch mine. Still, it seemed inexcusably rude to interrupt the interaction after all of those texts. I brought her to orgasm with my hand and then lay there for a few moments before slithering out of bed to go to the bathroom.

Mercifully alone behind the closed bathroom door, I splashed cold water on my face and avoided the mirror. I considered how to get her out of my apartment without being a complete asshole. I considered the possibility that I was already an asshole. I spat into the sink and then pressed my hands against my face, as if I could smear it away and start over.

Here I was, again. There wasn't anything extraordinary about my situation except that I felt ready to do something about it. Well, almost ready. A few weeks later, I decided to spend three months celibate.

"You'll want to use some discernment when deciding who to talk to about this. I mean, making such a big deal out of three months of no sex," my mother, a therapist, cautioned me over the phone. "There are people who—"

"I know," I said. "Of course I know that. Hang on, I'm about to run the blender."

"What's in your smoothie?" she asked, but I didn't attempt to answer over the machine's roar.

The problem with making a radical personal decision is that it pales in comparison to most things one might consider radical, like political revolution, religious conversion, suicide, or even divorce. A personal revolution is entirely subjective. Veganism, parenthood, sobriety, and, yes, three months of celibacy are attempts to induce a dramatic change in one's life, a fact they share with political revolution, but on a different scale. A shift can be radical and ordinary at the same time. Or meaningless, when removed from the context of a life.

I didn't say any of this to my mother because it would have been patronizing and unnecessary. She has made many radical personal decisions, including living in a commune, escaping a cult, raising her baby (me) vegetarian in the 1980s, two divorces, one religious conversion, and several dramatic career changes. She wasn't refuting my decision, only pointing out the obvious with her usual unvarnished honesty. It had been she who most persistently recommended that I take a break in between relationships over the years, and she who knew better than most the reasons why I ought to.

More relevant to our conversation was the feeling of pressure inside me that had been accumulating for years, and accelerating over the past six months. We imagine the need for change manifesting in blatant ways because that's how it is represented in movies and memoirs and TV commercials: a eureka moment that requires little discernment. *I must leave my spouse! I'm queer! I can no longer toil as a cog in this machine!* For me, and I think most people, it is less specific and more atmospheric, a recognition of the air quality rather than a strike of lightning. Perhaps there are some who recognize the first signs and change with haste, but I am not one. I cling to the habitual. I avoid inconvenient truth. I interrogate intuition. I let the pressure build until the discomfort of staying the same grows greater than my discomfort with changing.

When I was younger that pressure took the shape of what I called "free-floating anxiety," as if anxiety were a weather system or airborne disease that I had randomly encountered, rather than an internal response to my external life conditions, a result of my own choices. Anxiety, one therapist told me, is a secondary emotion, a response *to* emotion. Buddhists calls this the *second arrow*. I don't know what Catholics call it, probably guilt.

Whatever I called it, it had returned, a cloud bank of fear that pressed dully over the whole sky. It was worst in the mornings. Since getting sober, I'd woken up happy most mornings, but now it took an hour to muster enough gumption to face the day. I was flinchy and tired and easily disgusted. My shoulders throbbed, tightened by anxiety's winch while I slept. I had nightmares so gruesome they felt rude to recount. I chewed my nightguard into pieces. I was clearly depressed, a state that makes me feel like an animal masquerading as a human in human clothes, because we are all that and depression is more honest than happiness. I knew from experience that my depressions are usually situational. Drugs don't help, only change does.

All of this to say: I felt feral and sad and couldn't explain it, but I knew that something had to change.

"It's got strawberries, frozen banana, spinach, protein powder, and soy milk," I told my mother, taking a sip through my smoothie straw. "A *lot* of spinach."

"Yum," she said. "You can put so much spinach in a smoothie without it tasting like spinach; it's amazing."

"I know," I said. "The color is so bright but it just tastes like nothing."

D ON'T YOU THINK you should take a break?" my mother asked me when I was thirty-two. I had just ended a three-year relationship with a woman I think of as my Best Ex. Our relationship had been my healthiest ever. A year into it, she became very ill and our lives upended. A year later, I could change a PICC line dressing with the efficiency of a trained nurse. After two years of crisis and caring, she began to show improvement, but we were over. I still loved her and couldn't bear the thought of abandoning her, so I stayed until I eventually kissed someone else. This failure to conduct myself with integrity at the end of our relationship remains one of my greatest regrets.

Before my Best Ex, I had not been single since my first relationship at fifteen. I had been preoccupied with one person or another since I was eleven years old.

"A break is probably a good idea," I told my mother. I did not divulge that I had already begun an affair with the person whom I betrayed my Best Ex by kissing. I knew that I was probably using the dopamine of a new infatuation to anesthetize the pain of my breakup, but reasoned that after such a hard two years I deserved a little fun.

The worst two years of my life followed. All of the wisdom I'd ever gleaned from experience and therapy sloughed away and I was smooth and stupid as an egg. I tolerated emotional pain that now defies credulity. That relationship was more painful than kicking heroin, than the migraine that split my skull at sixteen and the spinal tap that followed. I would easily choose a daily spinal tap for the rest of my life rather than relive our time together. Still I chose her, day after day, for two years. Giving up that kind of attachment can be harder than giving up a drug, I found, at the end of it.

The contents of this book begin where that nightmare ended. I would not have ventured into celibacy had I been less ravaged. In the early days, however, I was not ready to admit this. In my recovery community, people often say that one's bottom gets lower the longer one is sober. That is, the deeper we get into recovery, the clearer we can see the wreckage of the past. It was always worse than we told ourselves as we lived it. I have long struggled to face the depth of my own hurts. I tend to minimize my wounds until I am a certain distance from their cause. At first, I minimized the stakes of my celibacy, of changing myself, because it made it easier to step toward that challenge. I preferred to think about celibacy in terms of self-actualization. I needed more time for everything, didn't I? I did not want to admit that my life might not be worth living if I did not change. That I might not survive another round of such debasement. That what I had called love might be something else.

It is not easy to stop a twenty-year habit. This habit began when I was a child suddenly inside a woman's body, and I had been yoked by the desire of others for most of my life. However painful, however limited my power, it was simple. Though I was capable of changing myself in many other areas, when I became unhappy in love I changed my partner. It is easier to change the hardware than the operating system. Changing your own operating system is a slow and painful work. I'd done it before. It is an act of creation and the imagination sputters to envision the unknown. What would govern me if not this old familiar moon, looking new every night?

.   .   .

My friend Jenny and I met at the new café on Bedford Avenue to work together. It was full of attractive people in their twenties and thirties who also came there to work because they didn't have room in their apartments. Or they worked better with the gentle pressure of other people's presence. Back then, I focused more easily with a companion nearby. When I worked alone in my apartment, the feeling that I was missing something gnawed at me. It may simply have been a function of living in New York City, where I paid so much in rent that I wanted to justify it by constantly having the unique experience of living in that specific place. That is, of course, how all of those pretty people got there, why that café existed, how that neighborhood—Bedford-Stuyvesant—had been so radically gentrified since the late nineties when I arrived in New York. Most radical shifts are the result of cumulative personal decisions, intended or not.

After a couple of hours spent staring on our laptops at adjacent tables, we broke for lunch. I had spent those hours reading about the Belgian beguines and Dahomey Amazons, hurtling down the rabbit hole of female celibacy, a new habit of mine. I was supposed to be completing edits on my second book. One way of describing the book is that it detailed the violence with which revelation must occur to me in order to puncture my resistance to real change. Another is that it told the story of that ruinous two-year love affair and performed an autopsy on my abandonment issues. It had been just over a year since that relationship ended, a year in which I had furiously worked on the book. The writing had served a dual purpose, as it often did: it was simultaneously a means of avoiding the emotional fallout of the events I described and also processing it.

Jenny was working on a book, too. She had beautiful curly hair, a raspy voice, and was one of the funniest people I knew. Over our exorbitantly priced grain bowls, I explained to her that I planned to spend ninety days celibate. Jenny had been single for almost three years at that time.

"Something needs to change," I explained.

Jenny thoughtfully finished chewing her mouthful of farro and swallowed. "So, you're going to give up sex for *three* months?" She laughed richly, like a villain in a children's cartoon and then concluded: "Fuck you, Melissa."

"There are different kinds of celibacy!" I insisted. I wanted to elaborate that being involuntarily celibate was so very different from choosing abstinence, and to describe all the various kinds of celibacy I had been reading about—the beguines and the mystics and the Shakers and the Amazons—but it all rang pitifully in my mind. It occurred to me that making a study of my experience was a strategy that helped me to approach a challenge, but I ought not mistake my motive for a rhetorical one. Jenny wouldn't be fooled. In the context of her life, my celibacy was ridiculous. That was as true a fact as the radical nature of it in my own life. Being a memoirist had instilled in me a tolerance for the contradictory truths of personal experience. So I said nothing and laughed with her at myself.

After lunch, I went back to reading. I often tried to substitute an emotional pursuit with an intellectual one. In our sessions, my therapist incessantly interrupted my analytical discursions to ask annoying questions like, *But where do you feel this in your body?* This was what I paid her for and I hated it. Writing itself was also a form of procrastination, a way to replace one kind of work with another. Autobiographical writing in particular was a form of intellectualization and aestheticization that still led, ultimately, to a confrontation with emotional truth. I was so averse to confronting my emotions that I needed to be boiled in them ever so slowly, like the proverbial frog. A slow-boiling pot gets the job done eventually.

The beguines interested me in particular because I was looking for maps. In the thirteenth through sixteenth centuries, these orders of religious laywomen spread through northern Europe like a beautiful contagion. The beguines lived in semimonastic communes called beguinages, each with their own self-designated rules. They spent their days among the poor and worked in service as nurses, social workers, and teachers. Though celibate and unmarried, they took no vows, did not give up their property, and could leave the order anytime. They traveled, preached, and lived more independently than most women in the western world.

The beguines saw celibacy as a route to freedom rather than a deprivation. For many, I imagine, it was itself a freedom. Exempt from the servitude of marriage and motherhood, their world and their futures grew far beyond the circumscribed limits of female life at that time. At least until the men of the church realized what freedom they enjoyed and began persecuting them, ultimately stamping out their centuries-long movement and attempts at its historiography.

I liked the idea of *choosing* celibacy, not as a last-resort treatment of my depression, not as a deprivation, but as an attempt to grow my world. I was haunted by my romances in the years since Best Ex and I broke up. Not only the worst one, but interludes like that with the curator and its sad, predictable plot. What had felt thrilling and expansive for much of my life had not only led to the greatest disaster of my adulthood, but also, through repetition, circumscribed my life. I scrolled back in time and saw that, especially in the months since those apocalyptic two years, I was drawn to the bright promise of sex and romance, only to find it soon tasteless like that cheap gum I used to love as a kid, chasing the bloom of acid sweetness piece after piece until my jaw ached.

As I walked home, it began to rain. It was March, the ugliest time of year in New York: trees barren, snow melted to reveal defrosting layers of garbage and dog shit. The warmth of Jenny's company began to wane and my anxiety returned. The filthy street became a mirror. Two men stood smoking outside of a bodega and when the smell seared my nostrils, I badly wanted a cigarette. I loved smoking. I had loved it since I was fifteen and taught myself to inhale with a stolen pack of Marlboro Lights.

No one in my family smoked and they looked upon the habit

with disgust, but I understood before I ever took a puff why a person would smoke. A cigarette provides both hunger and satisfaction, organizes a day into a series of resolved plots: the rising desire and its perfect fulfillment. It offers a trail of breadcrumbs to follow through the chaos of life and its many unmet desires, its less predictable pleasures. Quitting smoking, which I had done many times, triggered a fear that there would be nothing left to look forward to. This feeling passed if I stayed stopped, though it didn't diminish my love for smoking. Even during years-long stints without cigarettes I pined for them like an ex with whom I was still a little in love. As one of the addictions slower to kill me, I picked it up periodically and flirted with full-fledged smoking.

I did not stop to bum one from the smoking men or to buy a loosie from the bodega. I kept walking. I distracted myself with thoughts of how people who stop smoking in the UK say that they "gave up" cigarettes, whereas we say that we quit them. It seemed to indicate a fundamental difference in relationship. To quit something is to leave it, to remove oneself from the site of it. We quit jobs, gambling, biting our nails, and sometimes people. To give something up is to relinquish it, to hand it over to some other, better keeper. To free one's hands for other holdings. It is more surrender than departure. I had not really *given up* smoking, only quit it, temporarily.

For years, I had a glittery bumper sticker on my car whose voluptuous font read: *Don't Quit, Surrender,* one of the more sanctimonious twelve-step slogans. Best Ex and I—both sober for years—had put it there for laughs, but over time my reading of it became increasingly earnest, especially after we broke up. Our breakup was messy and agonizing, which felt like a betrayal of how great our love had otherwise been, an extension of my more local betrayal of her. Our relationship was beyond my skill level, really. The more time passed, the clearer it became that I had been punching over my weight. I was not up to the task of being a good partner in the face of our challenges. I did not end things when I should have. I had waited to stop loving her. I had tried to quit without surrendering, without giving her up. Eventually, the sticker started to feel pointed, as though I were being trolled by my own bumper, so I scraped it off with a razor.

I had quit many things. As a younger woman, I was always leaving. I never even told some jobs that I had quit. I just stopped showing up and never walked down that street again. Once, I quit a yearlong relationship that way. There is a word for this now: ghosting. In 1998, no one was complaining about it on the internet, so it remained unnamed. The act of naming has materializing power. Now, we know how many ghosts there are. Back then, I thought it was only me. It was easier to feel like a specter when I was the only one, to believe in self-erasure, to not think of my exes and their hauntings. This kind of quitting shrank my world. You can erase only so many streets before you are confined. Then I would move and start over.

As I aged, it seemed that I was always giving something up. Sometimes it felt relentless, but I knew it was also proof of growth. In my more honest moments, I suspected that I would eventually arrive at this oldest drive, this most compelling distraction: love. Still, once arrived, it felt too big to face. I was in such a shaken state—racked by nightmares, still reeling from disaster.

I began to wonder with some dread if giving up love and sex for a spell might not be enough to disrupt my patterns, to prevent the worst from recurring. If I did not change myself constitutionally in that time, my old routines would be waiting for me intact on the other side, pretty as an unlit cigarette.

I CAN'T QUIT YOU, BABE, sang Robert Plant on the classic rock station as I drove to work, *so I'm gonna put you down for a while.* It had been only two weeks, but everything seemed to lead back to my celibacy, including the radio's persistent characterization of love as a disease, an addiction, a form of bondage. This perception is called the Baader-Meinhof phenomenon, or frequency illusion. The most commonly given example is when one learns a new word and it suddenly appears everywhere. There was less illusion in this case, however, because the majority of songs on the radio really are about love, and the majority of songs about love characterize it as a total nightmare. Or, at best, as a manic fantasy that clearly has nothing to do with the beloved and everything to do with the singer treating them like a rag doused in ether. *Hit me, baby, one more time,* indeed.

I remembered the clinical term for it: *limerence,* which I'd discovered and been briefly obsessed with as a teenager. Coined by psychologist Dorothy Tennov in her 1979 book, *Love and Limerence: The Experience of Being in Love,* limerence refers to the state of obsessive romantic infatuation, especially when the subject has yet to possess the object of their obsession, or even to confirm that their feelings are reciprocated. It could refer to a simple crush, or obsessions at the more pathological end of the spectrum. The Jungian psychoanalyst Robert L. Moore theorized that limerence is a genetically driven condition, and others have suggested that those who are chronically afflicted suffer low serotonin levels, similar to people with obsessive-compulsive disorder.

My responses to all sources of the hormones that might treat such a disposition—dopamine, endorphin, adrenaline—suggest that I am one of these people. My childhood reactions to television, sugar, praise, mood-altering chemicals, and, yes, romantic infatuation were epiphanic. I hadn't known I suffered until I met relief. The tastes I developed for them were nothing short of fiendish.

As a teen, I already recognized myself in Tennov's descriptions of that heady intoxication, the secret truth that "despite ideals and philosophy, you find yourself a player in a process that bears unquestionable similarity to a game. The prize is not trifling; reciprocation produces ecstasy." I had already enjoyed that ecstasy and understood the thrill of the chase, how irresistible yielding to it could be. But my other obsessive pursuits did not possess that game-like quality, did not satisfy the thrill of the chase, of competition against myself. Infatuation provided the satisfying high, but also a sense of accomplishment. I was good at being in love, good at securing the affections of my love object. Over the years, however, my pride gave way to ambivalence, and then shame. Finally, at thirty-two, that once comforting form of control had led to my demoralization. F. Scott Fitzgerald famously said: "First you take a drink, then the drink takes a drink, then the drink takes you." Love was not a drink, and my pursuit of it did not fit perfectly into the rubric of addiction, but it had taken me.

I turned off of the highway and took the familiar turns, passing strip malls and pizza shops. As I pulled into the campus parking lot, I smelled the salt air through my cracked window. I taught at a university on the Jersey Shore whose campus sprawled around a majestic building that was the former summer home of Woodrow Wilson, the twenty-eighth U.S. president, avid racial segregationist and anti-suffragist. It was remodeled by its subsequent owners—the brothers who owned the F. W. Woolworth Company—in the style of Versailles, an over-the-top gesture that from a twenty-first-century vantage point looks quintessentially nouveau riche, and quintessentially New Jersey. It served as Daddy Warbucks's mansion in the film *Annie*.

In the footsteps of those dancing orphans roamed my students, burnished by tanning beds and clad in tiny shorts. One of the few notable alums (though he had not actually graduated) was a cast member on the reality show *Jersey Shore*. They were obedient and innocent and somewhat spoiled, still living at home with parents who paid too much for their private education. Over the years, I came to think of them privately as "America's children," with a little disdain but mostly affection.

It was a good job for which I was grateful. I had been working since the day I turned fourteen and at thirty-six still mentally broke down my salary to weekly amounts. Prior to being a professor, I worked for the longest stints in food service and the sex industry. This job, in addition to paying more and furnishing benefits, was the least humiliating one I'd ever had, and one of the only in which my pay did not increase with my willingness to exploit my sexuality.

I was interested in the concept of "a life's work" and believed that one's life's work was whatever pastime one devoted the greatest number of hours to. My teaching job granted me an awareness of all the years I had spent leveraging my body for financial security. I did not want self-exploitation to be my life's work and was chilled by the possibility that one might not recognize their life's work until it ceased.

That night, I taught a graduate class that was devoted to a semester-long study of lyric forms. We met in a classroom in the university library. There were a disconcertingly small number of books in the library, but there was a beautiful marble staircase and massive floor-to-ceiling windows. The building was designed by the same architects responsible for the New York Public Library on Forty-Second Street. It was a Beaux-Arts-style mansion replete with

Palladian arcades and Ionic columns in its marbled interior. The exterior was white stucco and the windows adorned with the green-and-white-striped awnings of an Italian villa. My class was held in the chestnut-paneled former billiards room.

Everyone said that the mansion had been Peggy Guggenheim's summer home, which turned out to be untrue, though for years I imagined her bringing Samuel Beckett up that marble staircase and fucking him in one of our classrooms or the rare books room. I liked teaching in the library because it was beautiful and because I felt connected to Peggy Guggenheim. In addition to dynamically influencing the art scene in mid-twentieth-century New York City, she had also fucked whomever she pleased. Consequently, she was viciously slut-shamed by the whole art world, which supposedly did not cause her to feel ashamed but did cause her to move to Venice, Italy. I had been viciously slut-shamed in middle school and, unlike Guggenheim, had felt tremendously ashamed, a feeling that lingered and still arose sometimes in my adulthood.

That night in the former billiards room I tried to explain the lyric *I* to my students, the way it, as the text I had assigned them explained, "sounds the status of the 'human' itself—an animal with a past," and how "its character or ethos also sounds the historical truth of a linguistic community—those who share a particular experience of trauma that produces 'humans.'" They mostly stared at me, uncomprehending, except for the one or two whose eyes flickered, lamps lit by understanding and interest.

"The lyric *I* is not just the speaker of the poem," I told them. "It is not the poet. It is the voice of experience, a voice that includes the reader, that speaks out of a collective first person—a kind of first-person plural." Some of them, I knew, did not have a firm enough grasp on pronouns or point of view to contemplate this grammatical metaphor. Though these same students loved to write first-person narratives in the second-person point of view. *You, you, you.* Not to address the reader directly, but to include them, to include everyone, really, in their descriptions of experience. They did it when they spoke colloquially as well: *It's like when you,* they said. They said *you* to mean the *I* that is *we*. It was a trend I noticed in speech, theirs and mine. In a way, it was an example of the lyric *I,* the collective, an acknowledgment of shared experience, or a wish for it.

I quoted the poet Edward Hirsch, saying that lyric poetry is "a highly concentrated and passionate form of communication between strangers" and felt that they were with me, at least emotionally. They liked to talk about passion. All of their poems were love poems. We would get to the love poems, but first I had hazed them with this long and difficult article about lyric poetry. Half of them wouldn't have finished it and the other half wouldn't have understood it. I was chewing it for them like a mother wolf, breaking it down into language that they could digest.

I did not feel maternal toward my students, nor did I cultivate a motherly relationship to them, but I loved the way their faces brightened with understanding when I got it right, when I lit their lamps not only with the right words, but with my passion for the subject. The key was to teach the subjects that lit my own lamp.

Part of making the students love a text was circumnavigating their first reactions to it. Even if they *loved* it, or thought they did, it was often a false love, driven less by comprehension and appreciation of the work itself than whatever they projected onto it.

"There is a difference between how you *react* to a text," I told my students at the beginning of every semester, "and how you *analyze* a text. You can be attracted to or repelled by the content and still think critically about that response, about your own relationship to the text. Our work is that of practicing such discernment, of teasing apart a *feeling* from comprehension." This process revealed entry points into the text that weren't visible before, obscured by the reader's first emotional response to the content, or to the experience of being flummoxed. As in love among humans, we cannot appreciate a text until we really see it, and in order to see it we have to get out of the way.

.   .   .

The history of celibate women, for instance, turned out to be over-whelmingly populated by religiously devout women. Voluntarily celibate women throughout history had mostly made that vow as one to God. My first reaction to this was disappointment. I wanted celibacy to be, well, sexier. Though I considered myself a spiritual person, religion remained uninteresting to me.

My Puerto Rican father and his brothers grew up in a small New Jersey town. At the Catholic school they attended in the sixties, their teachers were Dominican nuns, many of whom were sadists and rac-ists. They caned children's knuckles with rulers and hung them by their collars from coat hooks in dark closets. My father's loathing for the Catholic Church is complete and uncomplicated. He raised my brother and me to believe that people of religion were dangerous fools, duped by the literal reading of an ancient book of fairy tales, who had weaponized it for centuries to torture themselves and others.

What are religious people? he would ask us.

Sheep! we would answer.

And what are you?

WOLVES, we would cry gleefully, and howl.

I carried this bias until I got sober at twenty-three, when other sober people told me I must develop a conception of a higher power in order to stop doing heroin. Though my father had been partially correct in his judgments of the church, a little scrutiny revealed the hubris of any individual assuming they knew better than seventy thousand years of human observance of faith in something greater than themselves. That humility made it possible for me to develop a concept of a higher power—I had only to look at my recovery com-munity or to nature—but it didn't make religion any sexier to me.

The prospect that some of my new role models might be the beguines, an order of medieval religious laywomen, was hilarious as well as surprising, though its very unexpectedness gave the idea cre-dence. No younger version of me would have chosen it. I had only recently begun making different choices. I could not use the past as a metric except to measure the distance I grew from it.

What I did think was sexy, mere weeks into my celibacy, was the idea of celibate nuns fucking each other. That wasn't why I kept reading about them, but from the moment I began to, I hoped to encounter some evidence that they hadn't given up sex after all and in fact were gleefully having it with each other.

Here's the thing: the women of history had so many good reasons for choosing celibacy. The beguines did not just quit sex, and it is likely many did not quit sex at all. They quit lives that held men at the center. If they gave up sex, they did so as the cost of that freedom. Surely, it was no sacrifice for some. Some must have dropped it like an anvil. To put God in the center of their lives required freedom from men. Which is to say that freedom from men required that they put God at the center of their lives. In practice, it meant putting each other, and themselves, at the center.

In this way, celibacy was part of the long tradition of all feminist practices. I am interested in a broad definition of feminism. For me, it is the prioritization of justice, the wisdom of lived experience, and a critical examination of social roles that deems any life practice "feminist." Like many women throughout history, the beguines did not use the word *feminist*, nor the rhetoric of feminists that I grew up reading. As Patricia Hill Collins explains in her landmark text *Black Feminist Thought*, a consideration of feminism outside of white, dialectical conceptions must challenge the definition of "intellectual." Collins uses the example of Sojourner Truth, a formerly enslaved woman who could neither read nor write and nonetheless is reported to have offered "an incisive analysis of the definition of the term *woman* forwarded in the mid-1800s" and pointed out the conflicts in her identity as a "woman" and as a Black person, thereby exposing the social construction of the concept of "woman."

Most of the beguines were not intellectuals in the academic sense, either. They had no concept of feminism, because no such concept existed. They were not educated or middle-class. They were intellectuals in the sense that they thought critically about their own identities and their roles in society and challenged those definitions by electing to live in a manner that disrupted them. The same could be said for countless other groups and individuals across history, including women who lived in "Boston marriages," spinsters, and the many gender disruptors across time and place.

My interest in these figures long predated my interest in celibacy. I had been interested in feminist lives for as long as I could remember. I had never once, however, considered how many of those lives and the aspects I ascribed to them as *feminist* overlapped with and were facilitated by practices of celibacy.

The most obvious of these were the ones who explicitly made the connection, the radical feminists of the 1970s and '80s, like Shulamith Firestone, who called herself a "political celibate," echoing the concept of "political lesbian." Firestone published her best-selling *The Dialectic of Sex* when she was twenty-five, and the text has the gorgeous moral certainty of a twenty-five-year-old, which is hard to sustain as one ages. Among many other things, Firestone wanted to abolish gender, capitalism, monogamy, childbirth, and the nuclear family model. Her main argument was that all injustice stems from gender ideology, and eliminating concepts of gender would solve most other forms of oppression. She was a kind of visionary for her once radical hypothesis that one day "genital differences between human beings would no longer matter culturally." That day, of course, has not arrived for all, but it is on its way in my community, along with many of her other once outlandish ideas. Less prescient was her claim—ignorant in exactly the way of so many white feminists throughout history—that racial oppression would be solved once gender was abolished.

Emily Chertoff wrote in an *Atlantic* article after Firestone's death: "The radical feminists died off because they were inflexible, but we accept a number of their ideas today—ideas that in the 1970s were considered immoral, laughable, or twisted. Firestone was a radical biological materialist, but in her fervor she at times resembled a martyr or a saint." Fresh from my reading about martyrs and saints, I had to agree. Visionaries often share a tendency for extremism and fervor, an obsession with purity. It takes that kind of passion and conviction to live against the grain of what we are taught and how we are disciplined. Though I had always been passionate and convicted, I knew I did not possess that kind of maniacal fortitude. That was okay with me. I didn't believe I could forge a path to a new society; I just wanted to change myself.

Though intellectually I preferred Firestone, in practical ways I had been more of a Helen Gurley Brown–type feminist. A proto-sex positive activist, Gurley Brown was interested in liberation *through* sex and fun, while Firestone was a mentally ill hermit; no one found her body for a week after she died. Her life read a bit like a cautionary tale against the rigidities of radicalism. Why not have some pleasure with my feminism? An integrated approach made more sense to me than wholesale divestment, anyway. I wasn't going to disassemble the patriarchy on my own, nor in my lifetime. That kind of asceticism seemed neither fun nor sustainable. I was interested in liberation, but also in love.

As it turned out, psychic liberation wasn't simply a matter of will. I had a hard time successfully selecting what parts of compulsory heterosexuality I wanted to abstain from and which I wanted to indulge. Living in proximity to oppressive structures made it hard to resist them. As Firestone writes in her *Dialectic,* love "becomes complicated, corrupted or obstructed by an unequal balance of power." Even in relationships between women. Or when that imbalance was present only in my own thinking or habits. In the words of a more contemporary feminist, Sara Ahmed, "When you leave heterosexuality you still live in a heterosexual world."

This was the impetus for the feminist separatist groups like Cell 16, started in Boston by Roxanne Dunbar-Ortiz, and The Furies in Washington, D.C., which included the lesbian novelist Rita Mae Brown. They, too, recognized the difficulty of psychic liberation while embedded in the dynamics of the oppressive culture. The first issue of *No More Fun and Games,* the zine of Cell 16, included a short missive by Ellen O'Donnell entitled, "Thoughts on Celibacy," which ended with the line: "In reaching out in physical love, there is still the desire to mold the other person's energy under the guise of togetherness." This sentiment rang so true to my experience that the hair on my arms stood as I read it.

That first issue of *No More Fun and Games* also included a manifesto written by Dunbar-Ortiz, a career activist who subsequently took an active role in the American Indian movement of the 1970s. "The myth has persisted that the American Woman is free," her manifesto reads. "She is about as free as the descendants of the African slaves." Cell 16 credited the Black Liberation movement as an inspiration for their group while acknowledging that women were oppressed even within that movement. "How can men liberate anyone when they are not themselves liberated?" wrote Dunbar-Ortiz. "They are not free. They are too bound by their own need to own another."

There is an irony to this acknowledgment that Black women could not be liberated within a patriarchal anti-racist movement, as it fails to recognize what many Black feminists have: that Black women can be no more free within a movement led by those who are still identified with white supremacy. The feminist separatists were overwhelmingly white and, like many white feminists of preceding generations, not all shared Dunbar-Ortiz's commitment to racial justice. At that time, even she seemed to consider women's liberation *analogous* to racial liberation, not synonymous with or dependent upon it. It's easy to see the relationship between the swift disbandment of these groups and the development of intersectional feminist ideologies by anti-separatist Black feminists like the Combahee River Collective, whose 1977 statement reads:

[W]e are actively committed to struggling against racial, sexual, heterosexual, and class oppression, and see as our particular task the development of integrated analysis and practice based upon the fact that the major systems of oppression are interlocking. The synthesis of these oppressions creates the conditions of our lives. As Black women we see Black feminism as the logical political movement to combat the manifold and simultaneous oppressions that all women of color face.

Men hadn't been at the center of my life for a long time. Most of my friends, lovers, and students were women, nonbinary, trans, and queer people. I had not given up sex to get freedom from men, though many of the things I wanted freedom from were inaugurated by them and are perpetuated by the social structures that privilege them. I had given up sex because my life had fallen apart and I needed to change. Had I also done so to put myself at the center, like the beguines and radical feminists? My celibacy was certainly not a holy or pious act, though I imagined that giving up sex would allow me to live in greater service to others, even if those others were only my future lovers. Interrupting the patterns in which my romances were entrenched might lead to better relationships in the future, an outcome that also served me. I hoped that in the short term giving up sex would free me from the preoccupations of love and romance. Even as a single woman with no children, I craved time. I wanted more time to write, to dance, to think, to sleep, to read, to meditate, to exercise. I marveled at people who had *hobbies*. It's hard to have a hobby while juggling multiple obsessions.

This all sounds very rational, and the factor that most drove my endeavor was not rational. I felt it in my body like physical hunger, tugging on every cell. It felt *biological*. A pressure like that of sickness or fatigue. It was a desire that had finally grown stronger than its opposite, but was yet unknown. What did I want when I wanted the absence of something? It wasn't really time or a hobby. I had no reference for the object of my hunger, and that was a strange condition.

In my quietest moments, on the drive home from work, my body humming as I belted out a song about love, and just before I fell asleep or after I woke, I was merely *an animal with a past.* I sensed how much I didn't know yet. I understood that an animal could be very hungry and not know for what, only in what direction it lay.

A ROUND THE TWO-WEEK MARK, my friend Ray came over to help me move some boxes. She was more than a decade younger than me, the youngest friend I'd ever had. Until my mid-thirties, my friends and lovers were always older than me. I loved being the precocious baby, the recipient of doting smiles.

Ray knows the feeling of being the precocious baby. We had met the previous summer in the queer section of Riis Beach through a sober friend and exchanged numbers after learning that we were neighbors. A few weeks later, we arranged to attend a local recovery meeting together. Moments after she entered my apartment for the first time, the room shifted as if I'd been struck by a spell of vertigo.

Ray is beautiful, with poreless olive skin, floppy Justin Bieber hair, and a body carved by obsessive hours at the gym, but it wasn't her beauty that caused my vertigo the first time we hung out. It was no passive effect but a power she exerted. She *smoldered* at me with a gaze so intimate that I looked away, disarmed, and offered her a selt- zer. It was like the moment when a mood-altering drug kicks in— the smear of lights and judder of guts—just that uncontrollable, a greater power grasping the helm of one's body. I steeled myself and the vertigo stopped. She'd caught me off guard and I wouldn't let it happen again.

I had recognized Ray's charisma when we first met on the beach, the light that emanated from her. Lots of people have it, and I didn't give hers a second thought, as I wouldn't any other observable quality in a new person, because I did not intend to sleep with Ray—her age placed her so far outside the realm of my consideration that I was not even tempted. I could see that she was attractive and you could say I was attracted to her, but there was a resolute boundary in me that foreclosed the possibility of sex with someone so much younger than I.

So it is not an understatement to say that I was shocked when she spun the dial of her charisma upward and it did its sudden work on me. People with this power are savants; like those with a genius for music, mathematics, athleticism, or photographic memory. They can hone their talent, but it is a God-given set of instincts, often paired with the tendencies of addiction, which also include hyper-focus and relentless appetite. Like many animals, we evolve to attract the things we hunger for.

As an adult, I'd had little experience being the object of sexual magnetism, because I was usually the one exerting it. In those first moments I felt like a magician whose assistant had disappeared her. I was struck with the uncanny sense that I had encountered my younger self. *So this is what it feels like,* I thought. I hadn't imagined my machinations were so obvious and I felt retroactive embarrassment. My pride in this ability had been so misplaced. Seduction had felt like control to me, like power, but my need had been so transparent. *Want me,* it begged.

In the intervening year, I had studiously ignored Ray's smolder, which waned enough for us to become friends. It was not her magnetism that attracted my friendship. She was gifted at more than the art of seduction, was funny and kind, and driven by appetites I understood.

After she moved the boxes for me, we shared a bag of unsalted almonds on my gray sofa and she told me about the neuroscience study that she was working on with a famous psychologist who specialized in brain and body mechanisms involved in affect, emotion, and motivation. All day in the lab, Ray took videos of people making facial expressions that were then analyzed by a computer that calculated the emotions expressed, according to Paul Ekman's famous research on facial expressions and emotion. Ekman theorized that there are six primary emotions and that the facial expressions associated with these emotions are universal across time and culture: enjoyment, sadness, anger, fear, surprise, disgust, and contempt.

Though Ekman traveled to communities outside of the United States during his research, his original data sets used almost entirely static faces, so Ray's study intended to evaluate the reliability of Ekman's research using a data set of dynamic, moving faces. Ray invited her friends, ex-girlfriends, and strangers to the lab to make faces, which she videotaped and ran through software that analyzed the emotions expressed. The study also tracked the neurological response to visually observing these changing emotional faces. So Ray's subjects also looked at the other videos she had taken while she tracked their brain activity for markers associated with emotions. She found that her subjects' brain activity mimicked the emotions expressed in the photographs. That is, seeing sad faces potentially generated sadness and angry faces anger.

After she updated me on the lab gossip and her research, we stared at each other on the couch and contorted our faces (tragically sad! aggressively surprised! so angry!) for a while before lapsing into laughter. I wondered what the face of desire or longing looked like and to which category it belonged, but thought better of asking Ray.

I considered the infinite feedback loop of beholding a face of desire, how it generated further desire in the seer. Or a face full of worship. Did it create reciprocal worship? Did it also transmit that feeling about the subject themself? That is, if someone looked at me as if I was perfect, worthy of worship and desire, did it make me feel so about myself? I'd read about the emotional mirroring parents do with their infants. *You are loved,* their faces say, and so the child's brain develops around the belief, *I am loved/lovable.*

I remember lying in bed with a boyfriend when I was twenty-four. This man expressed his adoration freely, showered me with compliments, and stared at me with the face of desire. I had an acute hunger in me that seemed to be for these things. When he offered them, however, it frustrated me. I felt the shallow space inside me that absorbed them. Like a hungry ghost with an empty belly and needle-thin mouth, my hunger could never be sated. When we kissed I would open my eyes to see him staring at me with what you might call love. The sight of that soft gaze sometimes made me want to punch him, other times for his weight to grow so great that it would obliterate me. The visual proof of his love made visible my own insatiability. The fact of my own insatiability prompted an existential dread at the far edges of which lay nihilism. If being a lover was ultimately the plight of a hungry ghost, what point was there in anything?

Though reductive, it made sense that the person who craved the worshipful face of a lover failed to develop their brain around the fact of their lovability. If a parent doesn't mirror adequately with their infant, the infant is likely to develop an insatiable hunger for love and its mimics. Developmental psychologist Mary Ainsworth, who famously piloted studies on attachment theory, might assign that person an "insecure attachment style."

Sitting on my sofa eating almonds with Ray, I felt a familiar disappointment that I didn't have this excuse. Despite our family's challenges, there was no question that I had been loved well as a child. Enough to render my hunger for proof of lovability something of a mystery.

I once explained to the therapist I had in my twenties that the common denominator I'd observed among the famous and otherwise very successful people I'd met was that they all had an insatiable hunger for love and validation. It seemed clear that one needed an inexorable emotional ambition to sublimate as professional ambition. Those with less to prove are less eager to work ceaselessly and to sacrifice other pleasures. I confided in my therapist that I sometimes worried I would not be as successful as I hoped because I lacked such a drive.

"I don't think you have to worry about that," she said.

It was an unseasonably warm day, so we moved out to my stoop to enjoy the sun and people-watch while Ray updated me on her dating situation. For the last year she'd been in a long-distance relationship with a woman in Wyoming. Her Wyoming girlfriend also had a Wyoming girlfriend. The Wyoming girlfriend's Wyoming girlfriend had been the source of a lot of strife in their relationship, and, among us, a lot of wisecracks about her name, which was Canyon. Ray's girlfriend had recently moved to New York and devoted herself full-time to Ray. This is what Ray had been longing for, and despite or perhaps because of that fixation, it had proved a tremendous disappointment.

"All we do is fight," Ray moaned.

"Where is a Canyon to swallow her when you need one?" I said.

"Seriously." Ray laughed. Then she told me about a bridesmaid she met at a wedding recently. "She's not my usual type, but our chemistry is unparalleled."

"How would you describe your usual type?"

"I usually go for girls who are real disruptors. Tattoos, assertive, academic, a little older." She stopped and a flush crept up her neck as we both realized that she'd described me. "Anyway," she added, "Bridesmaid is working corporate America. She's really pretty and smart, but completely basic. Like, she wears UGGs and drinks pumpkin spice lattes. And she's proud to announce it."

"What's your chemistry like?" I asked.

"I mean, it's all about her worshipping my body. Not my usual deal, but it's pretty amazing."

"Yeah, it is," I said, withholding my own points of reference. Then I told Ray that I'd decided to spend ninety days celibate.

"Cool, cool, cool," she said, nodding in her characteristic way. "Are you thinking of it in terms of addiction? Ninety days and all."

"I don't think so? I mean, it definitely has a little bit of the -ism in it, a little compulsiveness, but it's definitely not fully fledged addiction. I've tried to stop being in relationships before and failed, which is"—I shrugged to acknowledge this familiar marker of addiction. "But the sense of unmanageability," I added. "It isn't on par with that of my past experiences of addiction. It isn't life-ruining, or health-ruining, but it is super consuming, and has sometimes been unmanageable in the past." I believed this as I said it, and did not think of the two recent years I'd spent ruining my life and health in the name of love. I was still not ready to face this greatest impetus.

Recovering from drug addiction taught me that ninety days is a good length of time to detox from something and that abstinence is the only way to really know if you're addicted. Detoxing subtracts the acute urgency and therefore loosens whatever denial and rationalization have been supporting your habit so that you can see the thing more clearly, which was part of my goal.

"I mean, it's definitely an emotional high," Ray said. "Sex, but even more so seduction." Ray and I had discussed this topic and our similarities around it at length, without ever acknowledging our dynamic. Occasionally we treaded into this kind of meta-territory, and that afternoon the thought occurred to me that I hadn't been completely honest with myself about the satisfaction of her attention, which was no longer smoldering but far from entirely platonic. As a ridiculous man once said to me, *What's the harm in a little friendly fire?* I didn't know.

"Right," I said. "I mean, in some relationships, I've definitely qualified as a love addict. I've spent a lot of my life getting high on seduction. But our society has a fucked-up and compulsive relationship to love and dating and sex, so it's hard to separate my own relationship to relationships, you know?"

"Totally. I mean, at different moments in our lives, that addictive part of us can activate in response to literally anything, right?"

"Anything," I agreed. "I've had it the longest in response to people, food, and drugs, but I can wear out a good song like an eight-ball."

"Honestly, pretty regular shit," she laughed.

"Right? There are so many more interesting things one could be addicted to."

Then she told me about a girl she once met in a treatment center who identified as a vampire. This girl would look up cutters in online forums and meet with them to suck their blood.

I reciprocated with a story about a woman I'd known when I first got clean who called herself a she-wolf, but in a literal way, not a woo-woo, crystal-loving way. When she was alone, she would crawl around her apartment on all fours and eat without using her hands.

Ray volleyed back a description of a woman she knew who was obsessed with growing fungus on her skin. She would compulsively wet her hair and then lie in bed until it dried and then repeat.

Finally, I told her about the regular I had as a dominatrix who needed five women in the room in order to come: one to insert a catheter while jerking him off, another clamping his nipples, another clamping her own nipples, and one pretending to shit in a bedpan in the corner. He always had some off-the-beaten-path porn playing on the wall-mounted TV, too. Still, with everything in place, it had looked like an uphill battle.

"That was a late-stage situation," I said.

"I think you're all good," Ray laughed.

"Drug and love addictions are pretty banal, right?"

We finished chuckling and then sat in silence for a few minutes, watching my neighbors trudge home from work.

"Hey, wanna share a cigarette?" Ray asked as she pulled a yellow pack out of her pocket.

"Oh, definitely."

M Y CHIROPRACTOR was gay. I knew this because I spent a good part of the morning after my session with him sleuthing online to find out whether or not he was gay.

No one had laid their hands on my body for weeks. His touch was perfunctory, careful but detached. I was a mechanism and he the mechanic, unconcerned with any response I might have to his touch other than in the alignment of my spine. His only expectation was that I not perform any response at all. It would be inappropriate for me to indicate pleasure at his touch. In this sense, chiropractic adjustment was the opposite of sex. Its unspoken contract of stoicism created a wonderful privacy in which to experience physical sensation.

It wasn't sexual pleasure that I felt when he enfolded me in his crushing embrace and listened for the telltale crunch of my vertebrae, or when he donned the latex glove to painfully prod the roof of my mouth, but it was pleasure. My body opened like a struck note and rang as he dug into my pelvis and stared with concentration at the wall, trying to *see* me with his fingertips.

I did not find him sexually attractive. He was a man and beyond that a blond. Blond people, particularly men, did not arouse me; they were like tow-headed eunuchs, though I was capable of recognizing and appreciating their beauty aesthetically. My chiropractor was fit, clean, and fragrant. His hands were always dry and firm. He had a sensible disposition and I trusted him.

Given all of this, why should it have mattered if he was gay or not? Still, it did. Our perfectly neutered dynamic freed me to enjoy our sessions without reservation. Confirming the impossibility of *his* enjoying it in a sexual way gave me full permission to luxuriate in the element of his touch that was not sexual but did include an element of the erotic. I was curious about this new pleasure that could not ever result in sex. This eros that did not erode, but nourished with its longing.

That morning I had been reading about Saint Catherine of Siena, and after my chiropractic session I wondered if she ever felt that pleasure when she performed the laying on of hands. Did the healing surge in both directions, like Ekman's emotions, the warm skin of the dying spurring the blood to rush joyously beneath hers? My chiropractor must have known a version of that exchange. Healers must find their work nourishing or it bankrupts them. Teaching is sometimes healing work, and I feel nourished by it. I also know how it drains. Whatever his experience, I felt healed by my chiropractor's touch. I left our sessions full—not empty, as I often had felt after sex. There was no cost to my pleasure or healing in that office beyond his ninety-dollar fee.

The beguines were healers, too. They tended to the sick and infirm in their communities for no pay and were relied upon to give last rites. That service must have paid in other currencies. As celibates, they surely sought other forms of touch. Did they lay hands on each other for healing, for pleasure? Some of them were undoubtedly queer, whether they had the words or will to name it or not. Some of them must have been lovers (again, against the odds, I hoped to find evidence of this). But the ones who weren't, did they know this freedom, too? This pleasure that allowed one to keep all of herself for herself. To walk away not empty but full.

.   .   .

I suspect that the last cis-man I dated was the last one I will ever date, a title he may or may not appreciate holding. We got together just before my tryst with the curator. He was an old college friend who had been in town from California for the weekend. When I called another friend to complain about a bad date with a woman, she told me to call him.

"Call him and have him come fuck you," she said. "It will make you feel better."

This sounded unlikely, unlike me in every way.

"How do they do it, the ones who make love / without love?" wrote Sharon Olds. "These are the true religious, / the purists, the pros."

"I don't date men anymore," I reminded my friend.

"So what?" she said. "If I remember correctly, you're capable of enjoying sex with men. You can stop if you don't like it."

Was that true? One of the things that I remembered about sleeping with men was that it was hard to stop even if you didn't like it. It felt easier to just keep fucking them, because then you wouldn't have to emotionally clean up afterward. It was easier to keep fucking them than to find out how awful they might be when sexually thwarted—a potential I knew was hard to overestimate. Masculinity was a glass vase perpetually at the edge of the table.

My old college friend was a feminist, I reminded myself. I'd always thought of him as a nice guy, by which I meant that he wasn't terrible. The bar for cis-men was basically underfoot.

Why not, I thought. *I'll try something different.*

It was as easy as my friend had promised: I called him and he came right over. The sex was just all right. His cock was shapely and hard, and I liked the feel of it on my thigh as he sucked my nipple. There was a thrill as he penetrated me, owing in some part to novelty. Within a couple of minutes, however, I recognized the familiar tedium of being thrust upon. I knew what came next and it was not me. Still, I dutifully turned over onto my hands and knees and let him fuck me from behind. It took a few more minutes for me to realize that I was waiting for it to be over. It took another few to work up the gumption to tell him to stop. Then, before I could speak, he sputtered to a finish and there was no need.

Even when I watched pornography featuring men, I wanted to disappear them as soon as I came. Sometimes I gently closed the computer before I finished my orgasm, as if I wanted to leave without the actors noticing. To my dismay, the Last Man assumed that he would be staying over. I was very sleepy. When he curled up against me as big spoon, I yielded and leaned into him. This was a position I was accustomed to, having been shorter than all of my recent sleeping partners. They had been women, though, and his relative immensity quickly made me feel claustrophobic and overheated. His body hair prickled and I was shocked by the profusion of sweat. A person only wants to be drenched in the sweat of someone she loves, and not always then.

The next morning, I pretended to leave for work so that he would leave with me. After we parted ways at the café on the corner, I walked home. As I closed the apartment door behind me, the pleasure of solitude was so great that I closed my eyes and leaned back against the door with a sigh. I drank a glass of water and made my bed. My bedroom, having been intruded upon, felt sanctified in his absence.

After he went back to California, he started writing me letters. He wrote me a letter every day for the next six months, an act that now sounds deranged, though at the time it charmed me.

While in a sanitorium for his tuberculosis, the French theorist Roland Barthes fell in love with another patient. Though the man was straight, Barthes wrote him letters every day for six months. I do not think the letters convinced the man to love Barthes. The ones sent by my old college friend did the trick, however. Like Catherine of Siena, who is considered one of the greatest Italian letter writers of the fourteenth century, he was a very good writer of letters. That, combined with the four thousand miles between us, was a powerful aphrodisiac.

He started coming back to New York every other weekend. After a few months, he asked me why I had not introduced him to any of my friends.

"Are you ashamed to be dating a man?" he asked.

"Yes," I answered.

While dating the Last Man, I fantasized about having a baby almost constantly. I was thirty-four. The obsession was so powerful that I assumed there was a hormonal factor at work. I pictured infinitesimal messengers scrambling through my body like so many Paul Reveres, sounding the alarm of my waning fertility, but it turns out there is no such endocrinological explanation. It is simply the consequence of the powerful cocktail of societal pressure and nature's ultimatum. Still, when I think of our sex, I think of it as the last gasp of my biological imperative.

I am all but certain now that I won't ever have children. When I let go of my interest in biologically creating a human, my desire for children disappeared entirely. I felt shocked by this. Perhaps I had never wanted to be a parent, only an incubator. I hadn't wanted to miss anything, especially profound corporeal experiences. There is a lot of emphasis in U.S. mainstream culture on what women will miss by not having children, as opposed to what we will miss by having children, which seems at least an equal amount. A cursory investigation made clear to me that there was much to be missed and cherished in either direction. Every life contains joy and sorrow, and parenthood is no deciding factor in which of these prevails.

The Last Man would have been a good father, I thought. But whenever we spent more than one day together, I couldn't wait to get away from him. His need for my attention emitted a very high-pitched whine, like a mosquito audible only to me. When I broke up with him, he tried to talk me out of it.

"You'll regret it," he sputtered. I almost laughed in surprise, but restrained myself.

"Maybe," I said. "But I don't think so."

"You're making a colossal mistake!" he shouted.

Sometimes I still roll the phrase around in my mouth like a lozenge: *A colossal mistake.*

I N THINKING ABOUT my exes, I decided to make a comprehensive list of them to review during my celibacy. I had learned the power of taking stock through an inventory by way of twelve-step programs, each of which prescribed a variation on the process. My inventory would combine elements of what I'd learned in recovery with my own devised form.

I did not want to merely take "a break," as my mother had suggested for years. A break implies a return to the preexisting conditions of one's life. I did not want to feel better temporarily. I wanted to change my life. In order to do so, I knew that I needed to change myself. Inventorying my history of love felt like a good beginning. I would start with the series of relationships I conducted just before starting my celibacy and move back through time, write the story of each relationship with as much honesty and thoroughness as I could muster.

The mere act of scanning my own memories was tedious in its repetition. I kept making the same kinds of mistakes, like falling in love, or something, with the prolific writer of letters, or sleeping with people whom I wanted as friends. I did not know exactly how I wanted to *be* different, but I was interested in making different mistakes.

"Throughout life, all of love's 'failures' resemble one another (and with reason: they all proceed from the same flaw)," wrote Barthes in *A Lover's Discourse*. In my case, I assumed it was more than one flaw. My life had always more or less functioned as a treat-based economy. For many years, and still to some extent, I lived for the next reward. A bag of heroin, a drink, a flirt, a cigarette, a cookie, a kiss. Mostly the objects of my obsession had occurred in a descending order of lethality. An arc, really, beginning in childhood with books, food, secrets, and approval. In my late teens and twenties it advanced to drugs, tattoos, and the more extreme ends of sexual and romantic intrigue. Then it circled back to food and approval. Finally, I was left with exercise, art, and intrigue.

After years and years of food obsession, I finally more or less ate when hungry and stopped eating when full. It was the sort of miracle that arrives only after decades of therapy and often not even then. The miracles of women are always more labor than magic, I was discovering. In addition to taking a celibate vow, Catherine of Siena drank pus from cancerous sores of the dying, sat for days in ecstatic rigidity, performed self-flagellations, and starved herself half to death for most of her life. Her rewards were exemption from marriage to a man and the liberty to preach like one. She mockingly referred to the Pope as "Daddy," and scolded him publicly. By the time she finally did starve herself to death at thirty-three, she was one of Italy's leading ecclesiastical authorities and statesmen. Though unschooled, she was one of the most prolific writers in church history. In the Middle Ages, at least, celibacy had often been the bedrock upon which women's sovereignty was built.

I was not as interested in male celibacy, or any kind of punitive or forced celibacy. The male monks, unlike the beguines, could not live among the poor, or anyone, and remain celibate. It was the great struggle of their lives. Even cloistered away in hair shirts, they took to raping female donkeys and molesting novice monks. For them, celibacy was a punishment, a great deprivation, cause for a war with themselves. They had no freedom to gain, only freedom to lose. Having nothing left to gain could be a vulnerable position, though not one for which I had much curiosity, or sympathy.

My position was not one for which all would have sympathy either—not my friend Jenny, nor most of my exes. I could not expect everyone to see the difference between deprivation and surrender as meaningful.

Celibacy itself was not my work, anyway. It would simply make space for whatever that work turned out to be. It was easy to frame my relationship to romance within the paradigm of addiction, but I knew it was more complicated. Love and sex were not just "treats" that I chased through my life to the exclusion of more unprecedented pursuits. I knew my romantic history indicated an underlying relationship to power, escape, and that bottomless need that my old therapist had been so sure I possessed. I was not looking forward to discovering all of this, but I could make a list, so that is where I started.

TIME HAD ALWAYS FELT in short supply, and it began to appear that I'd simply been splurging it on romance. A month into celibacy, I had more time than ever. Over the first month, I'd met every freelance deadline on my docket, caught up by phone with everyone I loved, cut off half of my hair, bought six pairs of shoes, donated three garbage bags of clothes, organized my whole apartment, and run forty-five miles. It remained unclear what I was running toward. My anxiety had lessened but I still felt pursued. Flashes of motion darted in the corners of my vision.

On one of my runs, I passed a man sniffing a bag of heroin in the gray light of early morning. I knew it was heroin and not some other powdered drug because his skin hung on his bones like wet laundry. Addicts wear their addictions differently, and dope, while it empties the eyes, weighs heavy on the body. I still remembered the taste: musty and bitter in the back of my throat.

I had not so much as flirted with anyone in four weeks. Did my celibacy preclude flirting? That seemed extreme, but also correct. I was uncertain whether this was something a person (me) could fully control. My uncertainty already felt like failure. The feeling of failure ratcheted up my anxiety, which remained worst in the mornings, a haze that wore off as the day progressed.

I had woken up to a text from a date of a few weeks ago. I knew that I should tell her I wasn't dating anymore, but I did not. Instead, I turned off my phone and read a depressing memoir about sex addiction. Throughout the book, the narrator fucked so many men, but never mentioned getting a yeast infection or a urinary tract infection or any kind of sexually transmitted infection. I was sure she had excised those details. I considered it a missed opportunity, narratively speaking. The physical symptoms of addiction are some of the hardest to ignore and are often the addict's route to confrontation with the truth, thereby anything resembling an epiphanic moment.

I had never thought I was a sex addict. It had always been the emotions that got me high. ("They do not mistake the lover for their own pleasure.") What were the physical symptoms of emotional addiction, I wondered. When I was addicted to a person, I had wept all the time. I cried so much during those two years that the skin around my eyes peeled away, as if my body were attempting to exfoliate down to another, more reasonable version of me. My hands were perpetually sweaty. I kept changing the tone of my text alerts—from a cheep to a ding to a whistle to a strum—because after a few days of whatever sound was pinging, I developed such a powerful fear response that I worried what all that adrenaline was doing to my heart.

I kept busy, also, by working on my inventory. The practice of making an inventory was one that I had learned to rely upon in sobriety, a fundamental part of the hygiene for addressing a resentment or behavior that I wanted to change. As I wrote in the floppy spiral-bound notebook I had designated to this task, I felt tempted to categorize my romantic and sexual history as an addiction narrative. As a memoirist, I was good at assigning narrative to experience. Addiction had a familiar narrative, one that, however tormented, was appealingly simple to resolve. But this was not simple. Love was not a drug from which I could practice perfect abstinence. Also, it seemed unfair to call a socially conditioned behavior an addiction. Wasn't that just adaptation? Civilization, even. Capitalism had us all addicted to consumption. Unfair did not mean untrue. I could have blamed patriarchy for almost everything and been righteous. The issue wasn't whose fault it was, but how to get free.

The next person on the list was one of the more embarrassing ones. The previous summer, seven months before my celibacy began, I had intended to take *a break*. I brought this intention to an artist residency in Vermont. Though artist residencies are known fields of sexual pursuit, I told my friends that I was planning on taking *a sexual sabbatical*. It was cute and not enough to override twenty years of conditioning.

I brought an ugly pair of clogs to the residency, as if they were a prophylactic. The first week of the residency, I wore the clogs to daily yoga classes. I woke up at dawn to write. I walked in the woods and abstained from the freshly baked bread that they served at every meal. I inhaled its yeasty perfume and felt virtuous and in control.

Then I began an affair with a painter. She was twenty-five years old, with long limbs and a razor wit. Such a thing would have been inconceivable at any earlier point in my life. The boundary that prevented me from being tempted by much younger people had never wavered. I had exclusively dated people older than me. Well, I was not *dating* the twenty-five-year-old, I said, mostly to myself.

One night, I lay across her lap while she fucked me, a position that I had enjoyed with other lovers. I liked to be cradled, to feel precious, somewhere between an armful of flowers and a dish of steaming food set before a ravenous diner. As she fucked me in the perfect dark of my studio, the irony of being held like a baby by someone so much younger than I was leapt through me with a sudden chill.

After that, I started eating the bread in the dining hall. Soon, I was eating hardly anything but the bread, great slabs of it at every meal, slathered in salted butter. I began smoking cigarettes with the twenty-five-year-old and sleeping until midday. I did not wear the clogs again. My last act before leaving the residency was to toss them in a dumpster before I drove away.

The twenty-five-year-old came to visit me once in New York,

a few weeks after I returned home from the residency. I took her out for dinner at a popular but remote Thai restaurant and when we walked onto the crowded patio, I scanned the room for familiar faces. I realized that I was ashamed to be seen on a date with someone so young, not only by people I knew, but also by strangers. I had rarely ever felt ashamed of the people I chose as lovers and here was the second instance in just a few months.

A few days after she left New York, I called the twenty-five-year-old to tell her we couldn't see each other again. I had been careful to warn her the whole time that it couldn't ever be serious, so I hoped it would be an easy phone call. What twenty-five-year-old heeds a careful warning? I certainly hadn't.

"No!" she shouted into the phone when I told her, sounding more like a child than ever before. I felt embarrassed for us both.

During my affair with the twenty-five-year-old, I sometimes soothed myself by thinking of Colette. I had read the French novelist's most famous volume, *Chéri*, as a teenager and been instantly infatuated with its protagonist, Léa, a forty-nine-year-old courtesan. Léa is a great beauty who leads a life of luxuries common to her class in early-twentieth-century Paris, at the end of the Belle Époque. She lives in a silk-laden apartment, sleeps in a heavy brass bed, and takes baths drawn by a faithful lady's maid who prepares "a large cup of reduced chocolate with an egg in it" for Léa's dinner. Her days are spent writing letters, calling upon other rich middle-aged courtesans, reminiscing about her colorful past during which she entertained lovers of all genders, and sleeping with the eponymous Chéri. She exhibits no shame in her social status nor in the fact that her lover, a friend's child whom she watched grow up, is half her age. The book contains no hint of the humiliations and dangers that I now know are implicit to the lives of many sex workers, no matter the country or time period.

To sixteen-year-old me, living in the late twentieth century in a small town in the United States, Léa's sounded like a life beyond my wildest dreams. After I learned something of Colette's own life—which was also rich with Parisian extravagance and sex with lovers of all genders, including plenty of much younger men—the boundaries between it and those of her characters blurred in my mind (as they had during her lifetime). Colette's life sounded even more appealing to me than Léa's. To have all the fun, money, and sex, and also be a prolific and famous writer? Many of my literary heroes up until that point had been men, partly the result of having come of age in the internet-absent early nineties, partly because female artists with notorious appetites are rarely glorified. Colette was a role model that truly suited me.

The pleasures of the Belle Époque provide the setting of *Chéri*, however, not its subject. It is a novel about heartbreak, aging, and sexual abandonment. At sixteen, I had no reference for any of that, so it was the opulent settings and sexual freedom, the shamelessness, that stuck with me, even after I experienced those pleasures for myself. First impressions, if not consciously reconsidered, often far outlive their relevance.

So, at thirty-five years old, when I lay in the arms of my much younger lover and the shame crept through me, I did not think of the final scene of *Chéri*, when he walks away from Léa and she stands waiting, heart buoyant with pitiful hope that he will turn back and look at her, see her as he once did, which he does not. Instead, I thought, *What would Colette do?*

I T HAD BEEN seven years since my first book was published, and I needed fresh author photos for the new book's jacket. I hired a photographer I'd known for years, an East Village fixture in the punk dyke scene. She was fifteen or twenty years older than me and we had always had a flirtation. She radiated the kind of brazen, erratic sexual energy that would be repellent in a man but was fun coming from her. As I chose my outfits for the shoot, I imagined the familiar once-over I knew she would give me. I went big on my eyeliner and folded a bunch of black shirts into my bag.

"Hey, babe." She smiled when I arrived, and invited me inside. I had forgotten how she opened every door like it was the door to her bedroom. Truly, if she were a man I would have laughed in her face, but instead I felt my nipples harden.

Her apartment was classic East Village and rent-controlled, so nothing had been replaced in thirty years. Its wooden floors were buckled and had gaps between the slats in which decades of grime had settled. Everything in her bathroom was yellow as an old tooth. All of this notwithstanding, it was a big flat with great light and windows that overlooked Avenue A. Most of the city's denizens, including me, would have killed for it.

There were screens and lights set up by the windows. She offered me a glass of water, and as I sipped it we caught up. I told her that I was spending three months celibate.

"Oh, wow, I should probably do that," she said, eyes wide, and laughed. I laughed, too, as if we both found the prospect hilarious. Behind my smile, doubt needled me. I worried that it was a joke, me trying to change my life in three months. Certainly, it sounded like a punchline to some. When I imagined committing to a longer stint, however, my resolve faltered. If I aimed too high, it would only undermine my chances of following through. But then why did I keep telling people about the celibacy if it embarrassed me? I tossed it up like a shield against sex, but it often moved the conversation in precisely that direction.

Over the next hour, she shot me looking out the window, staring into the camera, and sitting in a wooden chair. I had been photographed many times over the course of my adult life, but it never became comfortable. I liked attention but was no exhibitionist. I squirmed under the lights and the gaze of the camera, its black blinking eye. Experience and photographers had taught me to resist my instincts, to soften and open toward the impassive lens. I knew my angles, but I had never gotten good at posing. I performed better if there was a person behind it with whom I had chemistry. That was probably why I'd booked this photographer. I also loved to watch women manipulate equipment with expertise, and as she moved around me, *click click,* I started to enjoy myself.

When we finished, I descended the crooked staircase that deposited me back onto the sidewalk. I felt wrung out and a little high as I rejoined the churning stream of pedestrians. I wanted a cigarette.

A week later, when the photographer sent me a link to the photos, I saw that my mouth was parted and my eyes soft. The woman in the pictures looked slightly scared, and slightly scary, too. The affect seemed appropriate for a book jacket—we like our authors a little scary and our women a little scared—but the images made me uneasy. I sensed that they exposed something I shouldn't reveal to the world: the private mechanics of my flirtation with the photographer. The look on my face had nothing to do with the book.

I thought of my clothes and makeup that day, the angle of my shoulders. I wondered how they all might have been different if I were thinking not of the photographer but of the book. I recalled all the photographs that had ever been taken of me, the thick catalog of my attempts to synchronize my appearance with the desires of each viewer. An archive of images meant to represent one kind of work while doing another.

Later that afternoon across a plate of vegan wings, my friend Nora's eyes glittered above her pink-flushed cheeks and lips. Her pupils gaped and I guessed that she was in love even before she told me about the new woman she had begun dating. She had met the lawyer months before, she explained, but it hadn't taken. Then the woman invited Nora and some other friends for an adult sleepover on the solstice. Something about the way she said *friends* gave me pause.

"Wait," I asked her, "were all the other friends her ex-girlfriends or something?"

"No," Nora clarified. "But they were all interested in her romantically."

I made a suspicious face and urged her on. That night, all of the women wrote something they wanted in the new year on a scrap of paper and then burned it. Nora wrote the lawyer's name and the name of the university where she had just interviewed for a tenure-track job. Despite the fact that she hadn't yet defended her dissertation, she was offered the job a few days later. Not only that, but she and this woman had also begun dating. She now spent weekdays writing her dissertation in her small suburban apartment with her cat and adoring beagle, and weekends at the lawyer's high-rise apartment in Manhattan. Nora looked high as hell when she told me all of this and envy struck me hard. I wanted to be in love and rapt with possibility, too! Never mind that the lawyer sounded like trouble.

Nora and I had met in our master's program, after which she segued into a PhD. Her nimble intellect and creativity quickly made her a rising star in her field. The job she had been offered was a rare opportunity for someone at her career level. Not for the first time, the implicit fact of her ambition surprised me. Nora had long lustrous hair, the face of a cupid, and the appetites of a hedonist, though it took years for me to see the last. That kind of voracity was counterintuitive in someone so kind and with such a gentle affect. In our MFA program, she was a diligent student who enrolled in supplementary literature classes far beyond what was required by our curriculum. I wasn't surprised to learn that she'd been the valedictorian of her high school.

During graduate school, we'd both taught for a nonprofit college preparatory program on the weekends. One weekend, we took the teens to a Six Flags amusement park. While I bought a bag of cotton candy, Nora joined a line with the students to ride the park's terrifying new roller coaster. I shook my head enthusiastically when she beckoned. Despite my own voracious appetites, I have never experienced physical terror as a form of entertainment. I won't ride anything more daring than a Ferris wheel.

I watched raptly as she exited the serpentine queue and was strapped into a medieval-looking apparatus meant to keep her from being ejected into the clouds. I tried to keep track of her blue shirt as she was tossed around by the enormous contraption, the squeal of fifty screams surging and waning as the snaking device climbed and twisted and whirled and shuddered and dropped. My beautiful friend emerged from the experience with tousled hair and that same starry look in her eyes, like she had a crush on the roller coaster. I was shocked when she joined the line again, and again, and again. She must have ridden that perverse machine five or six times, as many as the afternoon would allow. By the time we left the park, she was in a state of ecstasy, a rapture that I recognized, though not on her. I understood that I had met an integral part of Nora that day, one that we shared, each in her own way.

S IX WEEKS INTO my celibacy, a big national writers' conference was held in Los Angeles. Thousands of writers descended
upon the sun-bathed city like sickly ants from under the log of
winter. For months, I had been planning a fundraiser for a feminist
literary organization on whose board I served. It had been a lot of
work—feminist activism, unlike our fantasies of it, consists mostly
of administrative work—and I was looking forward to the dance
party that would conclude the evening. The last woman I had kissed
would be there. She was the final person I dated before my celibacy
began, and I had only recently ended our affair, which, like that with
the curator, had mostly been conducted over text, punctuated by a
few make-out sessions.

A few weeks before the conference, she texted me to say that she
had booked a room in the hotel that was hosting the fundraiser.

You're welcome to join me there, she wrote.

I already have a room at the conference hotel, I said. *And I've decided
to spend three months celibate.* Embarrassment washed over me, yet
again, as I sent the text. This announcement seemed less offensive
than reminding her that our affair was over, but only nominally less
horrible overall.

Okay, she responded. *Good luck.* It was possible to infer any number of things from this response and I considered them all, which left me feeling indignant and self-loathing.

She was a fellow writer whom I'd met in a professional setting. I had instantly developed a crush on her, though it was less sexual than intellectual, which is often the way my crushes began. She was attractive, with dark hair and soulful eyes, though not my type. Her mind was my type: sharp and ruminative, laced with wry humor. The kind of person whom it thrills me to make laugh. The desire to impress smart women has always been an aphrodisiac.

During our first conversation, I tried hard to shine. A few weeks later, I invited her to lunch. I did not consider my intentions, whether I had invited her to lunch in order to woo her as a friend or a lover. I simply wanted to see her again. I didn't always know in the early flush of liking someone if I wanted to kiss them or not. Maybe it would have been possible to discern this if I had tried, but I did not.

We lunched at a little Mediterranean place in the West Village and ate fresh yeasty pita with hummus, and dolmas that gleamed with olive oil and left a green pool on the white plate. We laughed a lot and had already begun teasing each other a bit by the meal's end. As we said goodbye on the sidewalk, she leaned in and kissed me. I was surprised by this and, I can see now, disappointed. The kiss instantly revealed to me that I had only wanted to flirt, in the way of new friends. I could have stopped her that day outside the restaurant and explained that I just wanted to be friends, but I had never said that to someone whom I liked as much as I liked her. There seemed only one way forward.

There was real chemistry between us, and so our texts were excellent. I did not restrain myself and our titillating banter soon punctuated whole days. It was a familiar pattern, or part of a pattern: the daylong distraction of our correspondence, the thrill of intimacy's advancement. Her wit sped my pulse, but when we saw each other again, our mouths didn't carry the same charge. As my pleasure in our physical interactions diverged from my pleasure in our correspondence, my anxiety grew. *Why not just stop?* I wondered later with frustration. I had all of the information and still I trundled toward that visible end. I was in a kind of trance, which would be a more sympathetic explanation if it hadn't been happening for twenty years.

A few days before the conference, she texted me again about the hotel room. A mixture of annoyance and fear swirled in me that she had seemed not to take my vow of celibacy seriously. I wondered if I would take myself seriously in this regard were I her, or anyone, and knew that I would not.

As my cab drove from LAX into the city, the sunshine evaporated my melancholy and replaced it with hope. For a few days I ate avocado at every meal and relished not flirting with anyone. It turned out that I enjoyed parties celibate as much as I did when there was the prospect of romantic attention, but not for as long. Staying in a hotel room alone was delicious and every night I hurried back to luxuriate in the crisp white sheets and cable channels, paid for by my university.

On the final night of the conference, the fundraiser was plagued by mishaps but the DJ was good and I danced until my feet throbbed. I had stayed busy all evening, but clocked the presence of the last woman I kissed, especially as the crowd thinned. At the end of the night, she was one of the few attendees who remained to help us clean up. As we cleared half-empty Solo cups from the tables, she leaned her shoulder into mine.

"Come back to the room," she whispered, and I saw how drunk she was. I shook my head and crossed the room to tie up the trash bags that hulked against the wall. Still, she stayed. We both lingered, along with a few others, until all of the chairs were folded and stacked, the trash bags lugged into the service elevator, and the floor swept. The last of us crowded into the elevator. My chest buzzed with fear that she would ask again in front of my colleagues, or make a scene when I did not follow her out of the elevator. I desperately wanted to avoid embarrassing either of us, so, though this now sounds insane even to me, when the elevator shuddered to a stop and the doors opened, she glanced at me and I followed her out. The dramatic irony is stunning in hindsight. I had so many opportunities to interrupt our progression: in the elevator, in the hallway, at the door of the room, that I chose instead to enter and watch her close the door. The room was dark and warm, a rumpled bed in the floor's center.

"Stay," she said, and reached for me.

"I can't stay," I said, and backed away.

"Stay," she said. She reached out and pressed her fingers to the side of my neck, attempting to draw me toward her.

I turned my head. "I need to go," I said. Still, I did not leave. Against reason, I stayed because I wanted her permission to go. I knew it would not come and still I waited.

"I just want to make you feel good," she pleaded, and her pleading was unbearable. It was an enactment of my worst fear. I knew that there was such a desperate and pleading part of me, that maybe it was the most honest part of me. It had gotten me here, somehow, and would not let me leave. I had done such a good job of avoiding her, this desperate woman locked in the far attic of me, every time but once. The memory of that exception filled me then, the sick feeling of that time when I had pleaded and begged and raged and humiliated myself with no apparent limit, a thousand times worse than the woman in that hotel room.

In its dark, the walls felt so close, suddenly. They pressed in on us like a shrinking box, inched me closer and closer to her, to that mirror that bore the most fearsome part of me. Terror and pity knocked together, vying for control. I wanted to apologize, to fall on my knees and beg forgiveness. I did not wish that desperation on anyone, least of all a woman that I respected, whom I had wanted so much to care for me, but not like this. I did not want to kiss her, but feared that I would if she did not stop begging, if only to make her stop.

"I need to go," I said, and it was almost a whisper.

She stood between me and the door then, the door that was also begging, I who was also begging, silently, *Don't make me push you aside.* I hated the thought of her waking to remember my hands pushing her aside. I would rather have suffered a mortification of the flesh than wake to such a memory, or ask anyone I cared for to wake up to such a memory, and I knew that the alternative was also a kind of mortification, a submission to something that would hurt me, not the lash of flagellation, but the lash that drove me farther from myself, that kept my body like a work animal who slept in a barn behind the house of my mind by treating it as such, an animal I could force my will upon. It was mercy to it over mercy to her, and I was heartbroken to choose myself.

As I shouldered her out of the way, I told myself that she was drunk and would not remember these final moments, and she didn't.

I barely remembered it myself, until I wrote a description of the scene in my inventory. I immediately recognized the experience as one in a long series of similar experiences that had begun with my earliest sexual encounters. This encounter had actually departed from the usual script, in which I stayed in the room and resolved the tension by sexually capitulating. Sometimes, I offered a sexual resolution before the other person even asked; a hint of their desire was enough for me to prioritize it over my own. There had often seemed only one way forward, whether I wanted it or not. This night marked the appearance of an alternate route, however hellish it had felt to choose it.

AFTER I RETURNED from Los Angeles, Ray and I went dancing at a club in our neighborhood. It was small and hot and played a lot of retro dancehall, my favorite music for dancing. Ray and I had perfected the art of dancing near but not *with* each other. The music we danced to was much too sexy for that. The space between us sometimes felt like a third body, the silhouette of how we *would* move together but instead moved around, drawing a picture of what we wouldn't do.

Afterward, we wandered around the neighborhood, sharing a liter of seltzer. The episode in Los Angeles had escalated my anxiety to its former intensity for a few days, during which I left the apartment only to teach and buy groceries. I ruminated on the obvious causal relationship between these events. I had not broken my celibacy, thank goodness, but it still felt like a kind of relapse. Dancing with Ray was a happy distraction.

As we made our way in the direction of my apartment, Ray told me that she had broken up with her Wyoming girlfriend. Their fighting ramped up after the girlfriend invited Canyon to Passover and not Ray. Finally exhausted, Ray had dumped her. The girlfriend showed up at the lab the next day with two pounds of Ray's favorite brand of dried mango.

"I think I had been so permissive in the relationship that she didn't take me seriously at first," Ray told me. "I tend to compromise and tolerate to a pretty far extent, and I did in that relationship. But when I get to done, I'm *done*. She hadn't seen me reach that point before."

I nodded, relieved that Ray was done with the Wyoming girlfriend. I understood that far place, how long it could take to get there and how irrefutable it was when I did.

I told her about my trip to L.A. and the incident with the last woman I kissed. "I didn't want to sleep with her," I told Ray, "and maybe I never even wanted to kiss her but couldn't tell the difference, because those means have been my most reliable route to closeness."

"Yeah, I get that," Ray said. "When I first started having sex with people, I think my relationship to relationships was my relationship to sex. And sex was something that I could get for myself, that I could, like, take from other people, too. It was all transactional. I was eating everything and everybody that I could."

This didn't fully characterize my relationship to sex, but I supposed, uncomfortably, that I had still taken something from my lovers: the emotional satisfaction of reeling them in and securing their attention. I thought of the flattened trances I used to fall into when I had binged on food or cocaine, which were equally devoid of self. The emptiness of gorging on something I did not actually want. The way that particular hunger was so *of* the body, but still dissociated from the body.

I thought of something my therapist once said: "You can't get enough of a thing you don't need." I had tugged at the riddle of its meaning for years, tested it against every kind of unhappiness. I couldn't get enough movie popcorn because it was terrible for me. I couldn't get enough money by overworking because I already had enough money. I could not get enough approval from a colleague whom I despised because I did not respect him. I couldn't get thin and fit enough because I still aspired to an absurd beauty ideal. I couldn't get enough attention from a woman I wasn't really attracted to because it wasn't romantic attention I sought. These desires were insatiable because no need could be met. Like fire, they grew when fed.

My relationship to love wasn't so simple, unfortunately. The pursuit of romantic love could be compulsive, but romance was also connected to something I did need: love. I wanted to change the compulsive aspects of my behavior but maintain that route to intimacy, reliance, partnership, and joy. The former thwarted the latter, but they were so entangled that I struggled to differentiate between them.

"Kind of empty, right?"

"Totally empty," Ray agreed. "I didn't have orgasms with other people for years and years."

"Me neither." Not for the first time, I felt repulsed by my orientation to the interests and esteem of others. I enjoyed sex most when my lovers seemed satisfied. There was nothing wrong with this except that I often failed to consider my own physical pleasure. That is, my satisfaction was almost entirely contingent on my partner's pleasure.

Years ago I had read about a study that found lesbians to have an outrageously greater number of orgasms during sex than heterosexual women. This gave me a self-satisfied zing of delight, as if I had given a correct answer on a game show. The reason offered for this was that women are socialized to be oriented to their partner's pleasure rather than their own. Reading this, my satisfaction dwindled. It was great that lesbians had co-opted the instinct for their own gain, however inadvertently, but still it depressed me to understand that we implicitly cultivated this instinct for men. Now, this interpretation seems overly simplistic. Lesbians aren't simply redirecting a conditioned instinct to please others. They genuinely find their lovers' pleasure arousing and unlike the typical straight male lover, they understand how often multiple orgasms are possible. My initial interpretation of the study seemed a likely symptom of my own compulsory efforts to satisfy the interests of parties I didn't care for.

"Hey, are you allowed to have orgasms during your celibacy?" Ray asked.

"I haven't decided yet."

She laughed. "Well you'd better soon, don't you think?"

In the days that followed, the long shadow of the night in that Los Angeles hotel room retreated, but I did not stop thinking about it. The interaction had stirred something in me much larger than the situation itself, which was not so unusual amid my personal history. The unusual part was that I had acted against that need to acquiesce to another's desire. It had been almost impossible. I had glimpsed how profoundly a proximity to another's wishes compromised me, tempted me to betray myself.

Had I always felt dread in the aftermath of such episodes? No. Sexual experiences that I acquiesced to in this manner were usually followed by a numb satisfaction, hardly an emotion at all. Whereas this feeling reminded me of the days after I watched a particularly haunting horror movie or read a disturbing book. It was right on the surface of me: a swirling oily fear.

By resisting my usual pattern and leaving that hotel room, I realized, I had made space for my own true emotions. It *was* frightening to confront the fact of one's own propensity for self-betrayal. It had been a narrow escape. The part of me who wanted to leave had only the thinnest advantage over that older instinct that compelled me to stay. This triumph implicitly revealed the countless incidents that preceded it, in which I *had* stayed. If leaving prompted such fear in me, then what feeling had staying prompted, all those other times? What backlog of horror was stored in my body, that I had not allowed myself to feel? It was no wonder that my "free-floating anxiety" had returned.

The link between these thoughts and the two years I'd recently spent in abject and relentless acquiescence could not have been more obvious. I recognized the connection, but looked away from it like a glowing doorway that I could not yet step toward.

T HOUGH I WAS fairly certain I was not a sex and love addict, I decided to attend a few recovery meetings to get further information. A part of me hoped to discover that I did qualify. It would be easier to have a single answer, to close the case and be prescribed a solution, a set of steps to follow.

Changing a fundamental part of one's lifestyle or outlook tends to pull the veil on unexamined beliefs, and deliberating over what to wear to my first meeting revealed my bias against femme fashion, as opposed to athleisure. I settled on a pair of joggers, a hoodie, and sneakers. My usual attire—form-fitting head-to-toe black and heels—seemed to evoke sex addict. As if hewing to a beauty standard that objectified women's sexuality signified something rapacious about the wearer's own relationship to sex? God forbid the people in the meeting mistake me for someone who belonged there.

I had often envied women who wore sneakers every day. I wondered if I'd be doing so, too, by the end of my celibacy. The prospect both excited and scared me. How much of what I considered my personality—"clothes look better on me with heels"—were symptoms of my orientation to the perceptions of others in general and potential lovers in particular? The answer to this was not yet clear, but already daunted me to contemplate.

.   .   .

On my way to the meeting, I got a text from a recent date. I hadn't had a great time with her, but still agreed when she suggested that we see each other again, partly because I found disagreeing disagreeable, especially when it could be postponed, and partly because I wasn't ready to eliminate the option yet. Hoarding romantic possibilities was an old and reliable source of comfort. It had begun to make new sense to me, as I wrote my list of lovers past. Hoarding is a symptom of fear, the fear of scarcity. When a comfort is fleeting, as that of romance was for me, it made sense to stockpile it. I thought once again of my old therapist's rueful assurance that I had enough hunger for love to fuel my ambitions.

I expected the recovery meeting to be attended by straight women who look like wrung-out dish towels and was surprised to find the cozy, wood-floored room in the back of the church full of vivacious women. Plenty of them wore all black and heels. They did not appear to have sold their souls to the god of heterosexual fetishism. A few even emitted a queer signal, though all were femme presenting. I sat in a folding metal chair with my Styrofoam cup of coffee, humbled by my presumptions.

The meeting's speaker, a white cis-woman in a blazer who was probably on her lunch break, spoke about never being single, getting off on being wanted by people she wasn't attracted to, having boyfriends she was ashamed to be seen with in public, and compulsively masturbating. She also referred to something called "rain checks," which, as far as I could tell, were when you kept a sexual or romantic option open, just in case, despite it being unappealing or inappropriate. "I always kept the back burner warm," she told us.

She spent the first year of her recovery totally free of dating, sex, flirting, and masturbation. This sounded extreme to me, although I remembered how in the early days of getting clean from heroin, total abstinence from all mind-altering chemical substances also seemed extreme. Sex and love lie in a less binary realm of addictions—

along with food, work, and codependency—whose objects cannot or should not be removed wholesale from one's life. Abstinence from these addictions is something that must be negotiated. After the speaker finished, she called on other attendees to share and I gathered from their contributions that every sex and love addict determined their own definition of abstinence based on their own particular set of troubling behaviors, though many chose, like her, to relinquish masturbation.

Despite my delight at being in a room of women willing to refer casually to their self-pleasure practices, my resistance was immediate. I had not even considered refraining from masturbation. It had never been a compulsive behavior, except perhaps during puberty. I wasn't interested in pathologizing healthy behaviors. I had decided to be celibate in an effort to simplify my life, not complicate it.

During the five-minute break halfway through the meeting, I smiled at the other women as I refilled my paper cup with watery coffee. I pulled out my phone and looked at the text from my former date and considered texting her back to explain that I was not interested. I considered telling her that I would be available in three months. Instead, I locked the screen and slid my phone into my pocket.

I mostly recognized when a behavior felt compulsive, when it had been sprinkled with the fairy dust of addiction. *Ecstasy* comes from the Greek *ekstasis*, "to be or stand outside oneself, a removal to elsewhere." At thirty-six, I knew when I was standing outside of myself. The ecstasy of orgasm was not that kind of ecstasy.

And yet, I was also in that room because I did not entirely trust my own perceptions. Compulsive behaviors are resilient, can bend perception for protection. A behavior that causes anxiety and also treats it can function like a psychological autoimmune disorder. Active addiction is a rationalization factory.

I could see how breaking the habit of issuing rain checks might be useful. I was even willing to consider that abstinence from flirting might be helpful for some. However, the idea of banning masturbation when it hadn't caused a problem stank of a little bit of what Foucault called "the hysterization of women's bodies," which is to say the deeply misogynistic practice of pathologizing women's sexuality such that it requires the medical interventions of men.

On the other hand, there were no men in that room.

When I got home from the meeting, I looked at the text from my date once more. Then I deleted it and blocked her number. Afterward, the empty feeling reminded me of turning off the television as a kid. As if all the light had momentarily been sucked out of the room. There was a flutter of terror. *What now?*

MY FIRST ORGASM was to the movie *Valley Girl,* starring Nicolas Cage, during which my grandmother lay asleep behind me on the sofa, but my first lover was the bathtub faucet. How did I even think to position myself under it, feet flat against the wall on either side of the hot and cold knobs? It wasn't a natural position; it was a natural inclination. After that, I experimented with all sorts of household objects and reading materials from *Valley of the Dolls* to *Rubyfruit Jungle.*

How comforting it was to learn, years later, of the "hydrotherapy" craze that took hold of European and North American bathhouses, beginning in the late eighteenth century. From Bath, England, to Saratoga Springs, doctors touted the water cure for the disease of hysteria, which had been literally plaguing women for centuries.

The word *hysteria* is derived from the Greek word for uterus, which Plato famously described as "the animal within the animal" and was believed to set out wandering around the body if it was deprived of a baby, drawn by powerful smells like a raccoon to garbage cans. Many men, from ancient Greeks to doctors who specialized in gynecology hundreds of years later, postulated that a bad case of Wandering Womb led to hysteria, that better-known affliction about which much has been written as far back as the fifth century BC.

Symptoms might include headaches, fatigue; any sort of melancholy, frustration, or anxiety; an excess or deficit of sexual interest with "an approved male partner"—basically, the expression of any response other than total contentment to the patriarchal structures that governed their lives or a failure to reinforce the androcentric model of sex that reigned (and still does).

Hydrotherapy most popularly featured a high-pressure shower or "douche" that massaged the pelvic region—sometimes in the exact configuration I discovered at eleven. According to an 1851 essay about an English spa by R. J. Lane, after treatment the patients often claimed to feel "as much elation and buoyancy of spirits, as if they had been drinking champagne." Common prescriptions suggested application of the water douche for four to five minutes, the same length of time in which researchers like Alfred Kinsey and Shere Hite later found most people able to achieve orgasm via manual masturbation.

Doctors of the nineteenth century claimed that more than 70 percent of women suffered from hysteria, thereby making it the pandemic of their time.

Despite my lack of neurosis around masturbation, I didn't get my first vibrator until my junior year of college, when a friend gifted me a pink Pocket Rocket. A bestseller for some forty years, it's the Toyota of vibrators: unglamorous, reliable, longitudinal. I used it for a decade, until its buzz grew so loud that it sounded like an actual Toyota in need of a new muffler, before sputtering out forever.

In my early twenties, my best friend and I lived in a series of Brooklyn apartments and shared a gargantuan vibrator that we christened "the Hammer of the Gods." It was roughly the size and shape of a human arm, hinged at the "elbow," with a blunt end where its hand would be. Whenever we felt moved, we shuffled into the other's room, unplugged it, and carried it to our own bedroom. We practically had to wear jeans when using it because the force of its vibration even on the lowest setting would otherwise render our genitals insensate.

The Hammer wasn't what either of us would've chosen (most likely a Hitachi Magic Wand, that more elegant powerhouse vibrator) but it had been a gift from a client at the dungeon where we both worked as professional dominatrices. That's where we met and where I learned how to talk freely about my own pleasure. When desire (or anything, really) becomes a perfunctory part of one's job, it's quickly shorn of whatever previous aura it carried. There's no room for the sacred or profane in shoptalk.

The gifting client would come in weekly for a session with his current favorite, moving on every month or so to a newer hire. His requests were predictable: he basically just wanted to get you off with a giant vibrator or to watch you do it yourself. It seemed like a good deal, getting paid seventy-five dollars an hour to be brought to orgasm, or to masturbate for a one-man audience whose opinion meant next to nothing.

Nonetheless, I only saw him once. I found it unbearable to be watched.

It makes sense that nineteenth-century men wanted the hysteria "solution" to be applicable only by them. They got to have it all: a model of ideal sex that served them alone in terms of pleasure and procreation, to medicalize women's pleasure, and to encourage women's dependence on them. This way, they could deprive women of the legitimate satisfactions of both social freedom and sexual pleasure, pathologize their reasonable response, and then charge them money for a modicum of temporary relief. What a coup, for men to convince us that being masturbated to orgasm in a clinical setting by them was a "cure" for the imaginary illness whose symptoms were our humanity, and that to masturbate ourselves (along with drinking coffee or alcohol, and a slew of other ordinary behaviors) was yet another cause of the illness.

How appropriate that George Taylor, who patented his steam-powered table vibrator in the late nineteenth century, called the cumbersome and expensive apparatus the "Manipulator."

Locked inside the bathroom as a teenager, hazy with steam and the sough of rushing water, I felt most alone. In the trance of orgasm, I forgot myself completely. I forgot the bath, the room, the house, the town—every context in which I understood myself. Without a self, a body is everywhere and nowhere at once. Pleasure becomes synesthetic, exploding like splattered paint across the sky of consciousness. It's a big bang of deafening thunder, the smell of lavender and salt.

"In this vision my soul, as God would have it, rises up high into the vault of heaven and into the changing sky and spreads itself out," wrote Hildegard von Bingen, the Benedictine abbess and mystic saint who had held my interest since those years when I first discovered erotic pleasure. My celibacy had led me back to her, and I remembered what had so enraptured me back then. I had no idea yet how important she would become to me.

Before Hildegard, my only impressions of nuns were gleaned from *The Sound of Music* and my father's frightening tales of Catholic school. While Hildegard may have embodied elements of both of these—her musical genius is still widely appreciated today and a cruel streak would have served her well—nowhere had I encountered an image of a nun so powerful as she. Hildegard was empowered in ways people recognized as masculine: politically, intellectually, scientifically, linguistically, and artistically, but she embodied these in a wholly feminine way. That is, her powers served only God, nature, and her community. She seemed to lack the colonizing impulse that accompanied such power in men. Above all, she was a visionary.

In her seventies, Hildegard described her lifelong visions in a letter: "The light which I see . . . is far, far brighter than a cloud which carries the sun. I can measure neither height, nor length, nor breadth in it; and I call it 'the reflection of the living Light.' And as the sun, the moon, and the stars appear in water, so writings, sermons, virtues, and certain human actions take form for me and gleam."

The aloneness of orgasm, the unbeingness of it, is similar in many ways to that of creation. When I am in the trance of creation, my self and its external contexts disappear, though sensation persists. The work becomes a mirror that reflects something other than the story of the self, something that disperses it to make room for a different kind of story.

Like that of most nuns, the goal of Hildegard von Bingen's celibacy was to relate to God. But God didn't assume human form. The only human forms in her abbey were other women, and she worked her whole life to make it so. At their inductions, she dressed them as brides in extravagant white silk, their hair flowing long and wild. She had passionate relationships with some, though allegedly she never had sex with anyone.

How then, did she write the first description of a female orgasm? How did she know the "sense of heat in her brain," or how "the woman's sexual organs contract, and all the parts that are ready to open up during the time of menstruation now close, in the same way as a strong man can hold something enclosed in his fist"?

It was hard for me to imagine that nuns like her did not give themselves pleasure. I had given myself orgasms without even touching myself, aided by only a pillow, or the force of my own mind. Perhaps they did not connect that phenomena with the misogynistic rhetoric of the church around women's sexuality that called it tantamount to evil. I liked to imagine they interpreted it as a holy gift, a vision, a fruit of devotion, the hand of God himself.

At the summer camp I attended as an adolescent, we played a game called Fishbowl, during which all of the girls would sit in a circle while the boys sat silently outside of it (in a following round, we would reverse positions). A female counselor would ask questions that the boys had submitted anonymously ahead of time. One of the questions the boys always asked was *What does a female orgasm feel like?*

Convulsion, we said.

A bright light flashing. A ripe persimmon, squeezed in a fist.

The mystics' writings supported my hope. Beguine Mechthild of Magdeburg writes of eating and drinking Christ in sensuous rapture, while beguine Agnes Blannbekin tells a bizarre story of conjuring the foreskin of Christ on her tongue and swallowing it, an act which wracks her whole body with orgasmic pleasure. She repeats it one hundred times. Catherine of Siena used Christ's foreskin as a ring when she wed him. Teresa of Ávila writes of an angel who "plunged [his] dart several times into my heart and that it reached deep within me. When he drew it out, I thought he was carrying off with him the deepest part of me; and he left me all on fire with great love of God. The pain was so great that it made me moan, and the sweetness this greatest pain caused me was so superabundant that there is no desire capable of taking it away."

Some of these descriptions read like straightforward erotica, Jesus fanfiction that is sometimes quite kinky and seemingly stripped of coy metaphors. Others, like those of von Bingen, seemed more like oneness with the world, a spiritual experience achieved through the body (as so many are).

The female mystics claimed a desire to *yield* to the divine, to disperse their selfhood into the universe. Superficially, these expressions appeared to reinforce a familiar edict for the feminine: to submit. But the mystic saints' descriptions of yielding often sounded nothing like submission. When the divine wrote through a person, her voice might more resemble that of a god than a supplicant. Artists find imaginative means of articulating our most stigmatized desires.

"I am the flame above the beauty in the fields," wrote von Bingen. "I shine in the waters; I burn in the sun, the moon, and the stars. And with the airy wind, I quicken all things vitally by an unseen, all-sustaining life."

The more I read about Hildegard and other women who lived in devotion to God and seclusion from men, the more I saw it as a harbor for ambition. Imagine a woman rich in talent, in possession of an exceptional mind, a woman who hungers for power and craves challenge. What hell for her to live in a society where nothing is expected of her, nor indeed allowed, but to breed and cook and clean and otherwise care for men who are her inferiors.

Hildegard claimed visions from early childhood, but no one particularly cared until she was forty. As soon as her direct line to God was recognized by men, she claimed that God had commanded her: "Make known the wonders you live, put them in writing, and speak."

In the High Middle Ages, women weren't allowed to write music in the church and certainly no one was interested in their ideas or stories, but Hildegard became one of the most powerful and prolific thinkers in history. She wrote copious religious and scientific texts, was an unparalleled composer and lyricist, and invented a secret language for her nuns to speak to one another. Her understanding of physical pleasure seems not to have hindered this, though entanglement with another person might have.

Perhaps the mystic nuns simply wanted to live freely among other women, to compose music and write and wear luxurious silks and let their hair flow freely. Proving an exceptional relationship to God was the single route to such freedoms. Yielding to the divine was the only way to avoid yielding to men.

I did not think a desire to be free precluded a relationship to the divine, or that either precluded erotic pleasure. The body was an instrument for all of these, but in every case, its retrieval from the possession of others seemed a first step.

As an adult, I had never been a light-candles-around-the-bathtub type of masturbator. I was more of an eat-a-bag-of-chips kind of masturbator. A procrasturbator. The most reliable time that I masturbated was in the early stages of writing something. It was a useful way to burn off the nervous energy of breaking ground on a new project, so that I could focus when I approached the page.

One definition of compulsion is *an act meant to relieve a mental obsession,* or some kind of distress. In that sense, my masturbatory practices qualified as compulsive. I was compelled by the anxiety of writing to watch a round of porn and have a handful of orgasms.

Despite my inclination to please, when lovers asked me to touch myself so they could watch, I always refused. I was shy, but that wasn't it. The prospect repelled me the way that client with the vibrator had. There was no performance to my self-pleasure and there was so much performance with lovers. Self-pleasure was the sole realm of true pleasure, unmediated or degraded by performance. To allow the gaze of a spectator to intrude upon that realm would have polluted it. It would have activated my internal spectator. Masturbating for a lover had more in common with sex work than with my private pleasure.

Unlike most other sex acts, I had never masturbated when I didn't want to. I had never followed a vibrator into a hotel room I did not want to visit. As a young person, self-pleasure seemed in direct opposition to my partnered experiences. Though I'd had plenty of orgasms with other people in my twenties and thirties, there was always an element of performance, of body consciousness, of other-orientation. The pleasure of a solitary orgasm did often feel like sunlight or thunder—elemental.

I'd had no internalized male gaze that directed my masturbation, and not because the activity was exempt from it; self-pleasure is a whole genre of porn, with copious subgenres. My masturbatory fantasies abounded with all sorts of hyper-patriarchal shit, but those images didn't dominate my consciousness or govern what I did with my body. This exemption was likely due to the fact that my practice of self-pleasure predated that of performance. It was a relationship I formed with myself before I ever formed a sexual relationship with another person. While I had built an image of myself out of others' esteem and others' desires, one that I monitored during sex with partners, I had another, truer self, that I could sense but not see, because I had not objectified her. I felt her in that private space, where there was no distance between the act and the self, the self and its image.

My need for celibacy had more to do with performance than it did with pleasure, I realized. I wanted to close the distance between that private self and the self I created in relationships, who was created by them. It was not physical lust that had compelled me from monogamous relationship to monogamous relationship. If my ceaseless entanglements were a result of the ways that I related to other people, then the goal of my celibacy was to relate to myself. The masturbatory me might serve as a kind of teacher, then. A reference point for pleasure without performance, for a self without a story.

A few days after the meeting, I decided that my celibacy would allow masturbation. My abstinence was about my relations with other people, not the expulsion or containment of desire. It was a space in which to tease apart the compulsive pursuit of "love" from real, sustaining forms of love. Sex with other people complicated that task. Sex with myself did not. Solitude could be sexy. In solitude, as in self-pleasure, the body opened. But if not to another, then to what?

That night I ran a bath. I dipped my body in the steaming water. As I lay submerged, the grit of salt beneath my thighs, breasts bobbing toward the surface, I listened to the hum of the refrigerator and the hiss of traffic in the distance. I watched my chest rise and fall with breath. I saw that most familiar hand, calling me home.

THE BOOK PARTY was in TriBeCa, the kind that's held in a private apartment whose owner is unclear, though it is clear that they are very rich. It was an unseasonably warm day, a harbinger of the scorching months to come. As I walked downtown from the train, I passed some Callery pear trees, *Pyrus calleryana*, which cover the city and when in bloom, smell unmistakably like semen. My body hummed with a seasonal kind of excitement. I had put on nice clothes and some makeup, and though I was not interested in semen, the Callery pear trees smelled of spring and possibility.

My friend publishing the book wore one of those dresses that looked like someone threw a beautiful piece of fabric at her from a distance and it landed on her body just right. I kissed her and shouldered my way across the loft, declining a stem of champagne and filling a paper napkin with cheese cubes. I did not recognize many of the attendees, but did spot a well-known lesbian in literary circles, who was at least twenty years my senior, seated on a pink sofa.

I parked myself on the other end of the sofa and when she struck up a conversation with me, something began to kindle. At first, eagerness warmed me from the inside. The interaction felt like a consummation of the excitement I'd felt walking to the party, under those blossoming trees. As we chatted about writers we knew in common and books, I imagined how it would feel to act on our lazy flirtation. I keenly felt the moment when my excitement at the chase would pivot into disappointment, because I was not truly attracted to my conversation partner.

As our talk bumped along, my listening face started to feel like a leering mask. The oil from the cheese slowly seeped through the napkin and slicked my fingers. The woman asked questions formulated to draw me out but did not absorb my answers, which beaded like rain on her glassy exterior.

It was the culmination of a pattern that had emerged over recent weeks. I had increasingly noticed when other people were on the make, chasing the high of another person. I had always been able to tell when someone who interested me was interested in me, but now I could detect their state of availability regardless of my own interest, or even theirs. I could tell if they were simply interested in being interested. I could locate that familiar radar from across a room, as if I'd developed an unpleasant sixth sense.

The *Pyrus calleryana* emits what is known as a "volatile amine" to attract pollinating insects, which are compelled by the scent of ammonia.

The woman smelled not of ammonia but of expensive cologne, and she was not across the room but leaning on her elbow next to me. Her gaze looked at me and through me at the same time. She was, as the etymology of *ecstasy* indicates, outside herself.

One of the early revelations of the past months had been that celibacy and ecstasy were not mutually exclusive. As there were plural celibacies, so there were plural ecstasies. The romantically interested person, the seeker of sexual intrigue, might be seen as embodying a form of Heideggerian ecstasy, wherein perception, or consciousness, is always split into subject and object. By Heidegger's measure, nearly everyone is in a state of ecstasy, and this "being-in-the-world," wherein all is subject or object, ought to be overcome.

The heightened ecstasy of the perceiver who objectifies with desire is something else. We have an amorous narrative for this state and hormonal explanations for the emotional component, though it was quickly becoming clear to me that a person in that state of intrigue or ecstasy was no more in love with their subject than a wolf in love with a rabbit, a grouse with an acorn, a junkie with the sudden taste at the back of her throat.

When I stripped away the great swells of feeling that obscured it, I could see how those habitually compelled by this ecstasy were almost robotic in their pursuit, like sex Roombas. Over the past three months I had observed this dynamic more often than I had participated in it, and I had come to understand that it was not a compliment to be pursued by a sex Roomba. The starkness of this fact disturbed me, as if I had suddenly recognized the smell of ammonia instead of heedlessly following it. As if I had just realized that money was nothing but paper.

Though excitement still fizzed in me on occasion when I encountered such people, the reality disappointed. The people I gravitated to, or would have were I not celibate, did not see me. They saw only a source of what promised to sate their hunger but never would. They were outside themselves, outside of the place where true empathy resides. Of course by *they* I also mean *me*, for most of my life. We had never been in this together; we had only each been alone in the same place, with the same goal.

Understanding this did not immunize me from further participation. If only self-knowledge induced change rather than insisted upon it. The desire to reconcile what I *knew* with what I *did* was emerging as primary motivation for my celibacy. It required more than abstinence.

As my inventory of lovers past progressed, it occurred to me that my survey might yield more insight if I exposed it to another set of eyes. I had also learned in recovery that committing my past actions to the page induced a more honest telling, but a witness further impeded my manipulation of the narrative. As a lifelong secret-keeper, confession had always appealed to me for cathartic purposes as well. On the rare Sundays during my childhood when my paternal grandmother took me with her to Mass, I had stared with longing at the confessional.

In my reading about Hildegard, I had learned something of the Benedictines. Like the beguines, their spiritual communities functioned upon principles of community, faith, and obedience, but they were formal Catholic orders and their monks and nuns took lifelong vows.

My father had taught me that religious people were sheep, yes, but also, as Robert Glück writes in his experimental novel, *Margery Kempe,* "When I was a child, belief attracted and repelled me, especially beliefs of Christian friends. Eating the body, drinking blood. Sexual sins whispered into hidden ears. The whacked-out saints, their fragmented corpses. Jesus nursing and the glorious fleshy ham." Like him, I found Catholicism the most erotic of the Christian traditions. It was so fetishistic, all that obsessive attention to the body of Jesus, mortification, the Eucharist (actual *transubstantiation*), Mariology and the Saints, and best of all, confession. Polarization is all tension, all eros. Guilt makes sex conflicted, and in my experience conflicted lovers are the most passionate in their yielding. The Catholic lovers I'd had were the most insane by far, but they were also sexual savants.

My reading about the Benedictines had led me to the work of Joan Chittister, a controversial icon in the world of contemporary Benedictine orders. The recipient of a master's from Notre Dame and a PhD from Penn State, she believed in abortion rights and had basically spent her career writing books about monastic life, spirituality, women's rights, and justice work that were intended for a readership beyond the church.

Every morning before my meditation and journal practice, I read a chapter from her classic text *The Monastery of the Heart.* Despite the fact that when friends came over I hid the book, whose cover looked exactly as you'd imagine a book of meditations by a Catholic nun would, it had proved surprisingly insightful. In the chapter on "Spiritual Direction and Counsel" she writes about mutual aid

and the importance of seeking guides who challenged us in loving but relentless ways. By identifying our spiritual directors, she
wrote, "we take our own soul into our hands . . . we become what
we choose."

I had always been driven by the desire to become what I chose.
I had dreamed of being a writer as a child and pursued that reality
with unwavering doggedness until I succeeded. I had wanted to be
a lover, too, for almost as long and with comparable commitment.
Hence, I found my perfect idol in Colette. In the way of most ambitions, I had never imagined the downsides of achieving my goal, only
the satisfaction. Now, I wanted to choose to become something else.

Chittister had cautions for the lazy seekers who "choose for
guides those who allow us to drift into nice, comfortable, secure,
superficial practices that promise quick fixes for the lack of genuine
spiritual life." She referred to "the complacent seeker" and, somehow most devastating, "the comfortable pilgrim," who "opens no
new or challenging paths that might challenge the self-proclaimed
guru around her." I did not want to be a comfortable pilgrim! I
wanted to be a rigorous pilgrim.

I decided that upon completion I would read my inventory to
someone else. A kind of "spiritual director." Someone I had known
for a long time. I had met them ten years ago and immediately
developed a crush. They were beautiful, with long dreads and a
raspy voice, quick to laugh. Over time, as I got to know them
through our shared community, my crush mellowed and the admiration remained. In the wake of that devastating relationship, I
had sought them out for guidance and we grew closer. I still felt
nervous around them because I wanted them to like me and because they told the truth more directly than most people. They
were a person whose integrity seemed to permeate every corner
of their life, which was why I had pursued their mentorship. They
were a fellow academic, though in another field, and, as Chittister
recommended, "someone whose life has been lived with love and
justice."

In many ways the same could be said of me. At more than ten years sober, I moved through most of my life with integrity. I knew that my comportment in love was under par, but believed my mistakes ordinary and my intentions good. I had been a loving partner to many and never, really, a scoundrel. I would be the first to admit that I was a passionate person, which came with some amount of drama, but wasn't that also a good thing? The dread that had driven me into celibacy, with its hissing undercurrent of shame, suggested different. I knew that if I wanted to be free, I needed to face it.

A S I WORKED my way back in time, the next person on my list was an age-appropriate music producer whom I'd dated for four months. I met the producer at the lesbian bar next to her studio in the West Village. She often worked throughout the night and would sometimes break to have a drink at the bar before it closed. I was dancing a lot at the time. Multiple nights per week, Ray and I would go out at 11 p.m. and dance until 2 a.m. I was still giddy with relief after the agony of that wretched two-year relationship, which had ended in time for the whole summer to feel like an enchantment: the heat luscious, time gone soft, my thoughts stunned and shallow after the shock of that harrowing.

The producer was beautiful, with golden eyes and long muscled arms. She had studied philosophy in college and played music on the side. She was kind, suspicious of money, and believed in ghosts. She also smoked weed and cigarettes every day and drank a fair amount of alcohol. She lived with a roommate and a gorgeous Persian cat who liked to sleep on her head and sometimes mine. There was often a punitive pile of cat shit waiting on the producer's bedroom floor when she arrived home in the early hours of morning.

Almost every time we had sex, I got a vaginal infection. When I started wanting to break up with her, the infections felt like a sign of our incompatibility. It was true that we were not compatible, but due to our divergent lifestyles, not some allergy of our bodies. The infections were more likely a symptom of the scented hand soap in her bathroom.

The first time I tried to break up with her, I couldn't bear how sad she looked. I backpedaled and said we should just spend less time together. A few weeks later, I suggested that we spend even less time together. A few weeks later, I floated the idea that we open the relationship. When I finally suggested for the second time that we end things, she squinted at me.

"You're terrible at this, huh?" she said. "Breaking up with people."

"Yes," I said morosely. "This was actually one of my most successful attempts."

I had stayed in some relationships for months and months after I knew I wanted to leave, until eventually I became attracted to someone else and kissed them. Of course, people in committed relationships are often attracted to other people. It doesn't necessarily mean that a breakup is imminent, or that kissing is, though in my case it usually did. I tried to will myself to remain in relationships beyond this point, but eventually my body would revolt. I never stayed past the first kiss—I don't have the constitution for a protracted affair— but also rarely had the guts or gumption to end my relationships without the imperative of infidelity. I am not proud of this, though I recognize that I have been conditioned by a history that stretches back centuries.

I was not bound to any lover by the thirteenth-century common law of "coverture," which persisted throughout the eighteenth and nineteenth centuries, in which marriage essentially erased a woman's sole legal identity, so that her rights and property were *covered* by her husband's. Breaking up with lovers would not render me destitute nor a social exile, but it sometimes felt that way, as if the stakes were inexplicably high. I would grapple for a rational estimation of loss to explain my dread, but there was none.

We laugh so often together! I might offer to my therapist or friends.

The implicit fear being that I might never laugh that way again. I feared this every time, regardless of the fact that I had always laughed with my lovers; I was a mirthful person, a joker. But how else to explain the terrible fear of leaving them? The specter of a commensurate loss must be somewhere, I reasoned. It did exist, but beyond the scope of my own life. It was less than one hundred years before my birth that women were allowed to remain legal entities after marriage and could avoid losing everything in a breakup. Sex beyond marriage guaranteed social ruination, and divorce was all but unheard of until the mid-nineteenth century, and even then it was exceedingly difficult for a woman to justify. While a wife's adultery was adequate reason for a man to divorce her, she must prove bigamy, incest, cruelty, or desertion in addition to adultery.

I had long known this history, seen the frothy period films that romanticize it and the tragedies inherent, just as I know my feminist history. Still, when I looked at the effort I'd devoted to justifying my desire to end relationships of a few months, my belief that I needed justification beyond my own desire to leave, I had to factor in the stakes of the past.

Perhaps even more compelling and difficult to prize out of one's consciousness is the narrative that accompanied the idea of marital love. Heralded by Jane Austen's novels, published at the threshold of the Victorian period, wifedom and motherhood were considered, in addition to the primary route to financial stability, the path to personal fulfillment and self-actualization. The combination of these imperatives, while no longer concretely viable for many of us, persists in an insidious legacy that had unexpectedly affected my queer relationships. Like Kelli María Korducki, I had "long suspected that women subconsciously accept some version of the belief that we're supposed to want secure romantic relationships more than anything in the world." Pair this prescription with my attraction to people who were unlikely to ever leave me and you have a recipe for agonized breakups.

.   .   .

The desire for internal change had spurred me on a campaign of external change, that convenient proxy. I had purchased a glorious and impractical white shag rug and a new bedframe.

Waking alone was one of the principal pleasures of celibacy. Every morning, I stretched my limbs out until I was eagle spread, then made sheet angels on the white cotton. There was no one to text who would be mad that I hadn't responded. Sometimes I ignored my phone for hours after waking.

Now that it was mine alone, I was becoming something of a bed fetishist. I had replaced the pillows and sheets, and ordered a new mattress. It arrived compressed in a box and when freed, swelled like a sponge until it covered the floor. Unfortunately, the bedframe required assembly and its instructions indicated that my new independence would not serve me in this task.

The producer and I remained on good terms after our breakup, so, six weeks into my celibacy, I asked if I could buy her lunch in exchange for help. She gamely agreed.

The bedframe was from IKEA and turned out to be missing an important screw. The slat apparatus was confoundingly complex. As we sweated, crouched over the motley picnic of parts, a special fury begin to rise in me, the one reserved exclusively for technical frustrations and being awoken from the brink of sleep. The producer maintained her cool—she was probably high—and sensibly suggested that we find a replacement screw. We walked to three hardware stores in the rain to find one of the correct approximate length. It took the whole afternoon with a break for pizza. Indeed, we laughed just as hard as we ever had while dating.

When we finished, I paid for her cab to the studio by the lesbian bar. As we hugged goodbye, she leaned in to kiss me on the mouth. I turned my head and her lips met my cheek. I returned the kiss to her cheek, as if that had been the intention.

Alone again, I lay on my new bed, tacky with dried sweat, ecstatically alone. In the lesbian Olympic games, peacefully assembling IKEA furniture with missing screws on a team with your ex would be an advanced category, and we would have medaled.

I was still riding high on this triumph when I met Nora for dinner a few hours later. She had finished her dissertation and we were celebrating her graduation. I kept asking about her new job and when she'd relocate to live near the new campus, but all she could think about was her girlfriend. They had graduated from the sublimity of infatuation to a rapidly alternating hot-and-cold cycle. At the moment, it was cold. Nora barely touched her celebratory charred brussels sprouts. Her eyes still glittered, but her focus had narrowed.

The week previous, Nora's family had traveled east to attend her graduation commencement. Experience had already taught her that combining her girlfriend with any other people she was close to yielded disastrous results. After agonizing over the issue, Nora had decided to protect that special day from the inevitable strife and chosen not to invite her girlfriend. It was an act of bravery and a grave underestimation.

The lawyer was furious and easily contrived a way to monopolize Nora's attention even in absentia. While Nora was at the ceremony, her girlfriend broke up with her in an avalanche of furious text messages. My friend spent the entire day drenching her regalia in cold sweat, feverishly typing on her phone in response to the onslaught of messages. She still remembers nothing else about that day, not the time with her family or the ceremony or the weather, only the gripping terror of abandonment, the device in her hand like a glowing portal to hell. Almost immediately afterward, when Nora had promised never to shut her out again, they reconciled.

I felt sick inside at this story, but chose my words carefully. "I know that kind of toggling," I told her. "The hot end is *hot*. Really mind-blowing sex." I saw the glimmer of recognition in her face. "But the cold end? Torment. It blots everything else out." I speared a sprout from her plate and popped it into my mouth theatrically. "It's the most alone I've ever felt," I said with an ironic smile.

She gave a surprised laugh and nodded. I'd embarrassed her a little, not because I'd brought up sex or divulged something private about myself, but because I had named something that felt so private, understood it with such little information that it suggested an ordinariness to what felt exceptional. We think of reinventing the wheel as drudgery, but it can as often feel like alchemy. Our ecstasy is so intense, we think, it *must* be unprecedented. A sort of wound from which no one has ever bled before.

The rest of that week, I kept returning to our conversation. I'd joked about that kind of ecstasy leading to "the most alone I'd ever felt." The joke was for my benefit, not hers. I had been writing my list in reverse chronological order, working my way into the past, and I had arrived at the place I least wanted to revisit. The maelstrom in which I had felt most alone. That story was no comedy, though it was rich in irony.

I spotted the glitter of Nora's eyes and narrowing of her focus, because, like the symptoms of a known illness, I intimately recognized them. I who had always felt so safe with adoring lovers, whose skin crawled at the prospect of feeling, or, worse yet, acting *needy*. Even in my most paranoid fantasies over the years, I had never imagined the depths of abjection my limerence would lead to. I dreaded facing them again.

My lover in the maelstrom had been tall with a dark curtain of hair and an agile mouth. We met on the heels of the years I'd spent helping my Best Ex navigate her illness. I was ready to leave, but it seemed too cruel an ending after our ordeal. Enter this charismatic woman who sent me flowers and fruit and poetic emails. I lost myself instantly.

I had described that affair in my forthcoming book, yes, but in doing so I'd had the mediator of aesthetics, of my own intellect. I'd had the specter of an audience. These elements had made me more honest, not less, but they also encouraged a degree of composure that my list did not require. The writer of a memoir is both the director and a character in her play, and thus enjoys refuge outside of its narrative. An author is the god of their story and must sustain the long view, the cool curatorial eye. I wanted my art to be beautiful, even when it described something ugly.

Inventorying my past, on the other hand, was a wholly subjective experience. My list was for no audience beyond myself and my spiritual director, who placed zero value on its aesthetics. The point was to ferret out the deepest buried bits of truth and I had no reason to curate or temper them with beauty, or to distance myself with objectivity. There would be no such refuge.

What transpired between my lover and me brought out the ugliest parts of each of us. I became my worst nightmare: a desperate, pleading woman who would have traded everything she valued for the fleeting comfort of another's affection. Who almost did just that.

Let's say that there are three kinds of ecstasy, though, of course, there are many more. Physical ecstasy, as in an orgasm. Mental ecstasy, as in the particular arrangement of brain chemicals (serotonin, dopamine, oxytocin, adrenaline) that produce a high. And spiritual ecstasy, which is primarily the ecstasy of self-forgetting, a total engrossment and devotion to something other than the self. I would categorize the total self-forgetting that can sometimes result from both dancing and writing under spiritual ecstasy, as did Aristotle.

"Perfect joy excludes even the very feeling of joy," writes Simone Weil, "for in the soul filled by the object no corner is left for seeing 'I.'" There is no corner left for seeing *I* in the mesmeric hypnosis of a toxic relationship, either. I hesitate to call that thrall a form of ecstasy, but it bears elements in common with all three of these definitions. It is a divergent strain, however, induced partly by the will and charisma of a person who wants to control another, and partly by the complicit aspects of the self. Like a drug, this ecstasy mimics the experience of true spiritual ecstasy, but it is poison. It draws from a well whose debt must be paid in suffering. I wonder how many of us who have been captive to this thrall share the hedonistic nature I recognized in Nora and myself. It is so much easier to control a person with enormous appetites. Scholars of limerence might postulate that we had early attachment trauma, or suffer from a genetic predisposition due to low serotonin levels. Either way, like a dog, or a rat, we are easily motivated by manipulation of the "food" source. We will stalk the source of our suffering with a fanatic's devotion.

Though I had been in the thrall of substances, had even used people like substances, I had never felt more disempowered than I did in that maelstrom. If all those years of feeling coerced by the desires of other people had stocked a backlog of horror in my body, then those two years were its culmination. I did not want to face it, but I knew that I must.

Though I avoided roller coasters, I did like being scared under the right circumstances. I'd always had a taste for well-written mysteries. Even as a child I had a sticky imagination and couldn't tolerate disturbing images, but made exceptions for the right mystery or BBC crime drama. My criteria insisted that they feature a female detective, tough and smart, but vulnerable in her own way; my favorite heroines all had a well-defined Achilles' heel. The crimes they solved couldn't be too horrific, preferably just a single murder. When a story hit the spot, it disembodied me in the most pleasurable way. I sat in a trance, waiting for my heroine to solve the puzzle, riveted and relieved of my own consciousness.

As I contemplated the backlog of bad feeling that I'd amassed over the years, I wondered if it wasn't the key to this pleasure. A mystery was a contained space in which I could vent my own horror—an Aristotelian sort of catharsis. The mysteries I chose offered a formula in which the enigma always found its resolution, and the female protagonist prevailed. Perhaps absorbing these narratives was yet another way I'd found to make one form of work stand in the place of another, harder kind. Perhaps it was another canny method of topping off my serotonin stores.

I would not categorize the pleasure of watching television among the ecstasies, though it is a form of standing outside oneself. In the early weeks of my celibacy, I indulged in long hours of police procedurals, but also well-written dramas and romantic comedies. A few months in, however, I struggled to stay interested in these favorite distractions.

Had the stories available for our entertainment always centered the overwhelmingly heterosexual romances and tragedies of marriage and parenthood? Even when the outlier show that featured a queer character as more than a gossipy sidekick or a punch line managed to get produced, it seemed almost exclusively concerned with the dating and sexual travails of that queer character, often in a mode dynamically indistinguishable from its heterosexual counterpart.

I scrolled through the infinite offerings and watched trailer after trailer. It was difficult to find a single show about a woman without children or a partner who wasn't obsessed with obtaining either of these things.

"As long as she thinks of a man," wrote Virginia Woolf, "nobody objects to a woman thinking." Her father allowed more room for her thinking than many late-nineteenth-century fathers, but only enough to realize how little she had, how constrained she was not only by her patriarchal society but also by the patriarch in her life. He died when he was seventy-two and Virginia twenty-two, and she imagined that if he had lived longer, "his life would have entirely ended mine . . . No writing, no books;—inconceivable." Still, his figure dominated her early works and journals, asserting itself at the center of her consciousness as he had when alive.

I was interested in the way that thinking of a man, or any person, can dictate not only the course of one's life, but also that of one's art. Liberation of the mind was essential to the liberation of one's art. I

supposed my growing cognizance of the television's myopic offerings and the attendant frustration were signs of my liberating mind,
but I had hoped that liberation would feel, well, more *liberating*.
Sometimes, it felt merely annoying.

·At forty, while her interest in friendship grew increasingly compelling, Virginia Woolf wrote to a friend that "*sexual* relations bore
me more than they used to . . . I have come to the conclusion that
love is a disease; a frenzy; an epidemic; oh but how dull, how monotonous, and reducing its young men and women to what abysses of
mediocrity!"

Of course, the stories of women had most often revolved around
men, marriage, and motherhood. It just hadn't bothered me this
much before. It hadn't bored me this much before. I had been able
to enjoy a wide assortment of treacly dramas, or sharp-witted and
predictable comedies, the way I was able to enjoy a delicious but
unnourishing snack, and with a similar voraciousness. *You can't get
enough of a thing you don't need.* There was pleasure in indulging the
entertainments I had been conditioned to absorb. Reinforcement is
more comfortable than subversion. I had always seen these as guilty
pleasures, a category of treat. But now, my abstinence from lived
romance was rendering me increasingly unable to forget that the
narratives I consumed reinforced the very things I hoped to expunge
from my mind. I could no longer enjoy what was making me sick.

When I was a dominatrix in my twenties, I used to enjoy indulging in celebrity tabloids. Before then, I'd dismissed such rags with
a sneer, but my colleagues left them discarded around our dressing
room, like slippery portals into a world where the diets of strangers
constituted headlines and only a tiny fraction of the female popula-
tion seemed to age beyond thirty-five, and eventually I succumbed.

After I quit sex work, I could not stomach paying for these
magazines, but still relished scavenging them among the free reading materials at the gym. I would climb the towering escalator to
nowhere while flipping mindlessly through comparisons of emaci-

ated starlets' abdomens. Who wore it better? Who had lost her man to a younger, more emaciated woman? Who had dared don a swimsuit after gaining five pounds? When I think back on this time, it feels like a memory of drinking poison.

I had always thought that I simply trailed off reading these tabloids, or maybe aged out of them, but it occurred to me that I stopped reading them at the same time that I stopped dating men.

Two months into my celibacy, *Vera* was one of the few shows I could tolerate. The long-running British crime series is adapted from crime novelist Ann Cleeves's books and stars the superb Brenda Blethyn as DCI Vera Stanhope, a curmudgeonly detective in her sixties who dresses like Paddington Bear. Vera lives a solitary lifestyle and probably qualifies as workaholic. She is happy, though, or as happy as she's capable of being, and that seems to disqualify her for a diagnosis of addict. A problem that doesn't cause suffering is no problem at all.

Vera seems not to have sexual interest in anyone. Her passions are for solving murders and eating biscuits. She is fat, charismatic, brilliant, disheveled, sometimes aggressive with her colleagues, intolerant of sentimentality and bullshit equally, and prefers to have a young male sergeant to boss around. She never expresses regret about not having children, in whom she is wholly uninterested but not unsympathetic toward. Now in its thirteenth season, each episode draws upwards of eight million viewers in the UK. Vera is beloved. She was one of the few examples I could find of shows with a female lead whose main preoccupation isn't men. All of the shows were about female investigators.

As long as she thought about murder, nobody objected to a woman thinking.

NEAR THE TEN-WEEK MARK, my anxiety was on the rise again and I knew it was a symptom of avoidance. It was time to get back to my list.

I packed the notebook in which I was transcribing my history of love and drove up to the Hudson Valley to stay with a friend. I hadn't seen this friend since I ended the two-year relationship that had overtaken my life. I called it a *maelstrom* because the experience was less like sinking into an *abyss of mediocrity* than being sucked into a powerful vortex. It represented such a radical departure from all my previous romantic experiences that no analogy seemed dramatic enough. "The Maelstrom" feels appropriately ominous.

The beginning of the affair was intoxicating. My lover was prone to grand gestures and expensive gifts, and I might have clocked these as warning signs had I not been so stoned on eros. My lover lived with another woman four thousand miles away. The first time I voiced ambivalence about our affair, she retreated so suddenly that I reeled. I was already hooked. I learned not to object, that the price of her adoration was complacency. In the early months, our time together consisted mostly of ravenous sex punctuated by romantic proclamations. It was thrilling to lose control so instantly, like a ride at the fair. But soon, the wild motions made me sick. I struggled to maintain other relationships, my work, my purchase on reality. No one wants to live on a ride at the fair, what torture. My life became smaller every day, until she filled it completely.

I had been avoiding the fact that I was still shaken. Over the first ten years of my sobriety, I had become a happy person, and, moreover, one who felt safe under my own care. Each year, the self-betrayal and abasement that addiction had brought seemed increasingly remote. Then I was sucked into the Maelstrom. Like a faithful companion who had committed a sudden act of violence, I had become untrustworthy to myself. My moods were riddled with the unease of someone under the care of an erratic guardian.

As I drove upstate, the traffic of the Bronx and Westchester gave way to dark conifers and unbidden memories of the last time I had traveled that route.

Edgar Allan Poe's 1841 short story "A Descent into the Maelström" is a story within a story, told by a tour guide at a Norwegian mountain peak. On a fishing trip with his brothers, the narrator explains, his boat was swept by a hurricane into a voracious whirlpool. One of his brothers was swept out to sea and drowned, and the other went mad at the sight of it.

The guide witnessed the vortex first as an abominable monster, then as a sublime creation. Observing the movement of the maelstrom's pull on different objects, he clung to a barrel and eventually was rescued. He explains to his audience that while he looks aged, with white hair and a haggard face, he is not old but was instantly transformed by the ordeal.

It was this story that introduced the word *maelstrom* into the English language. Poe based his Maelstrom on the Moskstraumen, a famous system of whirlpools in the Lofoten archipelago, off the coast of Norway, exceptional for its occurrence in the open sea.

I was shocked to find myself captive in such a maelstrom at thirty-two years old; its occurrence would have made more sense during the direr straits of my twenties, when I was already caught in a downward spiral of addiction. But like the Moskstraumen, whose odd location is due to a configuration of tides, local winds, and underwater topographies, my Maelstrom was presaged by the invisible topographies of my early life and precipitated by a series of local events that rendered me vulnerable to a powerful and unlikely phenomenon.

Six months after my escape, it was easy to personify that relationship as an abominable monster—not my lover nor myself but the centripetal force activated by our merging. This third thing had never enacted so fiercely in me before her, and has never since. I was terrified by my own desperation, my sudden willingness to beg. Still, I plunged ahead like a woman under a spell, more awake and more determined than I had ever been in my addiction to chemical substances. As Nicky Hayes writes of extended limerences: "It is the unobtainable nature of the goal which makes the feeling so powerful."

Now, at some years' distance, I can see with a more passive astonishment the magnitude of that power, the psychic physics that sprang a tornado in me. I know not to take any aspect of myself for granted. That vicious potential still resides in me and I revere it, as some people do their gods or volcanoes, in hope that it will keep its peace. But during my celibacy, I had no foresight of this. I had barely admitted to myself the wreckage.

As I drove to visit my friend whom I had not seen since the Maelstrom, the confident ease I'd begun to feel over the last month seeped away. I clenched the steering wheel and remembered sobbing so hard along the same highway that I had hyperventilated. I had cried incessantly during the Maelstrom, as if my body believed I could flush the spirit that possessed me out of those tiny ducts. For months after our breakup I'd still felt captive in it, frail as a sapling stripped by the wind. My hands had been damp for the entire two years and stayed wet throughout those early months of aftermath; I was surprised my own fingerprints remained. I had undergone fits of trembling while we were together, and six months out from our breakup I had still blanched at the sight of her name. As my car wound north, I felt my palms grow slick on the wheel. My body began to tremble, again, with retroactive fear, the harrowed sense of what I had survived. I could have died the last time I drove this road. I had been mad with pain.

As I passed through pastures dotted with grazing cows, I drew slow breaths and reminded myself that though I felt like Poe's guide at the summit—my hair gone white, my nerves ruined—I had survived it. I was in the process of restoration. I supposed, though, that one doesn't *restore* a house that has been demolished or burned to its foundation; one rebuilds. And if that annihilation is even partly due to some flaw in design, one does not rebuild in the shape of that ruined structure, but draws a new one.

As I neared my destination, this retrospective terror gave way to shame. This friend had last seen me in a sorry state. She probably remembered better than I did. A friend who has seen you in the throes of a maelstrom is similar to those who saw you at your addicted bottom. They have witnessed your worst, your most powerless. They have seen you in ways that you could not see yourself. This dynamic is the foundation of so much humiliation and intimacy. The same principle of vulnerability renders the back of the neck and knee erotic.

Once I heard someone say in a recovery meeting that an alcoholic would rather die than be embarrassed. I don't think it is only alcoholics, though we do have more to be embarrassed about. Aversion to embarrassment makes it incredibly hard to be vulnerable, and avoidance of vulnerability robs us of true connection with other people, the deep comforts of being known and receiving love.

I felt shy to see my friend as I pulled into her long driveway, but warmed at the sight of her familiar impish face. She had been my professor in graduate school and seemed not to have aged in the years since. After she made us mugs of tea, we sat on her porch and watched the light fade through the trees that surrounded her property. I was grateful for her gentleness when we revisited the past. She confirmed my insanity in the kindest of terms.

"You were . . . not yourself," she said carefully, staring out across her lawn where the fireflies had begun to blink.

When I thought of my last visit to her rambling, toy-strewn house, it was like remembering a bad dream or a horror movie: a madwoman careening around the curves of the Taconic Parkway, eyes flashing but empty—those of someone possessed by a demon.

The last time I had visited my friend upstate, my girlfriend had picked a fight with me just before I departed. Most times that I tried to spend alone with someone other than her went disastrously. My lover responded to her exclusion from these meetings as the lawyer had to her exclusion from Nora's graduation. I always ended up focused on her instead of the person I had meant to see. I ended up apologizing, without really knowing for what.

I didn't remember what her complaint had been that particular night—I never could, they were ephemeral as dreams—but I remembered the terrible drive north. I arrived in pieces and tried to explain my distress to my friend. Even through my haze I recognized what little sense she could make of my explanation. It was impossible to describe the Maelstrom to those outside of it, like trying to hold a pocketful of water. I remembered my effort to act *normal*, to play with her child and stay off my phone. I went to the bathroom every ten minutes and typed furiously, sweat drenching my chest and hands. I must have looked like a junkie with the shakes. By the time I went to bed in her guest room, my lover had stonewalled me. I wept myself to sleep, soaking the pillow, and woke with a salt-swollen face. We are taught that obsession is romantic, but at its far reaches it is not. It is hell.

That night, I tucked into the same bed that I had soaked with tears hardly more than a year earlier. I pulled my notebook from my backpack, drew a deep breath, and began writing.

I WOKE TO MIDMORNING SUNLIGHT on my face and found that the scrim of dread had receded, like cloud cover drawn back by the wind. Before sleep, I had written the events of the Maelstrom as simply and honestly as I could. The act of doing so had not been accompanied by the anxiety of avoiding it, but instead a sadness that deepened with each paragraph. How abject it had all been, and how relentless. Suffering was often monotonous. When feeling is acute, we need no novelty to compel us. I knew my relationship to those events would continue to change, that this was a bare beginning, but I'd begun.

Over breakfast, I told my former professor about my celibacy. She told me that she, too, had been in incessant relationships since her teens. She, too, had often felt in some deep part of herself that she needed a break. I described to her my quiet mornings, the inventory I was writing, and how I had begun to notice so many people drunk driving through their lives, getting high off of other humans.

"I'm happier than I have been in years," I told her, draining my last sip of coffee. I did not know this until I said it. That dread still clung to me like a shadow, but it was smaller, less menacing. More of a depressed sidekick, like Piglet, than a force of nature. "Being alone is a kind of ecstasy," I explained. Then I felt a little awkward, because she was married with a child and if that all worked out, she would never get a break, would never know the pleasure of aloneness until her child moved out and her husband died. It seemed rude to have brought this to our attention, as if I were a rich friend flaunting my wealth to a poorer one.

After we shared a long hug and I promised to return soon, I drove to a nearby art colony where I taught frequent writing retreats. On my previous visit, I had video-chatted every night of the retreat with the Last Man. I would have preferred to read myself to sleep in luxurious silence, but had felt obligated. One night, I hung up on him and then claimed a bad internet connection. I did not know how to say that I wanted to be alone. It felt cruel to admit this. When I thought about being alone, it was like imagining a glass of ice water when you are very thirsty.

The retreat before that, I had been in the Maelstrom. I spent the entire four days quivering with anxiety. I drove five miles in a thunderstorm in the middle of the night to get a phone signal so I could call my lover. I pulled so haphazardly onto the side of the country road to take her call that another car stopped to see if I was in trouble.

Do you need help? the driver shouted over the rain through a cracked window. I was in desperate need of help, but I waved them on.

I was amazed that I had not died in the Maelstrom. Over those two years, I spent a lot of time driving while highly distraught, often sobbing. Simply being a pedestrian in New York City in such a state is hazardous to one's life. Once, while texting with her, I walked into a street sign so hard that I feared concussion. Another time, I drove into a parked car across the street from my apartment and damaged it severely. I tracked down the owner, a kind woman in her seventies, and paid for the repairs as well as her taxis to and from the mechanic.

"What happened?" she asked me when I knocked on her door. "Did your brakes fail?"

"Yes," I said.

When I was addicted to heroin as a teenager, I used to drive with a hand over one eye to avoid seeing double. In hindsight, I think those were safer journeys than any I made in the Maelstrom. I have heard other sober people speak about driving drunk or high and killing other drivers or passengers in their own cars, and I have understood that there is no difference between us except timing.

In the summer of 1936, while speeding around a curve, the door of the station wagon that carried forty-four-year-old Edna St. Vincent Millay flung open and the poet, who had been leaning on the door, fell from the moving car and rolled down an embankment beside the road. I always imagined it as the Taconic Parkway, that dark and winding highway that leads to her former home.

Though the accident is well documented, there is no explanation of the circumstances that surrounded the event. Millay was not a subdued character—her life was punctuated by a string of dramatic affairs and decades of severe alcoholism. I assumed that her accident was caused by some combination of these. I could easily imagine having thrown myself from a moving car when I was in the Maelstrom, especially if drugs and alcohol had been in the mix.

For the remainder of her life after the accident, Millay, who had already been intermittently ailing, complained of chronic pain. Though her doctors could rarely locate the anatomical source of her suffering—a sore toe, shoulder pain that migrated to her lower back, fainting and fevers—they treated her with generous doses of morphine and occasionally Dilaudid. It was an unlucky turn of events, as Millay was already an alcoholic. The one condition reliably confirmed throughout her years of illness was an enlarged liver.

I began to have back pain shortly after departing the Maelstrom. During our first appointment, my gay chiropractor told me that it was caused by too much driving and sitting.

"Being a writer has broken my body?" I replied.

"Well, yes," he said.

"I suppose I haven't lived *lightly* in other ways," I added.

"We are not meant to live as we do," said my chiropractor. "Nor this long."

That made sense to me. Given the design of my psyche, I should have died years ago. I was a bomb set to explode in 2004.

The retreat was held at an artist colony named for the poet, who had been a kind of role model for me, more by way of her life than her poetry. The colony sat on an adjacent property to that of the farmhouse, Steepletop, which she bought with her husband, Eugen Jan Boissevain, in 1925, and in which she died in 1950. The writers who attended the retreat slept and wrote in the barn that Millay and Boissevain assembled from a Sears Roebuck kit. A path from the woods behind the building where I slept led to their graves.

As a teenager I immediately recognized myself in Millay, along with those more confessional New England poets, Sylvia Plath and Anne Sexton. In 1912, when she was nineteen, Millay wrote in her diary, "I do not think there is a woman in whom the roots of passion shoot deeper than in me." Many teenagers, especially teenaged artists, think the same of themselves. I certainly did. There are synonymous confessions in my diaries. By nineteen, I had already been in love with both men and women, and taken romantic pursuit as a central topic in my writing. Millay at that age had only an invented lover to whom she wrote passionate letters in her diary, but she would soon make up for that.

Vincent, as she was known by her friends and family, was a documented scoundrel. At least that's what she would have been called were she a man. While she was a student at Vassar, they held dances to which half the women wore suits and used male pronouns, but she usually played the girl.

Early in her college years, she wrote to an older male flirtation, "I had not realized, until I came here, how greatly one girl's beauty & presence can disturb another's peace of mind,—more still, sometimes, her beauty and absence.—There are Anactorias here for any

Sappho." I presume that she was writing about herself, a Sappho only in the practice of poetry, otherwise an Anactoria disturbing the peaceful minds of what her sister Norma once called "all those wonderful tall girl-boys for you to abuse as suitors."

"Beloved!" a classmate wrote to her over one winter break. "If only I could see you for a second I'm sure this chronic ache would go away . . . You haunt me beloved Vincent. I love you."

"Vincent was very definitely a person to whom others formed crushes, and attachments," another recalled of her. "They simply trailed after her."

When she broke things off with one college lover, Elaine Ralli, who subsequently suffered "a serious crack-up," Ralli confided in a friend that she "felt there was a ruthlessness about Vincent. That her work came first . . . She always thought Vincent had an eye on herself, her future . . . She felt it was her first love, and perhaps her only one: her poetry."

When I first read this in Millay's biography, I startled with recognition. How often did creative ambition and seduction arise together? I had always been aware of my own ruthless part. Even as a sensitive and eager-to-please child I understood that there was an amoral aspect of me, a potential that if triggered by the right circumstances would render me capable of anything. I was far from immune to regret or empathy, and would go to extremes to avoid hurting others, but I did possess an innate ability to so narrow my perspective with desire that I might behave temporarily without those sympathetic functions.

In a conversation with my therapist, I once described myself as a gremlin.

"You know," I said, "a cuddly and cheerful creature who, if doused with the right elixir, will transform into a monster."

The realm where I allowed this part the most freedom was in my creative work. Let my perception narrow, occlude my view of the world and all its people, because in doing so, another world opened to me. My oldest memories are of scribbling in notebooks and gorging on novels, never hearing my parents' call until they screamed my name.

I knew this function could be induced in other ways, too. That any subject on which I focused, for which I hungered, could induce it. To unleash it elsewhere quickly amounted casualties.

In "Ode to Aphrodite," which is sometimes called "The Anactoria Poem," Sappho writes:

> Some say thronging cavalry, some say foot soldiers,
> others call a fleet the most beautiful of
> sights the dark earth offers, but I say it's what-
> ever you love best.

Like Vincent, the Greek poet was diminutive, with an absent father. She loved women and is speculated to have had affairs with younger men. "Rarely since Sappho," wrote Carl Van Doren in *Many Minds,* had a woman "written as outspokenly as Millay." But beside Millay's lyrics, Sappho's are startlingly reverent. If Sappho in the absence of her lover experiences eros as "a delicate flame [that] runs beneath my skin," Millay experiences it "like a burning city in the breast." Whether flippant or anguished, Millay's poems reveal a more conflicted relationship to her own desires. "So subtly is the fume of life designed," reads one sonnet, "To clarify the pulse and cloud the mind, / And leave me once again undone, possessed." If eros was a noble muse to the Lesbian poet, it is a fume to this one. It is "the poor treason / Of my stout blood against my staggering brain."

The monster I'd become in the Maelstrom had been a kind of treason, and now I wanted to be less Millay and more Lesbian poet, more Sappho. She wasn't happy, but she was less pitiful in the end. At least we know little enough of her to believe so.

There is a painting of her by Charles Auguste Mengin that I had kept as my laptop's screen for years. Mengin was a French artist mostly known for the portrait, in which Sappho leans on a rock, the *wine-dark sea* and gray sky behind her. She looks absolutely exhausted, shadows beneath her eyes, her bare-breasted figure slumped, a lyre dangling from her right hand as if she can hardly stand to lift it, let alone strum another love song. Her gaze stares vacantly down, almost through the viewer, into her own mind. Mengin's Sappho is "Feeling Fucked Up," in the immortal words of Etheridge Knight's poem. "Fuck Coltrane and music and clouds drifting in the sky," her desultory face says, "fuck the sea and trees and the sky and birds."

It is a painting of the Romantic period and as such is meant to contain contradiction and embody dialectical tension, which it does. In it, I recognize the bond of sentiment and reason that has always made me particularly responsive to the art of that period. Reading about the Romantics, I see the trailheads of my own romantic ideals, the manner in which my self-conception blends aspects of the Romantic hero with Romantic Beauty. I have clung to ideas of fate and tragedy and powerlessness such that, at least in my twenties and in the Maelstrom, I might have been a character in a seventeenth-century French novel.

Sappho could have too, so exhausted and gorgeous is she in Mengin's portrait, ravished by love. I recognized her, this exhausted lover who had put romance at the center of her art and life. Could a woman have a crush on a figure in a painting? It was undeniable. Every time that screen alit, I thrilled to face her, felt the unbidden desire to rouse that gaze and make her see me.

Reading about these lovelorn poets had comforted me because the pairing of art and love was a balm. The fact that we still knew their names meant that love hadn't ruined them. Perhaps it had even helped secure them a place in history. I didn't care much about history's memory, but I did care about art. I did not want love or anything else to get in the way of my making it. A life harrowed by love was still worth living if one also spent it in the act of creation.

It wasn't complicated. I worshipped all these short women with abandonment issues who were also creative icons because they gave me hope for myself.

I had been noticing my role models. Most of them were women artists who were passionate and messy in love, like Vincent and Colette. I hadn't audited their relevance to my life since I was a teenager. I still loved their work, but did I still admire their lives? Love didn't ruin their art but it sometimes did them. I began to wonder what more my heroines might have achieved if not so consumed by romance. I wondered if I had been hedging my aspirations to avoid disappointment. That is, if being strung out on romance was my *goal*, then ruination would also qualify as success. I did not want to be ruined, though. The taste of it I'd had was plenty. I didn't think I'd survive another round. I considered what a more sincere list of role models would look like.

I'd chosen other heroes using this strategy. Before getting sober, I had cultivated a treasured collection of alcoholic and junkie role models that included William Burroughs, Billie Holiday, Charles Bukowski, Jean Rhys, Patricia Highsmith, Jack Kerouac, Chet Baker, Ernest Hemingway, and Marguerite Duras, who once said: "I drank because I was an alcoholic . . . I was a real one—like a writer. I'm a real writer, I was a real alcoholic." They provided me with a chorus of validation, evidence of the connection between addiction and art. If these train wrecks made what they made while strung out, why not me? Perhaps, I thought hopefully, the drugs facilitated artistic success. It was a logical fallacy, of course. I conveniently ignored the fact that Duras wrote *The Lover*, my favorite work of hers, while sober. There was no deficit of sources willing to endorse the claim that substance abuse enabled creativity. Addicts are rhetorical geniuses at such arguments.

Almost immediately after I got sober I realized that these artists accomplished what they did *despite* their long-standing addictions. I understood that their art would have benefited had they managed to get sober. I also realized that I no longer loved many of those art-ists' works, if I ever had. The stories that wooed me as a budding addict now read like repetitive tracts that could end only one of two ways: death or recovery. The travails of alcoholics became boring to me in sobriety because what I had found exotic and comfort-ing in those narratives was simply the predictable ruin of a disease with known treatments. The truly unexpected became possible only in abstinence, when the addict recouped their agency. I wondered what Vincent would have written if she'd lived past her addictions, and felt a surge of grief for that loss.

Perhaps this was the real motive for my course of study, all the reading I'd been doing: to find new idols. To build a lineage beyond those who shared my weaknesses. I did not want to hide in the sto-ries of other figures or to glorify my own failings for comfort, but instead to construct a future vision from the wisdom of the past. I told my students that art was a practice of *creation*, of conjuring, not a reiteration of the known. If a life's work was made of whatever labor one chose, wasn't lineage also claimed? I had already begun claiming mine.

AS I PACKED to drive back to Brooklyn, a friend texted me: *Are you single?*

Yes, I said. *But I'm celibate until the end of the month.*

I want to set you up with someone. A hot lesbian playwright.

Only a moment's hesitation before I typed. *Sure!*

A few minutes later, to my surprise, the prospective date texted.

Hello. Would you like to go on a date in the near future?

I'd like that, I replied after a few moments. *I've never been on a truly blind date—exciting!*

It's going to get even blinder, she responded. *When are you free?*

How does a date get blinder? I asked. *Are you going to drug me?*

Not even if you ask, she quipped, and I felt myself redden with embarrassment.

That was an awful joke. Sorry!

I love terrible jokes by good people.

You're going to love me. Watch out. God, had I always been this heavy-handed in my innuendo?

Hey, thanks for the endorphins, she concluded the exchange, and I felt indicted.

I set the phone down and noticed that my body was warmer. I had been recognizing how other people got high off flirtation, but I hadn't noticed the cozy superiority that had attended my observation, as if in my celibacy I'd developed immunity. Now it was I who sparked inside, the stranger a flint I'd struck myself against. How easily I'd slipped into the familiar current of seduction and out of myself.

As I reflected on my exchange with the stranger, my excitement curdled, as if I had cheated. Had I cheated? I was the only one who could say. For a fervent moment, I wished I weren't so alone in my own life. I wished there was someone else to ask, to tell me if I was full of shit or not.

I stared at the pad of paper on my desk, headed with the logo of the hotel I'd stayed at in Los Angeles. While texting with the potential date, I had written her name on the blank page. I had no memory of writing it. Now, underneath her name, I wrote the name of the date whose number I'd blocked. Underneath that, I wrote the name of the woman I'd flirted with at that book party. Then the photographer who'd shot my author photos. Below hers, I wrote *Sappho*. And then, *lol*.

It was always a question of how honest I wanted to be with myself. Did I really want to change, to live according to my own beliefs? Or did I secretly prefer to go on as I had been. I mean, why bother with such a project if I wasn't going to be wholehearted? The prospect of giving up *all* the pleasures of romance seemed downright sepulchral. But why was I actually doing this? Was it solely to avoid another maelstrom? To relieve my depression? I had already accomplished the latter, but knew I wasn't finished. The point of my celibacy wasn't merely to take a break, but to make room for change. I'd barely begun.

"Everything you write is about love," a friend said to me when I was thirty. It was a complaint, not a compliment. *So what,* I thought. Most of the great literature of history is obsessed with love. Most great music is inspired by love. Still, the comment disturbed me, because I had not noticed until she pointed it out.

As a teenager, I once encountered a book devoted to the astrology of birthdays. Each page featured a day of the year and offered an archetype to describe the people born on that day. My birthday's archetype was the Heartbreaker. Even as a teen, I felt a swell of relief at this. Not only did the pronouncement affirm my preoccupations, but it also reassured me. To be a heartbreaker precluded the possibility of being the heartbroken, didn't it? Now, this memory embarrassed me. I was so desperate to be relieved of responsibility for my own mind and conduct. Sometimes I still wondered what I would write about if I were not so busy writing about love.

When I was younger and eating disordered, I had spent most of my waking time (and some of my dreams) thinking about food. I used to imagine the time and energy I spent thinking about food, if it could be amassed, how enormous a resource it would be. I could write a book with it, I'd think. Similarly, the time I'd spent occupied by heroin—procuring it, ingesting it, withdrawing from it.

I had probably spent more time thinking about lovers past, present, and future than either of those other obsessions. I could have written several books with that cumulative energy. Arguably, I already had. I could have gotten a PhD. I could have had an entire secondary career, or a great many hobbies. I could have become a real activist instead of someone who only wrote about the things she'd like to change. Obsessive people don't have much time for interests extracurricular to their obsessions. A single interest can keep us busy for years, for a lifetime.

Still, I wanted to resist the temptation of binary thinking. My romantic relationships had frequently been sites of obsession and squandered energy, but they had also been the grounds upon which I had grown up, learned to care for others, practiced tolerance and patience, and experienced true intimacy. I did not want to dismiss my romantic history wholesale as pathological, only move toward those truer forms of love, and a more balanced life.

.   .   .

I left the little list of names on my desk. I stared at it intermittently while I responded to emails, made edits on my book, and continued my inventory of past love, and it stared back.

In season six of *Vera*, there is an episode in which a mother, having failed to prevent her adult son from taking heroin, doles it out to him while keeping scrupulous records of the amounts in a ledger. The images of that careful handwritten record chilled me. The mother character is despicable, but I recognized the appeal of such data-keeping, the comfort of a finite numerical record of a cycle over which one is powerless. The small taste of control it gives. The old fantasy that to recognize is to master.

There had been times when I kept track of my heroin use as well, carefully printed the dates and amounts as if my problem were one of disorganization. I have always interpreted my lifelong interest in lists as a similar expression: the relief of asserting some superficial order over the unmanageable. The reduction of the infinite to the singular column, the imposition of linearity. Even as a child, I made lists of human conquests, friends, crushes, desires, steps toward whatever end would quiet my hungers. My inventory was born of the same instinct, though I hoped that it would not be an empty gesture, like that fictional mother's ledger.

Millay's notebooks were filled with similar transcripts in the years before her death: columns of numbers tabulating the amounts of morphine she injected throughout the days. These records are, as her biographer Nancy Milford writes, "among the most troubling and pitiful documents in American literary history."

The poet's end was that met by many of my childhood idols: the sort of lonely death that awaits every addict if she lives long enough. The record scratch on the B side that I never played when I was young. At fifty-eight, a year after the death of her husband, and in the middle of writing a poem, Millay fell down a set of stairs at Steepletop and broke her neck.

"Beauty is not enough," she wrote in "Spring," a poem published thirty years earlier. "Life in itself / Is nothing, / An empty cup, a flight of uncarpeted stairs."

That weekend I had lunch with a psychotherapist who had written a very insightful book about love with a very bad title. A mutual friend recommended I read it and was correct in her prediction that I would find it helpful. The therapist and I met at Coffee Shop in Union Square. When I arrived, she had already secured a booth. She was a tiny person, dressed in a drapey linen outfit and artistic jewelry, and she epitomized a type of therapist that I like: small, wise, and bossy. I liked her immediately, though during our lunch she said many things with which I disagreed.

I told her how I'd been trying to see my relationship patterns through the framework of addiction. She waved her hand dismissively.

"You define yourself too much as an addict," she told me. "What is an addict but someone who is dealing with some unresolved element?"

"What are any of us but that?" I countered.

"Anyway, I think your sexual hiatus is brilliant," she said. "And that without it you'll keep doing the exact same thing."

"I've begun to wonder if three months is long enough," I confided.

She laughed. "Are you kidding me? Try starting with six months." She set down her fork for emphasis. "It has to be hard," she said. "If it's not hard, you're not doing it."

I bucked inside at this, but I enjoyed her certainty. I like women with strong opinions, even when I disagree with them.

"You know Ulysses?" she asked, as if he were a local plumber.

"Of course," I said, smiling.

She leaned toward me for emphasis. "You have to lash yourself to the mast," she said. "It has to be that hard."

I laughed at this. She was so dramatic!

"You know what I think is going to happen?" she said, leaning back in her seat. "I think you're going to get depressed. Really depressed. Possibly suicidal." She shrugged and popped an olive into her mouth. "Maybe not, but don't be surprised. There's something you must be hiding from. You have to give yourself space to do that. Without it you'll still be in prison. You have to let yourself wake up. It can't be a stunt."

Despite the fact that I found her words ridiculous and slightly offensive, they lingered in my mind all afternoon and into the evening, which found me in bed reading about Pythagoras. Would there be men in my new lineup of role models? Seemed unlikely.

Pythagoras is better known for his eponymous theorem, but he also founded a cultish school whose members were sworn to secrecy, vegetarianism, and celibacy, but the last only in the hot "dry" seasons of summer and fall. Winter, apparently, was safer for sex in its wetness. Conversely, early ascetics and doctors often believed that drying out the body was necessary for celibacy. Food that they deemed drying included many legumes, vinegars, salted olives, and dried fruit. As a secretive, celibate vegetarian with a taste for vinegars and dried fruit, the parallels pleased me.

It was too late to be reading about fanatical ancient mathematicians, so I turned off the light. I felt tired, but still blinked in the dark, stalked by the therapist's words. How closely they had echoed my own recent fears. *Was* it a stunt? I got out of bed to make a snack.

In addition to becoming a bed fetishist, I had increasingly stopped eating meal-appropriate foods at the appropriate mealtime. Instead, when I got hungry I assembled a plate of pickles and cheese, dried fruit and nuts, a sliced apple, maybe, at any time of day or night. In the middle of the night, I often wandered into the kitchen and ate pickles straight out of the jar by the light of the open refrigerator.

That night, as I stood in the dark kitchen, crunching a gherkin over the sink, I decided (again) that the psychotherapist was mistaken. She didn't know me at all. Even I was surprised by the ease with which I had adapted to this new reality. *When you're ready, you're ready,* I told myself.

I had always been good at new things, until they became difficult.

Later that week, I met a friend for dinner. He was a sculptor who had reached out unexpectedly and said he'd be in town from Chicago. Truthfully, he was more of an acquaintance with whom I had a lot of mutual friends.

The days were getting longer and I decided to walk the two miles from my neighborhood to the restaurant. As usual, I was early, and took a loop around the perimeter of Fort Greene Park. I watched a couple of dogs run in ecstatic scribbles across the grass and it occurred to me that my "friend" might think our dinner was a date. I wondered if I'd been aware of this possibility on some level since we planned it weeks before. I couldn't be sure. Well, I decided conclusively in that moment that it was not a date.

My dinner companion was a handsome trans man about ten years older than me and only a few inches taller. I paused at this and remembered a tall friend once telling me, in response to my preference for tall partners, how I shouldn't be allowed to date people more than six inches taller than me, in order to save the tallest people for the tallest people. I thought she would be proud of me for going on a date with this fellow short person. Then I reminded myself that this was absolutely not a date.

We had a long conversation over salty tapas served in miniature cast-iron pans. Mostly we talked about our work, while being mindful not to burn our wrists as we served ourselves. The sculptor didn't ask a lot of questions. As he described his latest project, I started to feel like a potential investor whom he was pitching. I got the lonely hunch that my dinner companion wasn't that interested in me. I sensed that he was *interested* in me, but not curious. We had no chemistry, though on paper we were compatible. We were both single queer artists with histories of attraction to people fitting our respective profiles. I wondered if that was enough for my dinner companion. It was hard to imagine making a limerent object of him. Maybe that was ideal. A relationship absent of obsession sounded tidier, if less exciting.

When the bill came, he insisted on paying.

"In the spirit of full disclosure," I said. "Are you trying to date me?"

"Yes," he cheerfully replied.

"Well, I'm celibate right now, so I'm not available for dating." I felt the familiar contours of these words in my mouth.

"When will you be available for dating?" he asked.

"In a couple of months," I said, though technically my ninety days ended sooner than that.

Outside of the restaurant, we shared a chaste hug.

"Talk to you in a couple months," he said with a smile. As we turned in opposite directions, I silently chastised myself. What kind of asshole waits until the end of dinner to say, "By the way, I'm celibate so this wasn't a date"? A person who wants to go on a date and doesn't think they should be on a date, that was who. An even better question: What kind of person lies and tells their dinner companion that they will be celibate for an extra month rather than admit that they don't want to date them? A person who ought to stay celibate.

In the morning, there was no getting around it. I extended my celibacy for another three months. This time, I would be clearer with myself about the definition of celibacy. There would be no ambiguous dinners, no flirting, no rain checks. I would put the work in to make sure it was not a stunt.

II

F IRST, YOU HAVE TO get the gaze right. Not stalker-heavy, but enough so they notice."

"Like this?" My friend, a playwright, glowered at me. I laughed. She was newly divorced, dating for the first time in a long time, and wanted to work on her seduction skills. I had to agree they were terrible. When I told her I was spending six months celibate because I couldn't stop getting into relationships, her eyes widened. Half of the friends I told started nodding before I'd finished my explanation while others rolled their eyes just as quickly. This friend immediately wanted tips.

"More like this," I said, and looked at her as I would someone who piqued my interest. Something activated in me, responded to a set of clues telling me how she wanted to be seen. I could not have identified these clues in language, or hadn't yet, but they were cognitively legible to me within minutes of our first meeting, more than six years previous. The ability to calibrate my gaze to meet that desire was one I'd honed much longer ago.

"Look," I told her, "but not long, just enough to graze them with your attention." When I was a kid my mother had taught me how to soften my vision when watching birds so they wouldn't feel the weight of my attention on their hollow bones. This was the opposite.

The concentration that landed like a finger, tapping, casting the line of desire until it caught, and tugged.

"Whoa," she said with a laugh. "Careful where you point that!" She looked at me in wonder, and I felt both proud and embarrassed. "Where did you learn that skill?"

I had always thought of myself as someone who innately knew how to activate this faculty, an intuitive seducer, but faced with the question—one I had been asking myself—I saw how unlikely this was. There was the fact of being a woman, a femme, and having been prescribed seduction methods my whole life by movies and TV. Still, many people are women, including my friend, and we all lived in this soup of sexual prescription, but only some of us know how to emit the smoldering atmosphere to reel someone in, whereas I could do it as if it were my job.

The server dropped our check and, after a brief tussle, I paid for our dinners. I always tipped big, regardless of the service, like most people who have waited tables. My ideal server basically ignored us and brought the food. They didn't have to do anything to "earn" their tip outside of their job description. I wanted to spare them that other kind of work, the kind that had, I realized, made me so good at seduction.

At my request, my spiritual director had given me a deadline: the end of the summer. I had been writing now for over a month. Like most inventories, mine grew repetitious as the notebook pages filled. There was a series of questions that I asked for each entry. Among them: *Where have I been selfish? Where have I been dishonest? Where have I been inconsiderate? Whom have I hurt? Where was I at fault? What should I have done instead?* Over and over again, I gave nearly identical answers.

The pattern that governed my recent years looked like this: I met someone I found attractive. Sometimes it was their mind; other times, their face. Sometimes the fun we had or the warmth of their attention. Early on, I detected an unevenness. I saw where my reservations lay. Still, we built a rapport, a flirtation, a fire that caught and we fed with witty text messages, long phone calls, and small gifts. *I'm not available,* I said, but my actions begged otherwise. *They are an adult,* I told myself. *I have given them all the pertinent information.* The truth: I knew I was being reckless with someone else's heart, or at least their expectations, but it felt too good to stop.

Sometimes, I thought, *I am in love.* Every time, there was a kernel of knowing inside me. A bud of nascent certainty that it would end, that I would be the one to end it. The *why,* even, layered in its fragrant darkness.

This wasn't always the pattern. When younger, I had less control. I wanted to be chosen. Though I was equally or more attracted to women, men had been raised to believe themselves choosers, so I entangled with them more often. Heterosexual scripts were so clear and loud; there was a beautiful simplicity to them. A relief in yielding to their small violences, in joining the collective movement toward that impossible goal: to be wanted, as if that were an endpoint, a place where we might arrive and set up camp. I mean, I did.

When I was young, each relationship was its own lesson. My lovers weren't my only teachers, though. I learned the art and uses of seduction in all sorts of places, including my actual jobs. As I plodded through the timeline of my history, other timelines emerged and I saw the knots where they intersected, the education they formed. I saw the way a life's work wasn't conducted in only one area of living. The self who grew out of that education came further into focus, and the manner in which she became me.

My first restaurant job was dishwasher. I dressed most days in a pair of faded overalls and green Doc Martens. Face rosy from the steam of the industrial washer, the bib of my overalls splattered with greasy water, I would peer out at the front of the house and watch the waitstaff, who held the glamour of low-level celebrities to me. Tidy in their identical aprons and T-shirts bearing the restaurant logo, they were all kind of hot in their own way, and the source of this was the skill with which they deployed charisma.

I watched them flit around the dining room, calibrating their affect to suit each diner. The ones with the tallest stacks as they cashed out at the end of a shift cultivated a flirtation with their tables that hit exactly the right note to release money. As if every diner were a slot machine played less by chance than by skill.

I want to do that, I thought. At fourteen, I already had a keen sense that I ought to appeal to other people, men especially, but "succeeding" at this had mixed results. Using my drive to be liked in a context whose endpoint wasn't sex and that promised material reward for success seemed a much safer forum. It turned seduction into a kind of game. As Tennov wrote of limerence: "Whether it will be won, whether it will be shared, and what the final outcome may be, depend on the effectiveness of your moves . . . indeed on skill."

At that age, I had called myself a feminist for years and a bisexual for almost as long. I had kissed a girl. I had also only just reached the far shore of a torturous two years. At eleven, my body had erupted. I went from athletic and unselfconscious to feeling ungainly and oversexualized. My body was an embarrassment and also a magnet whose drawing power I could not control. I remember once standing in the kitchen of a friend's house to call my mother on the landline. My mother never wanted me at this house and for good reason, the same reason that I loved being there: it was free of adult supervision and crawling with older boys.

A friend of my friend's older brother—a teenager whose face my memory has replaced with that of the actor Channing Tatum, because he was that type: an arrogant and beautiful white boy—ambled up behind me and softly kissed the nape of my neck. The back of my body turned liquid, from head to heel, melted gold, as if he were a god who had cursed me with pleasure. When I spun around, he winked and loped out of the room.

Nothing else ever happened between us—I was twelve and he

probably seventeen. His restraint has always seemed admirable to me, considering the lack of it that other older boys in that house showed. What a mind fuck, the revelation of that pleasure and the crushing disappointment of everything that followed, how numb I was to the hands that touched me and how powerless I felt to stop them.

I came up with a phrase to describe it decades later: *empty consent*. Until then, however, I never had words for those muffled hours in bedrooms and closets, strange fingers working against me like the pink erasers we used in school, the way they made my body a stranger to me, an object I couldn't set down but still tried, flung in the direction of anything that called. In the nineties, we just called it *fooling around*. Or we called it sex. If we said *yes* then it wasn't rape and there was no way to name how it froze us so much the same.

One memorable exception was Carlo. I met him the summer of that first dishwashing job. My shift had recently ended and I was sitting on a stone wall that overlooked the harbor nursing a soda. He hopped up next to me.

"We could be related," he said and looked straight into my face. Those are the only words I remember of that day. I was flattered by them because Carlo was beautiful. He had olive skin, a rosette mouth, and green eyes with lashes as long as a doll's. Also, he was right. I had all of those qualities, too, minus the lashes, though I felt far from beautiful. People had often commented on these physical attributes and how exotic I looked among all the Irish descendants that surrounded me, but it had never felt entirely like a compliment. Standing out physically is a liability for most children, especially if that difference locates one farther from whiteness or, for a girl, from traits seen as chaste.

Carlo and I had other things in common, too, I later discovered: our Puerto Rican fathers, sweet dispositions, and bottomless appetites. He was a couple years older than me and had gotten a head start on trouble. Years after our first meeting, I learned that my mother had once treated him during her clinical internship. He had joined a therapy group that she led, attended mostly by court-mandated teens. A soft look came over her face when she told me this. He had that effect on people.

Minutes into our first conversation, he led me away from that wall to a tent in the woods that belonged to some vagrant character whose name I've forgotten. There, we kissed for an hour or so among the dirty blankets. Carlo was a good kisser and he didn't pressure me to do more, two traits that differentiated him from other boys I'd encountered. My interlude with him in that humid tent was a good memory among many similar but unpleasant ones. Over the next ten years, we often crossed paths. I was attracted to him, yes, but I also admired the ease with which he had steered our afternoon. Like many of my crushes on boys, my attraction to him mingled with ambition. I wanted to kiss them *and* to be them.

Soon after that, I began making lists in my diaries. Beside tallies of books I'd read and words whose definitions I looked up, there were names. People I wanted to seduce. Not always for sex, because what I wanted from them was ultimately more subtle than that: to secure their focus, to make them *like* me. To cast a bit of glamour, a spell of protection. When I caught the flapping sail of their attention, I felt a swell of safety and power. For a moment, I soared. I wanted redemption, too, probably. That liquid pleasure without the risk. For that, I needed to be the one at the helm.

I FIRST WAITED TABLES at Café Algiers, a landmark Middle Eastern restaurant in Cambridge's Harvard Square that catered to Harvard professors and graduate students. I was seventeen and living in a semi-squalid apartment with three roommates in Somerville, among them my best friend. He was gay, a beautiful half-Lebanese, half-French hairdresser who taught me how to give myself a proper manicure and introduced me to crystal meth. We were the queer mom and dad of our circle, ordering pizzas and stirring chocolate milk from a mix for the kids who partied at our place every night. There was cat shit everywhere and someone always crashing on our couch.

Amid the wobbly octagonal tables at Café Algiers, I balanced silver pots of mint tea and plates of hummus, and practiced my approach. I learned that if my gaze was too clumsy, the men (and sometimes, thrillingly, women) asked *sotto voce* when my shift ended. If too subtle, they ignored me and left meager tips. The trick was to kindle the right feeling in myself—*I have something they want and I want to give it to them, but not yet*—to render the plates of food a symbol for something else, to exude an air of slight withholding, a little smug but available. I learned what all good salespeople understand: if you suggest that a person wants something with enough confidence, there's a good chance they'll believe you.

I was always good at reading people, and before this job it had been a burdensome gift. Under the surface everyone was so fraught with need and emotion; I didn't always want to know. Now this insight had a purpose, a goal to which I could apply it. Every shift was drill after drill, followed by immediate numeric feedback on the degree of my success.

I honed my skills quickly under these conditions. I could balance five entrées on one tray, instantly calculate a bill in my head, and tell if a diner wanted a server who treated them with mild disgust or like a long-lost family member. The scatterbrained nature that made me clumsy in life was steadied by the constant stream of necessity and discernment. Once I caught the rhythm of it, I didn't have to think and I didn't make errors. Which was good, because my livelihood depended on it: in 1997, the minimum wage for tipped employees was $2.13 per hour.

I had moved to Boston shortly before I turned seventeen. I still felt like that ungainly child, still hid my body in oversized clothes, mostly combat boots and overalls. Then I found hard drugs, which presented an easier way to leave my body and also to let it waste. I became thin and forgetful. I loved the scrambled feeling of a high and the scraped quiet of the day after it. Before then, clothes had been a disguise. I imbued certain items with magical thinking— they were the talismans that made me disappear. After my body shrank, however, I could wear anything. My body had drawn attention before, but finally it felt good. I began wearing high heels and shirts that bared a strip of abdomen, a pair of zebra-striped hip huggers that I lived in.

One morning, I walked from the Harvard Square T to Brattle Street for a morning shift at Café Algiers. I wasn't yet addicted to any one substance and had slept the night before. I was in a cheery mood as I sipped my coffee and watched the rising sunlight brighten the deserted blocks. It was just after 6 a.m., the only sounds those of birdsong, the hum of idling delivery trucks, and the occasional rumble of metal gates rolled up over the facades of shops. Outside of Cardullo's—a gourmet grocery that has somehow survived the creep of corporate franchises that long ago replaced most of the local businesses—I spotted Carlo.

In Boston we often partied together with a shifting group of friends. Carlo was quick-witted and kind, welcomed by everyone because he was always a good time. He had better dealer connections than I did and seemed to have friends in every social realm of Boston that might interest me and some that didn't. In the small hours, when others flagged or fell asleep, it was he and I who finished the last lines of coke or tried to get more under a pinkening sky. We had sex sometimes, too, and it felt companionable, something to do with a high or boredom that held little risk. He was one of the few casual sex partners whom I ever enjoyed. The years had only refined his looks and I still admired him. He was a person whose beauty eased his way through life, whose charisma ensured that people would always include him, want to please him, even love him.

When I called his name on that early morning, however, I barely recognized Carlo. His face was smeared with soot and his eyes flashed wild and empty. He smelled strange and his handsome features hung off-kilter. He was a picture of himself that had been crumpled and then flattened out again, ironed by someone's palm. When he looked up and saw me, then hesitated, I thought maybe he didn't recognize me, either. Now I know it was shame.

I had always assumed that Carlo and I had a similar relationship to drugs, that he also took nights off to live like a civilian. I didn't find out until years later that the nights I stayed in and slept he spent turning tricks in the Fenway and smoking speed.

There were eight or ten more jobs, each with their own demographic. The Greenhouse, another Cambridge institution where the regulars expected you to remember their orders and the female professors liked a dry little flirt. The Jewish deli where families came for brunch, the bakery frequented by moneyed lesbians, the Mexican restaurant that hosted a lot of tourists and bachelorette parties. My favorite patrons were always other food-service workers, folks just off a shift to whom I slipped free drinks and desserts, and who tipped extravagantly, as I did them. My least favorites were the worst of the men.

Whatever their differences, every restaurant was also a microcosm of larger social hierarchies. I once worked a brunch shift in Belmont with this guy who got high before work and then swanned around the room like he couldn't be bothered. People never got their water refills, and he didn't flirt with anyone except those he would have anyway. No matter what he did, at the end of the shift, his tips always rivaled or exceeded mine. Meanwhile, my earnings dropped if I missed a beat, smiled too little or too much. This was always the case: no matter what the quality of their service, male waiters got bigger tips from everyone, as if they had families to feed while women waitstaff were just keeping busy.

I remember a table I had during my brief stint at the Mexican restaurant. A big family, replete with a preening patriarch who emanated insecurity that he expressed by treating every woman in sight like garbage. I smiled through it, even when he patted my ass in full view of his wife, who then glared at *me*.

When things like this happened, a knot of shame and fury convulsed in me. I ignored it and imagined my tip—a ten or a twenty, even. I smiled at that vision and then directed it at the table. I remember that one not because the experience was exceptional, but because after they'd left, as I cleared their oily dishes, I realized that he had stiffed me. I seethed for days. It kindled a fire in me whose heat I still feel, more than twenty years later. It wasn't the money, but the humiliation. The trick of it: to treat someone like dirt and then withhold the small compensation for which they tolerated your treatment. It taught me what degraded characters some people have in the special and shitty way that only people who have worked in service understand.

.   .   .

This was the flipside of seduction in all arenas, as a woman: the potential for humiliation was ever present. What a thorny conundrum, to want to be wanted and hate being humiliated. Back then, I thought if I appealed in the right way it would offer a kind of protection. This was more magical thinking.

During a brief phase of club-going, I once brought a man home with me. When I took off my clothes, which I still only did in the dark, he squinted at me in the dim glow from the streetlight outside my bedroom window. Though he nodded appreciatively, I felt mortified. Later, in a rare moment of allegiance to my own wishes, I stopped our sex before he finished. I had had no orgasm, which was common, though I could have faked one. I did so regularly then, as a tool to end sex I wasn't enjoying. That night, I simply said I was drunk and tired. He sulked but I let him stay. It seemed the price of disappointing him. Now the idea of keeping an angry stranger in my bed sounds absurd, but back then, I only ever had a single *no*. Once I spent it, I was cashed and had to tolerate what followed.

An hour later, I woke to the slick motor of his hand as he jerked off over my body. Instinctively, I pretended to stay asleep, even when I felt his warm semen splatter onto my lower back. I lay still until I heard his breath slow beside me. Eventually, I fell asleep, too. In the morning I hugged him goodbye and then scrubbed the crust off in the shower.

I hoped that if I were good enough at seduction, as good as a man, like that guy with whom I waited tables or like Carlo—I would be invincible. My pockets would be stuffed with *no*s. I would no longer fear humiliation. Being wanted enough would unlock a doorway to everything else I craved. This goal and its underlying hope preoccupied me for decades, for so long that I forgot it existed. Hadn't I always just wanted to be pretty? Didn't everyone want to be wanted? No, I had craved safety. Freedom from a vigilance that exhausted me.

Maybe if I had been able to put words to it and share it with someone else, I might have seen it for the lesson it was. The one so many children are indoctrinated in from the moment of first cognizance. Maybe I would have seen that it compromised men and boys, too. No one has a pocket full of *nos*.

Over a decade had passed since I'd last seen Carlo. I arrived home one evening after teaching in New Jersey and turned off my engine. I often sat in my car for a few minutes after I found a parking spot to stare out the windshield or at my phone's screen. That night I saw the tributes on social media and felt my guts clench with sudden grief. No one said how Carlo had died, but I didn't wonder.

I had loved him more than could be measured by the time we'd spent together. He had been a kind of brother to me, a kind of twin. I sat in my parked car on that dark Brooklyn street and cried pitiful tears, tears full of pity for my old friend, and for past me. I wanted to call someone else who had loved him like I had loved him, but they were all gone, too. I knew that Carlo's beauty had not protected him. He had been loved, but not by all whose hands had reached for him. That desire had been no kind of protection, only a slow looting.

WHY DIDN'T I QUIT waiting tables? Well, I was a teenager for most of the years I worked in restaurants, and I didn't have a degree, or even a high school diploma unless you count the GED. Despite the tables that stiffed me, it was the highest-paying job I was qualified for by a long shot. Over time, exposure inured me to the inherent humiliations of the job. A personality will shape itself in response to the immoveable, wind its roots around anything.

The humiliations of waiting tables were also made tolerable by the satisfactions of being good at my job. I held less power than my diners in some intractable way, if only in that I was literally there to serve them, but I had a kind of power over them, too, one that they couldn't see and which increased with exercise. I worked them with the practiced ease of a salesperson, or a petty con artist, and they were my chumps, my suckers, my johns.

When I moved to New York in 1999, it was harder to get restaurant work. Upscale Manhattan joints wanted a résumé even from host-position applicants. My experience was decidedly downscale: diners, delis, brunch spots, and cafés. They were the hardest-working and the lowest-paying gigs, and they did not render me an appealing hire for positions that would enable me to pay rent in New

York. I worked a few months at a diner in the West Village, serving eggs and fetching jam, but I soon got into sex work, which paid a lot better.

As a professional dominatrix, I applied all the talents I'd hewn waiting tables. The beauty of sex work was in how the subtext of my seductive transactions became text. Before I worked with any client, we had a consultation in which he told me exactly what he wanted and I agreed to it or didn't. Of course, my demeanor in this meeting was informed by my instinct for what the client wanted. To my delight, there were many more of these patrons who wanted to be treated with disgust than in restaurants.

During the sessions themselves, I still relied upon my honed instincts for timing and intensity—although they had a script, there was still a lot to improvise. The work of it was also primarily that of seduction: the assessment of desire and how to draw it out, grow it, leave it wanting just enough. The main difference, and it was not small, is that I was paid well however the session went. There were tips, but I didn't depend on them. The humiliations were greater, but they weren't hidden. I did that work for almost four years, well into my first year of graduate school, which is a significant tenure in sex work.

I started adjunct teaching during my second year of grad school, which paid worse than either sex work or waiting tables. I got used to working on commuter trains and slowly built a different wardrobe than that I had needed for any previous job. Teaching was also a performance, but like sex work, I got a paycheck whether it was good or not. I was good at it, and the relief of not having to flirt with anyone to succeed was a revelation, however little I was paid.

I was grateful never to have been attracted to my students. It was easy to feel a sense of moral superiority about this, though I knew it wasn't earned. If I were attracted to my students and successfully resisted acting upon it, then I would have deserved some credit. I had simply always wanted to be the younger one. Which is why my tryst with the twenty-five-year-old and my sexual tension with Ray made me uneasy. They represented a sharp departure from my past inclinations. As I teased apart the knot of my anxieties, I saw that if I failed to make a radical change by choice, the aperture of my attraction might widen enough to include other nevers. Hence, my inventory.

In hindsight, I was surprised that I had tried to seduce only one teacher. It was in my last year of college. I attended a tiny liberal arts program that was part of a university with a radical leftist bent. By my final year, I was tired of listening to my peers hold forth in cozy seminar classes and I signed up for a workshop from the university's continuing education catalog.

It was a weekly night class, taught by a writer who had published one book of poetry. I'd never heard of him or the book, but it had been well received by critics. My professor was tall with a shaved head and an angular face. I liked him a lot, though I wasn't really attracted to him. He would sometimes mention his wife in class. In the years afterward, I told myself that he was a conquest, that I just wanted to see if I could. Now, a decade later, I saw that it wasn't true, or not the whole truth. I had wanted to be a writer since childhood. This professor praised my writing. He told me that I had talent, that I was the most talented student in the class. I believed he meant it. Of course, he didn't say these things in front of everyone.

Back in 2001, it was more common for a professor to invite interested students out for drinks after a class. It was also more common for professors to sleep with students, which was frowned upon by some but still mostly accepted. After our class, a small group would often move on to a nearby bar and share a few drinks. He and I were frequently the last two remaining at the bar. Once, we left together and walked through Washington Square Park. As we walked, I told him that I sometimes snorted heroin, which was a lie. I had been regularly shooting it for years.

"That seems like a bad idea," he said. I dismissed his concern and he did not voice it again.

The last time we went out for drinks was the night of our final class. He and I both got a little drunk, and at the end of the evening we shared a cab back to Brooklyn. As soon as my professor gave the driver his address, we began to kiss furiously in the back seat, as if we had agreed to it beforehand. While our taxi sped over the Manhattan Bridge he reached under my shirt and then my skirt. A few minutes later the cab pulled up in front of his brownstone. He removed his hands from me and smoothed his clothes. I could practically smell the panic emanate from him as he fled the car. I never saw him again.

I wrote to him the following semester, my last, to request a recommendation letter for graduate school applications. He did not respond. I called him a few times and got through once, but when I said my name, he hung up on me. I was twenty-one and did not understand his panic. *I didn't even want to have an affair with him,* I thought indignantly. I did not care if we ever kissed again. I had only enjoyed his good opinion of me and of my writing, and I needed a third recommender. I felt cheated. I was angry at him for being a coward and also at myself, because I knew that if I had left it alone, I would have gotten a letter. Perhaps even a mentor.

I had told the story to friends and lovers a few times over the intervening years and each time I had claimed responsibility. I made my younger self out to be the predator. When I wrote the story in my inventory, now a professor further in my own career than he had been back then, I saw how assigning myself responsibility for the incident had been a way of managing what, in the end, felt like an embarrassing misjudgment, as well as an abandonment. Better to have been *bad* than innocent. The truth was that I had been terribly disappointed by him. I never did find the kind of mentorship I now provide to my own students, and perhaps this explained why.

Over the years my anger waned. Eventually, I was the adjunct with one book that few had heard of. That life was grueling, even without a family to support. Still, no matter how demoralized, I could not imagine fingering an undergrad in the back of a cab. I knew that no student of mine, no matter how seductive, could have made a victim of me. I would always have been the one responsible.

In this episode, I saw the prototype of a pattern that emerged from my inventory. Like the last woman I kissed, I had confused my admiration for my professor with desire. I had mistakenly thought that sex was the closest I could get to him. I thought that if he wanted me I would be protected. Ironically, that approach had precluded all other forms of connection, as it so often did.

After I finished grad school and before I sold my first book, I went back to food service. I got a job at a small restaurant named after a spice. It was a much nicer place than any I had worked in before. There was a different menu printed every night and candles on the tables. The owner was the head chef, as is often the case in such restaurants. He seemed gruff during the interview, but I had known many grumpy chefs and was undeterred. I dug out my waist aprons and dressed in black for my first shift, thrilled at the prospect of a nightly cash payout.

Something began to waver in me as I took the first few orders. I still knew how to do the job, but a woodenness came over me when it was time to smile and wink and mold myself around the unspoken desires of strangers. Over the evening's course, my body's unwillingness to comply dismayed me. Luckily, the higher end the restaurant, the less affect is expected from its waitstaff.

At the end of the night, I made a small error. "What are you, stupid?" the chef shouted from behind the line. Chefs had shouted worse things at me in the past; abuse from chefs was a given in many restaurants and rated a pretty minor offense overall. But I was no longer inured to it. I had just spent two years at the front of college classrooms in which, however underpaid, I was treated with respect, even deference. I had ascended to a different realm of employment, where I was not required to use my body or my sexuality in order to get paid. Nor was I required to suffer these kinds of overt humiliations.

When I cashed out, I was left with more than I had ever reaped from a single restaurant shift. I zipped the wad of bills into my coat pocket and told the house manager that I would not be back the following night or any thereafter. I never worked the floor of a restaurant again. Sometimes I miss it, but I am always grateful for the privilege to have quit that life.

When I walk into a classroom on the first day of the semester, I scan the room of faces and feel their expectations swell in waves toward me. There is a way to hold attention, to respond and react to the desires of others—all performers know it, all seducers. I learned it not in the dungeon, but in the dining rooms of all those restaurants, the clatter of dishes wafting with the smell of garlic from back of the house. I learned to hear those other signals, to shape myself around them.

As a teacher, I do not want to implant knowledge in my students' brains, but to make them fall in love with a subject, an idea, a work of art, a practice. The best teachers exercise a charisma that hypnotizes their audience and induces selective attention both to the teacher and to the subject she teaches. Like the lover who captures the attention of the beloved and the actor on a stage, every performer is a Scheherazade, spinning stories to forestall a death. Part of what generates that charisma is a belief that lack of attention is a kind of death.

I did not like to think of myself as someone who depended upon the attention of others, though the very structure of my life indicated that I was, as that canny therapist had once intimated. It was impossible to fully account for the ways this dependence had shaped not only my relationship to work, but that to every person I encountered. Spending years thinking of people as slot machines to win by extracting their favor, knowing the security of my life depended on it, that humiliation was always a risk, did not set me up for healthy intimate relationships. It had taken me that long to understand that even on a good night the house always won.

H OW'S THE CELIBACY GOING?" Ray asked. We sat on the porch of the house she was living in, just a few blocks from my apartment. Everyone called it Chicken House because the front yard was fenced in to house a bunch of chickens and their coop. Chicken House had just gotten a new chicken who was small with fluffy white feathers that looked like fur. It was called a Silky, and it strutted around the yard like a tiny celebrity, somewhere between a stuffed animal and a dinosaur. It was impossible not to laugh whenever I looked at it.

"Good?" I said. "Good. Less anxious. I feel . . . as happy as I've ever felt?" I paused, surprised at my own words, which were true. "I think I could just stay like this for a long time."

"Happy or celibate?"

"Both, actually. But I meant happy." I shifted my legs on the wooden bench. The humidity had made them sticky. I was aware of the proximity of our bare thighs, the parallel distance of our hips, our shoulders, our breasts.

"What if you want to stay celibate forever?" Ray asked.

"Unlikely," I said, and shrugged. "But I guess I will, in that case."

Half of the time, Ray now lived a few hours away, on the campus where her mentor taught so that she could work as a research assistant on a massive new project. She was still seeing Bridesmaid, and going on other dates, too, but mostly focused on work.

"Do you miss anything?" she asked.

"Weirdly, no," I said. "I mean, I have lots of feelings, but not about missing sex. I still notice cute people, but after I remember that there's nothing to pursue, I relax. It's a relief, actually." I told her about the playwright who had thanked me for the endorphins and the sculptor, who had both recently circled back. Rather than issuing a rain check, I'd simply told them I wasn't available. The sculptor had been gracious and wished me well. The playwright had pushed back a bit.

When will you be available? she'd texted.

Not for the foreseeable future.

Are you involved with someone?

No.

What if we just get a coffee?

Whereas her persistence might have flattered me six months earlier, it now repelled me. Why pursue an unavailable stranger? It was a question I might have asked any number of otherwise reasonable people, including my past self, but the playwright's behavior now seemed unhinged. The discrepancy between what I knew intellectually and what I wanted had finally aligned. At least in this one small case.

When it was time for Ray to go to work, I jogged down the porch steps and waved goodbye to the chickens. It was a beautiful summer day, hot but not roasting-garbage hot, so I went on a long meandering walk, toggling between music and an audiobook. I had increasingly felt a spilling kind of emotionality, a state that I had sometimes reached on solo road trips or long flights, when I was alone for a stretch of time without distraction. I'd written my most heartfelt letters while on cross-country flights. I'd get hooked on some plaintive song and sink into the place where I had access to my truest feelings, the big ones I couldn't bear to feel all the time, or sometimes even when I wanted to. In that state, I thought about the people I loved and felt the most distilled measure of my affection, so pure that it took on a pained aspect, like touch in the moments after orgasm or upon a newly healed scar.

I had found myself slipping in and out of this state more rapidly over recent weeks. In romantic relationships, my emotions tended to consolidate around my partner. I felt longing and so I longed for them. I felt grateful and I was grateful to them. Whereas now, without such a focus, I simply longed, or gave thanks. I could direct those feelings toward ice cream or attention or friends, but increasingly I didn't. Instead of narrowing the scope of my feeling, I expanded it. A light that shone not on specific objects, but illuminated everything in proximity. I lay in the warm sheets of the morning and yearned. I walked across Brooklyn, past crowded stoops and sidewalk cafés and heavy-headed flowers in garden plots—fat peonies and blue hydrangeas—I smelled the blooming green of summer mixed with city-musk. In some moments every bit of life seemed to prove the existence of God. "It was odd, she thought," writes Virginia Woolf in *To the Lighthouse*, "how if one was alone, one leant to inanimate things; trees, streams, flowers; felt they expressed one; felt they became one; felt they knew one, in a sense were one; felt an irrational tenderness thus (she looked at that long steady light) as for oneself."

I had always thought that seduction would materialize divinity, that doorway cut in the shape of a body. What a cosmic joke that chastity had come so much closer. It gave me new respect for the mystic nuns who had achieved so many of my own aspirations.

In 1098, Hildegard was born as her mother's tenth child and, keeping with the tradition in noble families, her parents gave her to the church as a tithe. At eight years old, Hildegard was locked into a single room with Jutta, a disturbed teenager from a more respected noble family. Jutta, at fourteen, had chosen the ascetic life of an anchoress over the relatively social one of a nun. She would live secluded until her death, in a stone room adjacent to a Benedictine monastery at Disibodenberg, in what is now Germany's Rhineland.

The monks performed last rites on Jutta before she was locked into the room in which she would spend the rest of her life. Here, young Hildegard joined her and lived for thirty years. Through a small window, food and waste were passed, and the young women could observe services. The rest of their daily lives would have been filled with prayer, study—Hildegard learned to read the Psalter in Latin—and physical work like weaving and embroidery.

In later years, other young girls were gifted to the anchorage. When Jutta died, the thirty-eight-year-old Hildegard and her charges founded a new abbey of which the future saint was named abbess. Reading about the shocking deprivations of her early life, I understood the flowing hair of her nuns in a different way. Hildegard, likely traumatized by her early exposure to Jutta's self-harms, did not believe in mortifications of the flesh. Her writings suggest that Jutta was a harsh mistress to whom she was nonetheless faithful. How could she not be, to the only person whom she could access? But her work after Jutta's death speaks her disagreement with the brutality of her mentor's asceticism.

I often imagined the time just after Jutta's death. Hildegard would have been in her late thirties, only a couple of years older than I was. For thirty years she had been confined not only to a small stone-walled prison but to a self-conception defined not, as mine had been, by a string of besotted lovers, but by a single other person, a madwoman and sadist who came to rely on Hildegard over time, but did not *love* her by any definition I would recognize.

Imagine the glory of the first day, when that woman stepped out from the shadows of her confinement. How green the world would have been! The wood outside the abbey must have greeted her like a cabal of loving faces. I wept actual tears when I imagined it: the sunlight a warm and holy gaze finally cradling her starved body, the dew weeping from branches into her hair as she unbraided it.

It was this frame of reference I wanted to idolize now, not the drunks and love junkies of my youth. Hildegard lived for a different kind of love. The spiritual theory on which her faith rested was one she called *viriditas,* a Latin noun that indicates greenness, fertility, lushness, and all vital life-giving properties. The opposing half of this duality was dryness, "*ariditas,* a shriveling into barrenness." She called *viriditas* "the greening power of God," and understood it in both literal and metaphorical terms. It referred to the interconnectedness of all nature, including rocks, soil, plants, animal life, while "the soul is the green life-force of the flesh. For, indeed, the body grows and progresses on account of the soul, just as the earth becomes fruitful through moisture." It easily described my own sublime sense of the everythingness around me, which I recognized most pointedly in the greenness of natural life.

The concept of *viriditas* reminded me of a documentary about the abstract expressionist painter Agnes Martin. In it, the filmmaker had asked the artist about the first of her famous grid paintings. "I was sitting and thinking about innocence," Martin told her. "As a matter of fact, I was thinking of the innocence of trees. I thought it was quite easy to be innocent if you're a tree. And into my mind there came a grid, you know. Lines this way and lines that way. And I thought, my goodness, am I supposed to paint that? Nobody will ever think it's a painting." Still, she obeyed that vision and painted all six square feet of it. When she had finished, she offered it to the Museum of Modern Art and they took it.

Another woman who found her calling in midlife, Martin would have loved Hildegard. She probably did, in fact. She and one of her lovers, the artist Lenore Tawney, read Alban Butler's *Lives of the Saints* together when they both lived in New York City at the famous Coenties Slip, where Martin produced her most famous works. Like Hildegard, she was an artist with visions, though hers had a diagnosis: schizophrenia. She, too, found meaning and structure in artistic practice and in spiritual rigor. Influenced by eastern spiritual philosophies, Taoism in particular, Martin often denounced the use of intellectualism in artmaking. "The intellect has nothing to do with artwork," she told a class of students at the Skowhegan School in 1987. "A lot of people will think that social understanding or something like that is going to lead us to the truth, but it isn't. It is understanding of yourself." Though she was and continues to be seen as a kind of modern mystic, Martin belonged to no formalized religion.

"I read all about everybody else's religion before I settled on mine," she said. "It's a secret religion. You don't go out looking for converts or anything like that. Well, I guess I can tell you. It's about love, not God. There's no God but just love. That's all I'm going to tell you."

The simplicity of her religion appealed to me the way Hildegard's theory of *viriditas* did. It sounded like the beguines. Akin to many children of secular liberals, I had a deeply engrained distrust of duality, but also craved a simplistic fundamental belief that would guide my every action. As a child, I performed daily bibliomancy by pulling books off of our shelves at home, or in libraries and classrooms. I would slide my finger down a random page to land on a single line, hoping for words to live by.

You are either walking toward God or away from God, people in recovery sometimes said, and the words rang in me, plucking the string of that old desire. Reading of Hildegard's *viriditas,* I heard it again: *You are either walking toward greenness or away from it.* Hearing Martin's words, I heard it again: *You are either walking toward understanding of self or away from it.* Deep inside, I knew that the righteous path was often that simple. I had been thinking of this time as a dry season, but it had been the most fertile of my life since childhood. I had run dry when I spent that vitality in worship of lovers. In celibacy, I felt more *wet* than I had in years.

I WAS GETTING TOWARD the end of my list. As its chronology approached my teen years, a part of me relaxed. It was hard to imagine I'd done much harm at that age. If the urge to please in romantic relationships dominated much of my behavior as an adult, it had governed me entirely as a teenager. That fact seemed to preclude most forms of harm. Many of my early sexual experiences had been marked by empty consent. Though I balked at identifying with victimhood, my teens were the one time period in which I came close to claiming it. I couldn't fully admit this at the time, but I was looking forward to feeling a little bit justified for my romantic misbehavior as an adult. You can imagine my surprise when these expectations were upended.

In Boston, around the time I waited tables at the Greenhouse, I got into my first committed relationship with a man. A boy, really. We were both teenagers, living on our own for the first time. My best friend, the beautiful gay hairstylist, gave me the silent treatment for days after I started dating this boy. *I like you better as a lesbian,* my roommate sulked. But my first boyfriend adored me. He left flowers and packs of cigarettes on our porch, rode me on his handlebars to the hospital when I pulled a rib muscle from coughing with a case of bronchitis.

When I fell for one of his roommates a year later, I stopped answering his calls. I lived in Jamaica Plain then, a neighborhood that felt incredibly distant from Somerville, where he'd been able to walk to my place in five minutes. I had no idea how to break up with someone, so I quit him the way I'd quit all of my jobs: I disappeared. Eventually, he stopped calling, or at least leaving messages.

A year or two later I ran into him one winter day at the café-cum-ice-cream-parlor where he worked. I was in yet another relationship by then. We said cautious hellos and I asked if he had a cigarette. He joined me outside and we stood hunched inside our winter coats, backs to the wind that rushed down Mass Ave.

"Hey, we're cool, right?" I asked him, encouraged by his willingness to share a smoke with me.

He stared at me, incredulous, and I instantly understood my miscalculation.

"You broke my *heart*," he said. "I was sick, literally puking, for weeks. I didn't know if we were broken up until I learned that you were with someone else." I felt sick then, too, and managed not to remember this terrible correction until I reached his name on my inventory. How stupid I had been to think that the urge to please precluded harm. It was an urge driven by fear, not magnanimity. Self-centered fear leaves no room to care for another.

The list wasn't complete without my earliest romances, though until fourteen they were not sexually consummated. The inventory of my mistakes with men revealed the lessons I gleaned from them. It also revealed that it was the girls whom I loved more, at least by the definition I'd longest understood love.

My first best friend was Tanya. Until I was five, we lived in Springfield, Massachusetts, an old factory city known only for being the longtime home of Dr. Seuss. Tanya's family lived down the block, and she was the only girl of her parents' six children. Her five brothers had toughened her, and she practiced her toughness on me. I was a year younger than her and a devoted acolyte, Hildegard to her Jutta.

After Tanya was Jessie, a volatile but charismatic girl whose parents drank screwdrivers all day. After Jessie was Emily, who pinched my arms and legs so hard they flowered with purple bruises. After Emily was Ariel, who was like a competitive older sister, both protective and cruel. Then there was Tammy, who told me the other sixth graders were calling me a slut. Finally, there was Jessica, who would punish me with silence whenever a boy flirted with me, and who became the first girl I ever kissed.

As I wrote in my inventory notebook, I remembered sleeping through a recent appointment with my therapist. The following week, I had explained to her my anxiety about missing our session.

"I knew I had a late reading schedule for the night before," I said. "It made sense that I would want to sleep in. I should have just canceled our session."

"Why didn't you?" she asked.

"I guess a part of me fears that you'll be annoyed," I told her.

"Have I ever seemed annoyed?"

"Never."

"And so what if I am?" she asked. "You paid for the missed session. What's so bad about the prospect of my feeling a little annoyed?"

"Well, maybe you'll stop working with me."

"Have I given you the impression that our relationship is conditional upon your not canceling or missing sessions?"

"No," I had said. "I think it's an older fear than that."

In hindsight, it is easy to see the cruelties of those early romances, the machinations that I could not recognize as a child. Harder to describe is the devotion between me and each of those girls. The times we laughed until we peed our pants. The religious intensity with which we pledged our commitment to each other. The hours we spent murmuring on the telephone. The times they each said to me: *You can't tell anyone this.* Or: *You're the only one I trust.* Or: *I would die without you.* They all dominated me in a daily kind of

way, sometimes physical, but more often emotional. They threatened conditional love, and I was easily controlled by this method.
I feared abandonment and was macerated by adoration. Together,
we convinced me that I depended on them for emotional safety and
social acceptance.

Over time, however, cracks spidered into that belief and became
fissures. I remember once, in a rare divulgence, telling another girl
that I feared ostracization if I lost Tammy as a friend. The girl looked
at me, puzzled.

"No, it's the other way around," she corrected me, as if I were daft.
"No one really likes Tammy. You could be so popular if you weren't
always with her."

My chin dropped in shock at this information.

The girl went on, "She talks about you behind your back, too, you
know." The devastating oracle then wandered off and left me reeling.

Some version of this revelation played out with most of these
passionate friendships. It happened often enough that I began to
wonder if my beloveds were actually the more vulnerable half of our
dyads. They had always understood this, I think, and thus known
how important it was to control me. Though my loves could be
punitive, sometimes downright cruel, the power they held over me
was superficial. Whenever I saw this, my instinct was never to reject
but instead to protect them.

In one of my weekly sessions, I described this complex dynamic to
my therapist.

"Do you think you've imposed this fear of the conditional on all
of your relationships?" she asked me.

"Probably."

"It makes sense why you've brought such vigilance to all of them."

"In all of my long-term relationships," I explained to her, "this
thing happens after a year or two, where I don't want to be touched
while I'm sleeping. I feel sort of panicked and angry whenever my
partners try to touch me or cuddle me in my sleep."

"Why do you think that is?"

"Well, I'm wondering if it's a function of exhaustion. Like, I can't ever stop monitoring them, tending to the relationship. Sleep is the only place I get to stop. To be alone."

"That makes sense."

"I'm very good at convincing myself I'm dependent on things," I said.

As I wrote out the repetitive story in my notebook, again and again, I was tempted to make villains of those girls. Some of them had been horrible, but a part of me honored them. They had the ardency of Greek gods, whose stories I had always loved for their operatic passions and analogical genius—going on three thousand years old and they were still so easy to find ourselves in.

The beauty of the inventory was that its aim was to locate not blame but my own responsibility, to let those stories settle in the in-between space where all love ultimately lay: the field on which every person did their best, whatever the wreckage.

Distilled in my notebook, I saw the common instinct among my lovers and me, the implicit belief that love should be fought for and maintained. Certainly for women, its roots were sunk into the centuries during which our survival was dependent upon men's favor, upon our desirability as wives, but when I looked back at those first passions with other girls, they less resembled the coquettish prescriptions for girls than those of men. Our dramas were not those of blushing virgins but of troubadours.

People have always been falling in love, but, before the twelfth century, there wasn't much of a cultural story about it, nor instructions for an ideal procedure of it. Most stories in the early Middle Ages took the model of ancient Greek and Roman epics, tales of war heroism and love among men, parables that reified group loyalty over individual fulfillment. In the twelfth century, Church reforms shifted religious focus from a punitive and remote God Almighty to

Jesus, who had a human body and a message of love. Couple that with the advent of women's consent in marriage and the rise of literacy and the aristocracy, and the story of romantic love was born.

The troubadours were poets who traveled from village to village in the southern region of present-day France, performing their musical stories of courtly love until the popular pastime was taken up by singer-poets across Europe. "Good Lady," writes Bernart de Ventadorn, "I ask you nothing else but / that you take me as your servant, / so that I could serve you as a good master, / whatever my reward may be." This posture of subservience by the lover who wishes to possess his audience emotionally and physically was familiar to me.

What would I do without you? my first loves asked. *I would die,* they'd answer for me.

You'll never have to know, I assured them.

"If only I could see you for a second I'm sure this chronic ache would go away . . . You haunt me," wrote Vincent Millay's college paramour.

"Master," wrote Emily Dickinson in a mysterious unpublished draft of a poem, "open your life wide, and / take me in forever . . . nobody else will / see me, but you."

On some inchoate level, we knew these professions weren't true. It was a performance, a transaction not of divulged truth but of emotional comfort. I was given the pleasure of feeling necessary and worshipped, and I paid for this with the promise of devotion. There was pleasure, also, in the theater of it. Adolescent girlhood brought fresh nuances of disempowerment every day. How much better to perform the prostrations of a man consumed by passion, to cast the long shadow of implicit dominance with our small, rupturing forms. What a thrill to taste the worship of someone physically safe, relative to men. We were not aware of all this, of course. We had no idea where we had gotten those scripts, that they weren't authored by us. We knew only the swoon of our emotions and the satisfaction of such enactment.

Andreas Capellanus, in his famous 1184 text, *The Art of Courtly Love,* offers a list of detailed instruction for the aspirational lover. Among them:

2. He who is not jealous cannot love.
12. A true lover does not desire to embrace in love anyone except his beloved.
13. When made public love rarely endures.
14. The easy attainment of love makes it of little value; difficulty of attainment makes it prized.
19. If love diminishes, it quickly fails and rarely revives.
25. A true lover considers nothing good except what he thinks will please his beloved.
30. A true lover is constantly and without intermission possessed by the thought of his beloved.

Reading his list for the first time, I thought of all the songs that obsessed me as a teen. Concrete Blonde's "Joey," taped off the radio onto a blank cassette and played over and over, and Tracy Chapman's "For My Lover." All those anthems to enmeshment that made my guts twist before obsession with a lover ever did. I liked those songs by men, too, but there was a special allure to the women who played the troubadour. I went soft inside at the thought of a chivalrous butch. It is an echo of that feeling I knew as a girl. A combination, surely, of what I had been conditioned to want—to be pursued, treasured, hungered for—but with the physical safety and tenderness of women, whom I had always known more capable of emotional intimacy. Finally, the magical frisson of subversion. A man in leather on a motorcycle with greasy hair and a smoldering gaze could appeal to me, sure. But a woman? Be still my beating cunt.

The love story of the troubadour was absolute madness, of course. A recipe for misery. It was literal madness, even; the heroes of famous love stories were often stalkers, or, at best, morbid codependents.

It also offered a kind of permission, whispered across centuries on the pages of books and the crooning lips of entertainers, to those whose nature inclined toward obsession. *Go for it,* whispered seven centuries of love literature. If my drives were a heat-seeking missile, what better solution than to yield to their velocity, to point them in the direction of some approved object?

When the Maelstrom struck and especially after it was over, I kept asking myself, *How did this happen?* How did I fall prey to such an obsession at thirty-two, after all those years of therapy and sobriety? My inventory answered. It suggested that everything was always leading up to her, and to this. I did not regret that ruination. I could see the debt of my current clarity to that bottom.

The truth: there was no one else to blame. This drive in me had always been. It had made me an addict, this singular focus that had the power to overwhelm every other instinct, including that of survival. It would take me over a cliff and could turn anything into one.

As a kid, the only time I was allowed to binge on television was Saturday morning cartoons. My favorites were Tex Avery's Droopy Dog and sexy Red Hot Riding Hood, but of the better known characters, I had a soft spot for Wile E. Coyote. Coyote was the hapless protagonist of his skits, always trying to trap the smug Road Runner and always failing. Each of his Rube Goldberg contraptions backfired comically, and I found pathos in the grim resignation with which he opened his parasol as a boulder hurtled toward him. He was the rapacious predator, and also the underdog, the chump, the loser.

Partly, my sympathies were triggered because I rooted for the loser in every game, regardless of what team I claimed. I also related to Coyote. He looked like an absolute junkie: rangy and ragged, bloodshot eyes and greasy fur. Strung out on his desire for Road Runner, he was the hatcher of half-baked plans, a chronic underestimator, a real tweaker. Why didn't he eat something else? I understood why. Obsession made us stupid. Once that drive ignited, reason became a stranger. There was only hunger and new ways to chase it. I marveled at Coyote's ingenuity because I understood the relentless imagination of those whose perspective had narrowed straw-thin. Coyote was a hungry ghost, dying over and over.

Chuck Jones, who created the character for Warner Bros. in 1949, made him a "sick and sorry-looking skeleton" based on Mark Twain's description of a coyote in his 1872 book of travel writing, *Roughing It*. Twain's coyote was "a living, breathing allegory of Want. He is *always* hungry."

Once, walking laps around L.A.'s Silver Lake Reservoir, I spotted a coyote jogging along the inside of the chain-link that surrounded the water. He must have gotten in through a hole in the fence. Lean and haunted, he stared out at us passing humans, like, *How did I get into this hungry cage and how do I get out?* I had to turn away.

I described myself as a gremlin to my therapist, but the figure of a coyote is more accurate. A gremlin was a monster, but Wile E. Coyote, though a kind of villain, was also a slave, in bondage to his obsession. We associate villainy with power, but it is more often characterized by desperation. We are all capable of becoming predators if we get hungry enough.

To label the drive solely as one of addiction was reductive, though, and inexact. I believed that some biological quirk was its likely origin, be it a serotonin deficit or an inheritance of intergenerational trauma, but ultimately it didn't matter so long as I understood it wasn't a moral failing, or a life sentence. Addiction could be a consequence of it and certainly it could lead (and had) to moral failures, but the drive itself was something else, more capacious in its potential. The conditions that cause a tornado are not a tornado nor its wreckage; they are power inchoate.

The essay I had probably assigned to students most over my years of teaching was Annie Dillard's "Living Like Weasels." The magic of the essay is that it has almost no narrative. Dillard simply makes eye contact with a weasel one day on her usual walk around a pond. "If you and I looked at each other that way," she explains, "our skulls would split and drop to our shoulders." The rest of the essay is ostensibly an ode to the weasel, its "black hole of eyes," but really a bit of glorious thinking on instinct and how best to live. "We can live any way we want," she promises. "People take vows of poverty, chastity, and obedience—even of silence—by choice. The thing is to stalk your calling in a certain skilled and supple way, to locate the most tender and live spot and plug into that pulse. This is yielding, not fighting. A weasel doesn't 'attack' anything; a weasel lives as he's meant to, yielding at every moment to the perfect freedom of single necessity."

I had read the essay probably thirty times, and I always thought first that *yielding at every moment to single necessity* could be a description of bondage to addiction, poverty, survival under domination. Coyote yielded at every moment to his single necessity, and so had I as an active addict. So had I, as a lover, prioritized my limerent obsessions, no matter how fleeting, over everything else I loved. But Dillard wasn't describing the addict. She described the artist, I thought, though it could be anyone, "choosing the given with a fierce and pointed will." The key was choice. The difference between bondage to a single necessity and the perfect freedom of one was agency. Once obsession locked in, I lost the power of choice. But before that, I still had it: my perfect freedom.

I thought of Agnes Martin again. She had been plagued by psychotic episodes throughout her life but it still looked like freedom to me, because she had devoted it to art. She had never described her life as an unhappy one. She had suffered, yes, but also chosen the life she wanted, a life that would structure and direct the insurmountable forces intrinsic in her. If anyone could be characterized as in possession of a *fierce and pointed will,* it was Martin.

Wasn't it also that drive, that *fierce and pointed will,* that I had steered to the end of every book I had written? It had not awoken like some dragon the first time I shot heroin, nor with my first kiss.

As a kid, I read myself into a stupor. I lay on the floor of my bed-room, taping songs off the radio that made me quake inside, cracked my chest with faults I could still trace. I listened to the world news and knew that I could cry every day of my life and never run dry of sorrow.

What did people who had this thing inside them *do* with it if they didn't quell it with substances or direct it at other people? Was art enough? It hadn't been enough to prevent the Maelstrom.

Consider Margery Kempe, born in 1373, who *did* weep incessantly. She wept all over her village of Bishop's Lynn, wailing and railing for Jesus. She was ill over it, like a lovesick girl, like today's teens who film themselves weeping and upload their videos to the internet. Villagers, understandably, complained about Margery and her weep-ing. She was a disturbing presence, a nuisance. Maybe, a prophet. Almost a saint, but not quite. Instead, she is the unofficial patron of teenage girls.

I first learned of her when I was fifteen. By that time, I'd learned to suppress my tears, to plug the dam of my open heart. Then I fell in love for the first time. My heart uncorked like a bottle of cham-pagne. One day after school I wept for three hours while listening to PJ Harvey's "Oh My Lover" on repeat. Idols are often chosen for the narrative they offer to make sense of our suffering. In the Maelstrom, I carted Carl Jung's *The Red Book* around with me, des-perately hoping that my madness in the desert would also be the basis for my greatest work. Similarly, I was comforted at fifteen by the tears Margery had wept more than six hundred years before me, and the fact that her story was still read.

A lot of mystics wept ecstatically when they were teens. They began the practice of mortification as soon as they realized what their futures inside the sexual economies of hetero-patriarchy looked like, competing with the fervor of child athletes for the medal of sainthood. Catherine of Siena began fasting at sixteen when her mother tried to marry her off to her sister's widower. Years later, when asked how she did this, Catherine explained: "Build a cell inside your mind, from which you can never flee."

Margery was older when she had her spiritual awakening, already married to a man. Her life ruptured after she gave birth to her first child and she spent months consumed with visions of devils and demons who implored her to renounce her faith. She also had visions of Jesus, including those in which she was present at the Passion. These prompted her to quit sex with her husband, attend confession multiple times per day, and roam the streets of her village ranting and weeping profusely.

We know this because she wrote the first English autobiography, and in this sense, at least, she is part of my own lineage. Among other things, it describes the reckoning after her child's birth, her visions, struggles with erotic desire, failed business ventures, and eventually her vow to live a celibate religious life while still married. After she gave up trying to live like a normal person, she mostly made pilgrimages to holy sites, visited with the anchoress Julian of Norwich, and, like the beguines, was accused of heresy multiple times for preaching, which the church forbade women from doing.

There are many who say that she and most of the female medieval mystics were insane and undergoing psychotic hallucinations. Others say that her book and the writings of many mystics are evidence that this is not true, but perhaps in part a canny presentation so that they might speak in a time when women should not. Both might be true.

"I perform my story by lip-synching Margery's loud longing," writes Robert Glück in *Margery Kempe*. The book combines Margery's story with that of his own obsessive love affair with a younger man, L. "I kept Margery in mind for twenty-five years but couldn't enter her love until I also loved a young man who was above me," he writes.

The two narratives intertwine in his novel—sometimes Margery is Glück, sometimes she is herself, jumping time—and the text becomes a mimicry of the lovers blending and unblending, alternately confusing and ecstatic. "Jesus and Margery act out my love. Is that a problem? Every star in every galaxy spurts in joyful public salute to my orgasms with L."

Glück writes in tandem with Margery to tell his own story, and in collaboration with others, too, borrowing bodily descriptions from his friends. It is a tactic he uses in other books. He alludes to the writing process throughout *Margery,* which gives it yet another dimension of meta-narrative. *See what I must do to face this story,* the book insists. *How art is truer than memory.* I am doing the same thing here: building a linear narrative, grafting other stories onto it, folding time to see the patterns. If I suggest a single meaning it will be a lie.

"This novel records my breakdown," Glück admits. That was one of the reasons why I loved it. Glück had made a person his higher power, as I did, and set into motion his own maelstrom. My book recorded a breakdown, too. Like Glück's, it was full of tears and fucking. It presented love as "a human religion in which another person is believed in."

His book and Kempe's proved that such kinds of worship and passion were transhistorical. I had not only made a person my higher power, but had joined an ancient tradition of doing so. The difference between Glück and my worship, and that of Kempe, however, was Dillard's distinction: *choice,* and the successful exertion of one's will. Kempe chose her God and aligned her will with his. However antisocial she appeared, Kempe felt empowered by his grace, whereas Glück and I were slaves to the ecstasy of erotic obsession.

"I want to be a woman and a man penetrating him," Glück wrote, "his inner walls roiling around me like satin drenched in hot oil, and I want to be the woman and man he continually fucks. I want to be where total freedom is. I push myself under the surface of Margery's story, holding my breath for a happy ending of my own."

Oh, how I missed it as I read Glück's sentences. It felt like forever since I'd worshipped another body. My freedom from it was a relief, but when I slipped into the memory, my whole body quaked. At twenty-six, during her sexual awakening as a lesbian, Susan Sontag wrote in her journal, "To love one's body and use it well, that's primary . . . I can do that, I know, for I am freed now." I had felt that way for so long. I was sad to be changing my mind. If only all freedoms, once found, lasted forever.

The sexual hunger I'd been seized by in the Maelstrom was relentless; it had a purity to it. *The perfect freedom of single necessity.* It had not been Dillard's freedom, of course, but bondage. There was a beautiful simplicity to it, though. I had always struggled for control, and there was pleasure in forfeiting that power to someone so interested in it. Looking at that younger me, the one so numb and helpless, the broken promise of every attraction—I have sympathy for her later hunger, the gleeful gorging to have met, and met, and met. It *is* the ecstasy my body promised all those years before.

How lucky I had been to know it: body half moth, half flame, gleefully burning. I had flung myself against other bodies like a mystic in rapture, wet at both ends, face bright with tears. I had nursed the softest parts of women, made a sacrament of them no less holy than the blood and the body of any other savior. I wouldn't take back a moment of it. I wouldn't return to it, either.

I T HAD BEEN almost four years since our breakup when Best Ex and I made plans to share dinner and go to a mutual friend's play in the West Village. We hadn't seen each other since that tortured time.

When I saw her dear face and smelled her familiar smell—hair pomade and vetiver cologne—I could have burst into tears, but resisted. She had loved me better than anyone outside my family, and I still missed her every day. At her arm's quick squeeze, the still shaking part of me leapt out, grasping for the steady ground of her. I knew better than to let her see this. I was lucky she had agreed to see me.

I am still not proud of the way I left her. I jumped straight off the listing ship of our life together into the Maelstrom, which meant following a very hard two years with two exponentially harder ones. The latter were also my most selfish years, as if I were making up for the generosities of the previous crisis, or, more charitably, as if I had saved up my own crisis until my Best Ex was well enough for me to leave her.

Since then, we had tried to be friends, but it was a struggle. Some wounds are slow to heal. I was still riddled with regret, still a little bit in love with her. Though it had been four years, I hadn't moved on. Two of those years, I'd been captive in the terrible holding pattern of the Maelstrom. After that, I'd been manic with freedom, distracted by a string of sputtering romances, uninterested in digging for my grief.

It was one thing to get entangled with a twenty-five-year-old or a man. But it was another to betray someone I deeply loved, with whom I had built a life. That kind of breach was not just a betrayal of the beloved, but of the self. It necessitated a sort of dream state, a dissociation from love. The ecstasy of limerence, projected onto a new person. The mania of obsession precluded empathy and made it easier to break the heart of someone I loved. It isn't callousness that leads most people to cheat their way out of long-term relationships, but often its opposite. They grasp for the heart-anesthetizing power of new infatuation, which enables them to commit the necessary violence of breaking up. Or, their betrayal forces the responsibility upon their betrayed partners. Having done it myself, I am not without sympathy, but it is the coward's way. Whether ghosting or cheating or pleasing, avoidance in relationships was always selfish, I was learning.

The previous year, Best Ex and I had spent a gorgeous afternoon driving around San Francisco, where she'd been living at the time. I had told her about the Last Man, who I was then dating.

"Don't settle, buddy," she had said to me, gentle but firm, invoking the nickname we'd shared when we were together. I had wanted to retort that I wasn't settling, but I couldn't, because her words had made me realize that I was.

For this reason and others I was relieved to tell her that I was finally taking a break.

"That's good," she said. "That's really good." Her low voice reached into me and touched some part that still craved her approval. In that moment, I would have fallen to my knees and crawled across Manhattan if it would have earned me her forgiveness, but I knew forgiveness didn't work like that.

After the play, we wandered the maze of West Village streets and ended up facing the Stonewall National Monument in Christopher

Park, a little green enclosure across from the Stonewall Inn. There were candles and flowers everywhere. Earlier that summer, a man had walked into a gay nightclub in Orlando, Florida, and killed forty-nine people, wounded fifty-three others. We stood there for a while reading the tributes. Soon, tears streamed down both of our faces, for our dead kin and our past selves, for all the ways we'd loved and failed each other.

It seemed impossible to keep an open heart in this world, faced not only with my own harms, but those of strangers. Even as a kid it had seemed impossible. One might never stop weeping. To feel it all would leave no time for anything but grief. It made sense to keep the channel of one's heart narrowed the width of a single person, to peer through the keyhole at a single room rather than turn to face the world.

In those days, like now, it was hard to confront or look away from the news reports. There were earthquakes, a typhoon, a virus outbreak, and multiple civil wars with civilian deaths reported daily. In the U.S., a presidential election approached and the rhetoric of the candidates made me nauseated with anger. Had it always been this bad? I wondered.

I attended a protest in Manhattan and chanted for hours beside my friends and thousands of other furious New Yorkers. I had been raised to protest and remembered standing with my family in similar crowds as a child, hand-painted signs held up, but this was a different time. The politicians were more rapacious and craven than I ever imagined they would let us see, and this flagrancy foreshadowed worse. I waved my sign, monitored the ticking clock of my bladder, and struggled to believe that our presence would have any effect beyond satisfying the need to do something. Maybe that was enough. The will to go on wasn't nothing. Still, it depressed me.

"It's exhilarating to be alive in a time of awakening consciousness," writes Adrienne Rich. "It can also be confusing, disorienting, and painful." To have an awakening consciousness about the sickness of the society in which one lives or about the dysfunction of one's own life can feel like living in a roach-infested building. The situation is much worse than you thought. They are falling from the goddamn ceiling. Management won't acknowledge the problem. The other tenants are in denial. It can seem easier to just abandon it than spend one's energy battling the ongoing conditions. I understood entirely why history was studded with separatist movements. It is both psychologically and materially hard to divest from a society while participating in it.

Mother Ann Lee and the Shakers provide an unlikely but compelling example. Born in 1737, Ann Lee was raised in Manchester, England, a factory town in which half of all children and nearly that many women died in childbirth. Like most of her peers, Ann began factory work at the age of eight. She had already developed a profound hatred of sex, which she recognized as a compulsory duty for women that inevitably led to misery. As a young woman, she joined the Shaking Quakers, an ecstatic sect led by charismatic Mother Jane Wardley, who mentored Ann and preached the benefits of celibacy.

Ann's father forced her to marry at twenty-six, and from this juncture her story recalls that of Margery Kempe. After the death of her fourth child, Ann disavowed sexual union, naming it the root of all her suffering. Despite the protestations of her husband, Ann insisted and eventually he succumbed, converting to both celibacy and Shakerism.

Thus began Mother Ann's career as a preacher. She spread her gospel of celibacy and gender equality throughout the streets of decrepit Manchester, often landing herself in jail. She claimed a vision of Jesus Christ in which he named her his proxy on earth. Despite her criminalization, joiners rushed to Mother Ann, who promised women a sanctified path to freedom from sexual and domestic bondage. Eventually, she fled persecution and led her followers to the New World, where the Shaker community flourished with followers.

Dressed in gray garb like the beguines, the Shakers sublimated their sexual drives with ecstatic worship, wild frenzied dancing, arduous labor, and creative pursuits that gave us, among other inventions: the clothespin, the buzz saw, the flat broom, and their famous Shaker furniture. The problem with a celibate community is that it must consistently siphon members from the sexually repro-ducing community, and the separatism of the Shakers impeded this, especially after the death of their compelling, foul-mouthed leader in 1784.

I had no interest in following a charismatic leader or vilifying sex; a feature of Mother Ann's leadership was her vehement and sometimes lewd anti-sex sermons, along with her verbal humili-ation of members who tested celibate boundaries. Nonetheless, a celibate life committed to gender equality that consisted of peaceful industry, creative practice, and wild dancing sounded like a good one to me. I envied the conviction of Mother Ann, who seemed the embodiment of Dillard's *fierce and pointed will*. I didn't have to agree with her beliefs to recognize the freedom, force, and charisma of that conviction.

The only active Shaker commune that remains is Sabbathday Lake in Maine, which boasts two elderly members, but by the late 1800s, their numbers were already dwindling. The imminent extinc-tion of the Shakers made way for the movement created by a man once named George Baker.

George, who later renamed himself the Reverend Major Jealous Divine, known simply as Father Divine, was born in Rockville, Mary-land, to formerly enslaved parents. A handsome and diminutive five foot two, Father Divine was nurtured by the Black lay preachers of his Jerusalem Methodist Church, whom he idolized. After his moth-er's death, he relocated to Baltimore, where he confronted the urban realities of the Jim Crow era, and found harbor in storefront churches where he funneled his despair and anger into his talent for preaching.

Like so many of the subjects I studied, mystical experience awakened him to the belief that he was called to religious devotion.

Divine was convinced that he was the son of God, Jesus incarnate, and beholden to a staunch code of celibacy, positive thinking, and equality. Although he was and continues to be known as a civil rights activist, he diverges from other anti-racist activists in that he believed race, as well as gender, did not exist, and espoused an ideology of color-blindness rather than identity-affirming racial justice. Still, he worked to shared ends with Black activists and feminists, and succeeded to an impressive extent.

The young Father Divine left Baltimore in 1912 and returned to the South to combat Jim Crowism, a mission for which he was willing to risk his life. He inspired detractors, of course, but also attracted a fervent following of Black women who were drawn to the dapper and passionate little prophet for similar reasons that women had been to Mother Ann. During both time periods, many women's lives were characterized by domestic drudgery, sexual obligation, and the physical miseries of pregnancy and childbirth. Father Divine, like other separatists, offered freedom through sanctity. Such great numbers of women abandoned their husbands and children to follow Father Divine that a band of irate husbands and Black religious leaders protested and had Divine sent to jail, not for the first time. During his imprisonment, the press and new followers flocked to him.

By the end of the Depression, the Peace Mission movement, as Divine coined it, was officially restructured as a church. Adherents performed ecstatic worship like the Shakers, but their other primary form of sublimation was food: sumptuous banquets every night, attended by singing and praise. Again, aside from the wild religious assertions and cultish elements, this feminist society built upon principles of mutual aid, celibacy, and spiritual nourishment sounded downright utopian to me.

These concepts appealed beyond the west, as well. In 1937, Dada Lekhraj, a jeweler who lived in present-day Pakistan, founded the Brahma Kumaris, Daughters of Brahma. Like Ann Lee and George Baker, Lekhraj claimed visions: of Vishnu and Shiva, natural disasters, and an apocalyptic civil war. He sold his thriving business and began preaching a condemnation of sex as the root of all that ailed society. "I am a soul, you are a soul," he was known to repeat. Once again, women flocked to this message of gender equality and celibacy, and once again, men revolted. Wives who had joined Lekhraj's ashram were beaten, imprisoned, sued, and threatened with exile from their caste. Lekhraj was vilified and accused of sorcery. Eventually, he moved his ashram to Karachi and refined their structured communal life of sermons, yoga, worship, and work. Unlike the Shakers, Lekhraj understood that his movement would not survive without active recruitment of new members, and so proselytization became a tenet of their lifestyle. When their leader died in 1969, the Brahma Kumaris were already thriving internationally, and today the sect claims nearly a million devoted followers.

The Peace Mission movement, however, failed to maintain its numbers after the death of its charismatic leader in 1965. In the midst of a sexual revolution, celibacy was a hard sell without a compelling evangelist. Harder still was the blow of Divine's death after his lifetime promises of immortality. Today, at his estate in Pennsylvania, a small group of elderly adherents carry out his traditions, bereft of new followers.

Despite their obvious failings, these movements shared an understanding of the difficulty in divesting from the most harmful structures of society while participating in its sexual economies, out of which so many injustices spring and flourish. For this reason, separatism is the faithful companion of many celibacy movements. From the Shakers and the Peace Mission movement to radical feminist groups, to the medieval beguines, religious orders at abbeys and monasteries—people who want to divest from the structures of patriarchy and heterosexuality have understood that submersion in the active culture of oppression makes their work inestimably harder. The project of raising consciousness is hard under any conditions, and is especially daunting amid an onslaught of counter-conditioning. Unreasonable, even. The Dahomey Amazons lived inside their palace walls, Artemis in her forest, anchorites in their church cells.

I did not want to live in hermitage and was obviously not a charismatic cult-leader type. I'd never fantasized about being a leader of anything. I just wanted to make art, be useful, and avoid causing harm. I wanted to stop making other people my higher powers. I wanted to hold on to what peace celibacy had given me.

The feminist separatists appealed to me most, possibly because most of them were still having sex, often with each other. But they had failed even faster than the Shakers or the Peace Mission movement. Led by white feminists in the seventies, they hadn't considered the intersectionality of Black women's experience, how all feminists of color also need to collaborate with men of color to work for racial justice. Identity did not fall into categories neat enough to slice off of society. It would be even less realistic now, as the gender binary dissolves. The Michigan Womyn's Music Festival couldn't get their shit together and not exclude transwomen for one week annually; imagine a whole separatist society doing so. I wished that I could, that there was a working model to contemplate running off to, or in whose shape I could mold myself.

There were better ecological examples—off-gridders and so forth, but they were similarly flawed. That was a moot direction, regardless, because however radical a shift I wanted to make, I knew that it would not likely include roughing it. I was not a person driven by moral superiority and would not be satisfied by the pains of living within my own principles. I didn't even like camping.

The other common model I encountered in my study was that of people assigned female at birth who adopted celibacy in order to live as men. The Albanian sworn virgins and the Crow people's Woman Chief. Joan of Arc partially fit into this category. Some of these figures were undoubtedly transgender folks attempting to live lives in closer accordance to their true identities. Some just wanted more freedom. Joan wanted to obey her visions of Saint Michael and become a soldier. Regardless, I did not want to live as a man, nor would I need to be celibate to do so.

That left nuns. I'd been something of a hedonist, in practice if not ideology. But I understood that asceticism was not always the enemy of indulgence. All and nothing had more in common than either of them did with moderation. The deep desire for solitude, for *more* asceticism, appears in so many beguine and mystic stories. Saints are gluttons for punishment. Spiritual separatists were often political activists as well, but they all understand that they could get closer to God by making a life separate from society.

I could have joined a Buddhist monastery. Even as I entertained the idea, I knew it was no more than a thought experiment. I was tired and daunted by the work of keeping hold of my convictions. I was tempted by the comfort of the familiar. To retreat from society further would be avoidance. I had enough liberty to live with conviction. What I lacked was inspiration.

Plenty of people had done it. Many of the women I'd been reading about, for example. There were the artists and intellectuals like Agnes Martin, Adrienne Rich, and Audre Lorde. There were mystic activists, like Simone Weil and Etty Hillesum. Reading their stories, I understood that there was as much evil in human society now as there was during their lives, just as there was in the Middle Ages. It had never been easy to live against the grain of one's society, nor possible to do alone. I had it easier than any of my role models. My aspiration was modest by comparison.

I was late to discovering Hillesum, that less-known female diarist killed in the Holocaust. A teenaged depressive, Hillesum spent her early years ravaged by emotion, and "the feeling of something secret deep inside me that no one knows about." When I encountered her diary during my celibacy, the voice felt familiar. It is reminiscent of young Vincent Millay, of Plath's *The Bell Jar*—and would have been a strong candidate for worship by my own young self. But Hillesum's story radically diverges from the typical path of tormented female writer. She died young, but not a victim of her own hand or any addictive substance, except perhaps grace.

In 1941, at the age of twenty-seven, she began seeing the cultish psychoanalyst and palm reader, Julius Spier, who had studied under Carl Jung. Spier's style of treatment included "eroticized tousles" with his patients, descriptions of which make my twenty-first-century brain recoil, though Hillesum found him to be "gentle, good, and spiritually complex." Though not usually a part of his method, he became her lover. However offensive to our contemporary understanding of the boundaries between psychiatric patients and their doctors, there is no denying the great transformation their relationship inspired in her.

Spier introduced Hillesum to Rilke, the Bible, and other great works of literature that profoundly altered her worldview. Under his treatment, she underwent a true spiritual awakening. Though Jewish, her higher power was no Judeo-Christian god, but rather a conception of the internal divine, not unlike Agnes Martin's description of her own religion. Hillesum desperately wanted and in her awakening found what Rilke called his *Weltinnenraum*: a home within the self.

When the German Nazi roundups reached Amsterdam, Hillesum volunteered to work at Westerbork, a transit camp where Jews were interned before being sent on to Polish concentration camps. A month later, she refused the opportunity to flee, despite the insistence of her family. Another month later, they were all interned at Westerbork. In September of 1943, she and her family were deported to Auschwitz, where they were eventually killed. As the train left Westerbork, Hillesum flung a postcard from the train window addressed to a friend that read: "We left the camp singing . . . Thank you for all your kindness and care."

Hillesum was not celibate, but she did make a radical choice to live with conviction. Far from a *comfortable pilgrim*, she was a modern mystic. She wrote in her diary that mysticism "can only come after things have been stripped down to their naked reality," a reality that inexorably propelled her into active service. She lived Love, as the beguines did, felt a passion and sense of belonging to the world that was becoming familiar as I followed the trail of this new lineage.

"Ultimately, we have just one moral duty," reads her diary, "to reclaim large areas of peace in ourselves, more and more peace, and to reflect it toward others." From the charismatic spiritual leaders to the mystic nuns to radical activists to individual artists, it seemed the route to this reclamation of inner peace and conviction was the combination of agency and surrender that Dillard had so powerfully articulated. Every role model I encountered had chosen their *one necessity* and yielded to its *perfect freedom* over every other desire. They were not ragged coyotes but empowered by their obsessions.

M Y INVENTORY WAS COMPLETE. I planned to read it aloud to the person I had deemed my "spiritual director" but wanted to keep it to myself just a little longer. Some things do not become real until someone else sees them. Then, change becomes an imperative. *Nothing changes if nothing changes,* a friend and I said to each other often, half ironically. I wanted to change, just not yet. I feared what would become evident when I surveyed my past with a witness. I feared my own failure to meet that imperative.

I had been reading articles about confession in preparation for sharing my inventory with my spiritual director. My favorite described the Jewish practice of repentance, which unfolds in three parts: a change of heart, a decision to change, and the act of confession. I had had a change of heart, as evidenced by my celibacy, but had I made a decision to change? Must I first know what that would look like? I wasn't sure yet.

My last conference of the summer was in the Pacific Northwest, out on the Olympic Peninsula. First, I planned to visit a close friend in Portland.

On the plane, I read May Sarton's *Journal of a Solitude,* which opens: "Begin here. It is raining. I look out on the maple where a few leaves have turned yellow and listen to Punch, the parrot, talking to himself." *Journal* is an account of a single year of Sarton's life at her home in New Hampshire, from 1970 to 1971, during which Sarton was in her late fifties. Reading her ruminative entries—"I have written every poem, every novel, for the same reason—to find out what I think, to know where I stand"—I felt the giddy pleasure of recognition and wonder that this grumpy stranger, dead when I was fifteen, had articulated something so familiar in her journal before I was born. Her mixture of anguish, delight, self-appraisal, and a sense of the divine felt eerily similar to many of the writers I had been reading.

"It may be outwardly silent here but in the back of my mind is a clamor of human voices, too many needs, hopes, fears," she writes. "I often feel exhausted, but it is not my work that tires (work is a rest); it is the effort of pushing away the lives and needs of others before I can come to the work with any freshness and zest."

Sarton lived what I imagined as one possibility: being an older middle-aged woman and then an old woman, living in solitude, being in nature, writing, maintaining true relationships, having a sense of the sacred. She was not celibate, though, and her anguish was mostly linked to love.

After driving home from a weekend with her lover in the city, she writes: "Loss made everything sharp. I suffer from these brief weekends, the tearing up of the roots of love, and from my own inability to behave better under the stress." In response, she wrote a poem.

When my plane landed at PDX, I took out my phone, but no one awaited my report of having landed, so I slid my phone back into my pocket and felt suddenly minuscule, a seed in the wind.

Caitlin and her partner lived in a cozy house full of animals. They had a beautiful lady cat who rarely emerged but reminded me, when she did, of Léa de Lonval, Colette's beautiful middle-aged courtesan. Her green eyes had seen it all. There was also a wonderfully needy little dog, and an orange cat whom I adored named Fat Tony, who was weird in the way of all orange cats: intense and ridiculous.

For a week, Caitlin and I parked in cafés and worked on our computers, after which we sat on her porch swing and talked for hours. One morning, I woke up with abdominal muscles sore from laughing. Twice, we treated each other to vegetarian tasting menus at restaurants with overserious waitstaff and cartes du jour that resembled wedding invitations.

I had not visited her much for the past few years, not since before the Maelstrom. I had missed my friend. Caitlin had seen me through so many descents into and out of love, and never any other way. It was disorienting to visit her and have nothing else to do, no one to call and wish good night, no higher priority than to be with my friend. It was rich as custard, deep and satisfying in the way of a good poem or a hard afternoon nap, of which I took several during my visit.

We had met in grad school when we were both twenty-five and became instant friends, like children do. It was *easy* between us in a way that had made things hard sometimes, too. We were both Libras, both averse to conflict and adoring of each other so that frictions always had time to grow before we addressed them. Once, we had a rupture that lasted almost a full year, during which she avoided me and I avoided asking why. It was incredibly painful, and I was relieved when she finally explained that I took up more than my share of space in our friendship. We spent most of our time together talking about me, she pointed out, how I was falling in or out of love at any given time. I knew it was true.

It wasn't so difficult to change, in the end. I defaulted to self-centeredness, a symptom of my obsessive mind, which betrayed the truth that I was endlessly interested in her. How merciful to stop thinking of myself. Navigating that conflict had sealed our love further.

Our friendship, like all my longest ones, reminded me of Agnes Martin's 1963 painting, *Friendship*. It departed from her other enormous grids in its use of gold leaf, which Martin must have spent a fortune on before her work had earned her one. The technique she used, *sgraffito,* consisted of painting thin layers—in this case of red oil paint and then the gold leaf—and allowing each to dry before carefully scratching to expose the color beneath. She probably used a ruler and some bladed tool, like a scalpel. There are no perfectly straight lines in the grid that covers the canvas, and one can see the little bumps and digressions her blade made as she carved. The beauty of the painting is in this imperfection, in the texture, the layering, the visible hand and its consistence.

That was it, wasn't it? Love that one built by staying when conflict arose. It was so delicate, though. Not only as a conflict-averse person, but because one needed a partner who was also willing to stay. To step carefully around all the opportunities to hurt each other, like a room strewn with books. I had begged some lovers to do this work with me. I had also been the one to quit. My spiritual director once said, "Sometimes, people who blame their lovers for being afraid of commitment are actually the ones who fear commitment." Devastating. So far, I'd only managed to stay for the long haul with friends. A few times, I'd stayed too long with the wrong people. It could be hard to recognize the ones worth staying for.

In Caitlin's house, I slept in the sunny guest room and spent an entire afternoon reading Susan Choi's novel *My Education.* Like most of my favorite books, it was about romantic and sexual obsession, told from the point of view of a graduate student who has a blistering affair with a professor. "Had I been a doll," Choi wrote, "she might have twisted off each of my limbs and sucked the knobs until they glistened and drilled her tongue into each of the holes." *My Education* was a portrait of obsession, of ecstatic disempowerment. It described that erotic *single necessity* and an unhinging I knew intimately.

Once again, I felt grateful that I had never been tempted to have a sexual dalliance with a student, though Choi's sex scenes were fantastic and the trance of reading them so complete, so evocative of bodily experiences I *had* had, that every time I broke away from the page I shuddered, as I did in the first moments of waking from a dream in which I have relapsed and every time I walked through those sensors at the doorways of stores meant to catch shoplifters, absurdly fearful that I had stolen without meaning to, gotten high or fucked without remembering it until just that moment.

I closed my door to keep the animals out of my room, but every time I went to get a glass of water or a handful of grapes, when I returned Tony was sitting on my pillows, his back legs splayed open like a frog or a pervert. Sometimes he was licking the place where his testicles used to be. He looked up at me like I was the intruder. Our game delighted me and I always let him stay. Eventually, we'd fall asleep, the book on my chest, the warm loaf of his body pressed against my flank, a mobile of golden hairs twirling over us in the afternoon sunlight.

Of a dear friend with whom she discussed her tormented love, May Sarton wrote, "D and I are the same breed of cat, responsive and sensitive close to the surface. Willing to give ourselves away. Such people rarely lead happy lives, but they do lead lives of constant growth and change. Gerald Heard's saying 'he must go unprotected that he may be constantly changed' always comes to mind." This seemed particularly prescient from Heard, who became voluntarily celibate in midlife and was a friend to Bill Wilson, the founder of Alcoholics Anonymous.

On my last day in Portland, Caitlin and I went swimming in a lake whose bottom was silky, suctioning clay. At first it disgusted me, but I quickly grew to love the density, how it grabbed my feet and enclosed them in a mucky embrace. Her body draped over an inflatable raft, my friend drifted across the water with her eyes closed, face to the sky. Watching her, I filled like a pitcher with love from some inexhaustible tap. I thought of a few lines from a poem Sarton had written about a friend: "I recognize that violent, gentle blood . . . I would if I could, / Call him my kin, there scything down the grasses, / Call him my good luck in a dirty time."

ON MY DRIVE from Portland to Seattle, Nora called. She sounded far away and I couldn't tell if it was the connection or an aural perception of her emotional distance. I pulled over at a rest stop and removed my headphones to press the phone against my ear.

"Are you okay?" I asked.

"I don't know," she answered. Her tone sent a ripple of fear through me. She sounded opaque, like a picture of the future, changing with each new decision. I hadn't spoken to her in a long time, though I'd left a few messages. "It's about Walter," she said. "I have to send him away."

Nora had an enormous, beautiful feline named Walter who had been her companion for a decade. He was an eccentric beast who both mesmerized and scared me. Sometimes, when I stayed over at her apartment, he lumbered onto the bed and slept with me, which felt like being blessed by a minor god. Months ago, when he first met the lawyer, Walter had viciously attacked her, biting and scratching in earnest. Though, like all canny cats, he understood the power of a well-timed swipe, he'd never done anything like that before. Nora had worked to keep the two of them separated ever since.

As I stared through the windshield of my rental car at a swaying ponderosa pine, Nora explained that, having accepted her new position at the university, she needed to move. I nodded. The university was commutable to the city and given that she already spent most nights at the lawyer's apartment, she had asked the lawyer if they could move in together. She would commute to work or stay in a hotel on the days she taught, she had explained.

As she recounted this to me in her small voice, I said nothing, but the back of my neck contracted with fear. It was for her and also an echo from my past. Near the end of the Maelstrom, my lover had told me she was ready to come to New York permanently, to move in together. I had been lobbying for such a move for almost two years, but when she suggested it, that feeling struck the back of my neck. I was so tired. My stamina—both for the punishing work of navigating our dynamic, and for convincing myself that such efforts were the price of true love—was flagging. If only I'd had the strength to discourage her, I thought. To spare us both that final chapter. I wished I could go back in time, grip my own shoulders, and shake myself. Demand that I tell my lover *no*, a word I had been incapable of saying.

The lawyer had expressed ambivalence at first, Nora told me, but eventually capitulated. *I'm not going to be able to deal with my attachment issues if you move out of state*, she had explained. *I need you close by.*

I was already grimacing before Nora confirmed the final detail.

"I'm moving in with her at the end of the month," she said.

"Oh, Nora," I said. "Are you sure?"

"No. But it doesn't feel like I have a choice."

"You do," I said. I lowered my gaze and stared hard at a tree on a patch of grass beside the gas station, as if casting a spell. "I promise you do," I said.

My chest was clotted with dread, but I did not say more. Nora knew that everyone who loved her would be disappointed by this news. It had been hard enough for her to give me this update. Disappointment breeds shame, and she had enough shame in that moment. It was what made her voice sound like it was piping from inside a cave. I knew that sound, had heard it emit from my own mouth, my own cave, my own shame.

Nora also told me that, upon the lawyer's insistence, she would send Walter to live with her father before they moved in together. I understood that exile was a common sentence for those who served as mirrors before a person was ready to see themselves reflected. I had become estranged from almost everyone who loved me when I was an active addict, and again in the Maelstrom. My lover could not tolerate the presence of anyone willing to name the poison we combined into, and I could not tolerate choosing anything that caused conflict with her. Walter had been exiled for similar reasons. I knew I could be, too.

I also did not trust myself to see Nora's situation clearly. Much as I wanted to cast my celibacy as an intellectual endeavor, the truth was that it had been prompted by suffering, and my conversations with Nora had helped to clarify this. Her maelstrom so evoked mine that I feared seeing her as a proxy for my past self. Nora was also an *animal with a past,* one distinct from mine. She had chosen her path and would follow it to her own conclusion. I could not truly interfere. The only thing to do was love her, so I told her I did as we hung up the phone. In the silence that followed, I remembered that urge to shake my past self, to command her. I would never have responded to Nora that way, nor anyone else I loved. I understood that fury and panic had no power to dissuade a person in thrall to such an experience. I wondered if I could muster the same tenderness for my past self that I felt for my friend.

At the beginning of every class, including the one on the first day of the conference, I told my students not to use the words "good" or "bad" in their critiques of one another. Still, they did. Perhaps it would have been better to stop banning those words, which always failed, and to instead expand their meanings. The saints and mystics wrote a lot about goodness and badness, and sometimes badness was merely a synonym for human. The creature in us. The base desires, the essential selfishness of pursuing our desires regardless of the effect on others or the will of higher powers. I had always favored specificity and nuance over generalization, but could not ignore the uses of broad thinking when it came to radical change. That is, simple forms of abstinence required broad and binary definitions. One was either moving toward a drink or a drug or a fuck or moving away from those temptations.

In 1961, Carl Jung sent a letter to Bill Wilson, the founder of Alcoholics Anonymous, in which he wrote: "I am strongly convinced that the evil principle prevailing in this world leads the unrecognized spiritual need into perdition, if it is not counteracted either by real religious insight or by the protective wall of human community. An ordinary man, not protected by an action from above and isolated in society, cannot resist the power of evil, which is called very aptly the Devil. But the use of such words arouses so many mistakes that one can only keep aloof from them as much as possible."

In the same letter, he postulates that "craving for alcohol was the equivalent, on a low level, of the spiritual thirst of our being for wholeness, expressed in medieval language: the union with God." His words simultaneously dismissed any moral judgment of the addict and expanded the notion of evil to include addictive behavior. In the early years of my recovery, they meant so much to me that I kept a folded printout of Jung's letter in my wallet until its creases went soft and ripped apart.

I didn't really believe in *badness,* but his words had helped me to understand the dialectical impulse. There was a difference, a hierarchy even, among the actions we took to pursue our wants and "needs." What the mystics called evil or sin or even the work of the devil, I recognized as the desires I pursued without choosing. At least I did not choose them with my highest self, the part most aligned with the divine as I understood it. They were my "unrecognized spiritual need" being led "into perdition" by the temptation (and often capitalistic prescription) of more quickly sated hungers. For most, it was easier to eat a cookie or take a drug or even find a lover than it was to find God or "the protective wall of human community."

These two elements, I realized, often meant the difference between the bondage of addiction and Dillard's *perfect freedom of single necessity.* The person watched over by a loving God and community was more apt to have the agency to choose her single necessity. People in recovery often talked about aligning one's will with the will of their higher power. To some, God and community were one. Regardless, if one aligned their will with God and/or their community, it usually pointed them toward pursuits unlikely to annihilate them, like service or Love in the beguinal sense, rather than the dicier enterprises favored by the individual will, such as wealth, substance abuse, and consuming love affairs.

So many people fantasized about romantic love that would sweep them away, obliterate their agency and release them from accountability, a "tormenting, self-heightening pleasure, like a hail of hot stones," as I had. But no other human could exert that kind of power in love. It was a storm that rose from within, and which we projected onto a lover. After the Maelstrom, I was inclined to leave the hail of hot stones to powers beyond the human. I had begun fantasizing instead about love that left room for agency, a passion that I could choose, that would obliterate no part of me or my beloved. A love that God and the people who truly loved me could support.

On the last night of the conference, the faculty went out for dinner at a restaurant in town. The person seated beside me asked about an ex of mine and that led to an explanation of my celibacy. To my embarrassment, soon the whole table was attentive. This was not the first time this had happened. I hadn't expected the subject of celibacy to be conversational catnip to such a broad swath of people. Not since I was a professional dominatrix had my status so captured the interest of others. I did not keep a list of the people who sounded wistful when I told them that I was taking a break from romance, the people who said that they, too, had never been alone. If I had, it would have been long.

Conversely, I noticed how much people talked about sex and romance, not only on television, but in life. It was *all* some people talked about. It was all that some of my friends talked about. I became increasingly bored with these conversations. "But what about *you?*" I wanted to say. I was wary of acting as an evangelist for celibacy, though in truth I would have liked to prescribe it to many. My life was empty of lovers and more full than it had ever been. I wanted to read to them what Audre Lorde wrote in her essay "Uses of the Erotic": "Recognizing the power of the erotic within our lives can give us the energy to pursue genuine change within our world, rather than merely settling for a shift of characters in the same weary drama," but I compromised with the less sanctimonious act of assigning her essay to my students at the conference.

On the ferry to the airport, I sat on the deck and watched the waves rise and fall like soft teeth. The plangent cry of the ferry's horn rung over the water. "There's one thing I'm good at, and that's looking at the sea," Duras once said in an interview. Looking at the sea, I felt happy and lonely at the same time, and the loneliness carried a faint sense of accomplishment. I sometimes still worried that it had all been too easy and heard the echo of the psychotherapist's warning: *If it's not hard, you're not doing it.*

I N MY RECOVERY community, we often said that one ought to choose mentors who "have what you want." I once wanted what my old role models—Vincent and Colette—had: a life ruled by love and passion, whose pains and pleasures derived from the same sources. But I had wanted that life for half as long as I had lived it. Inertia sustained that pattern, but also fear. I had feared that I would always be ruled by my lower instincts, and my lovestruck heroines offered models of social integration and artistic success *within* such a lifestyle, even if it also stunted or eventually killed them.

I wasn't Colette, though. At forty-seven, Colette had slept with her sixteen-year-old stepson, on whom she based the character of Chéri. Nor was I Vincent. She had found her one true love and he had hastened her spiral toward addicted ruin and a lonely death. The only thing I still wanted of these idols was to write like a demon.

I no longer needed to romanticize my flaws because I now aspired to resist them and believed it possible. There are given and chosen lineages. I did not choose the family I was born into, nor the bloody legacies of my ancestors. I did not choose to be an addict nor a lover. But as an adult, I had the power to choose how I lived, how I loved, and what I created. *We can live any way we want,* Dillard reminded me. I did not have to choose idols who rationalized my flaws, who encouraged my complacency. I could choose teachers with higher standards. I could choose from the annals of human history. I could choose the passions of my old idols that hadn't killed them and leave behind the rest. I did want passion in my life.

Friendship was the realm in which intimacy with other humans seemed most possible, in which I was most capable of real, unselfish caring. It offered some amount of romance, but not passion. While I wanted a peaceful life, a useful life, I could not fully imagine channeling my passions into service and friendship alone. I wondered if further nurturing that *ruthless part,* my creative ambition, could satisfy my bottomless drive.

If I wanted an example of a life's work built on such a passion, I had only to visit science fiction writer Octavia Butler's papers at the Huntington Library, which I did. Butler had been a shy child who grew up amid the informal racial segregation of 1950s Pasadena. Severely bullied by her peers, she sought refuge in reading—first fairy tales, then science fiction—and in an oversized notebook where she scribbled her thoughts and stories. She eventually became the first science fiction writer to win the MacArthur "Genius" Fellowship. I was never an avid science fiction reader, but her novels singularly captured me. Their narratives transported, but also offered so direct a commentary on the flaws in human civilization and the human psyche that I understood imagination to be a necessary ingredient in social change.

I spent an afternoon sifting through Butler's typewritten pages and handwritten notebooks, which went back as far as her adolescence, when she began sketching out her first short stories. Butler wrote like a demon ever after, was more consumed by that passion than any for other humans.

Her pages were busy with plot outlines, character sketches, affirmations, to-do lists, and notes about her finances. Together they provided a map to a mind that was organized by creative devotion. I was awed by her singular commitment to her craft. The scrawl of her pencil as it announced: "I would like to write a horror story. I would like to write a story that is the genre equivalent of the roller coaster at Magic Mountain," or commanded: "No more whining. Do what you should be doing." Some of her pronouncements struck me so personally that I had the uncanny sense of Butler reaching through time, speaking across it directly to me:

"This is the story of an ambitious woman deliberately transforming herself," she said.

"Make it Clean. And Lean. And Powerful. And Real."

"Do what you fear to do until you no longer fear it."

"This is the story of a love affair . . . The final act is an act of love."

I believed that the passion for art had kept me alive, that it would continue to be the mill through which I spun much of my passion to good use. I also sensed an essential element that I was missing. I still had a longing with no object. I wanted no hail of hot stones, but to become that soul who, in the words of beguine Marguerite Porete, "is so burned in Love's fiery furnace that she has become very fire, so that she feels no fire, for in herself she is fire, through the power of Love which has changed her into the fire of Love."

If the beguines were any example, it is abundantly possible to indulge passion and not create wreckage. Surely they were directing their impulse for love and desire, but mostly they were living lives of great structure and purpose. They used that language to communicate *agape* rather than misplaced passion for a single human.

As Martin, who had also sublimated her fiery instincts into art, said in her Skowhegan lecture: "Your conditioning has taught you to identify with others, their emotions and their needs. I urge you to look to yourself. In our convention, it is particularly difficult for women, but still it has to be done. The purpose of life is to know your true, unconditioned self." There it was again: to align one's will with the will of a higher power. To find one's single necessity.

As the summer neared its end, I had a call with an Italian scholar, Silvana Panciera, who specialized in the beguines and whose fastidiously updated website had been an unmatched resource to me as I delved into the subject. However widely I read on the subject of celibacy, I always returned to them, these women for whom independence was the foundation upon which all else was built.

"The beguinal chastity," Silvana told me in her filigreed accent, "was not expressed by lifelong vows; it was a renewed promise. A vow is a forever decision, but a promise has to be renewed. But the goal is the same: for a deeper spiritual life, a deeper loving life." I knew that I wanted a deeper loving life. Did I also want a deeper spiritual life? It was spiritual, the manner in which I had stepped further into myself, my friendships, every activity from eating to sleeping to masturbating. I did not share this line of thought with Silvana, but instead asked why she was drawn to the beguines.

"Because I felt in them the root of my history," she explained. "The root of feminism . . . they made the first step toward independence." Silvana had been researching and educating about the beguines for almost thirty years, though she had studied sociology at the University of Leuven in Belgium. In 1994, when she was a student, she attended an exhibition at the Beaux Arts Museum in Brussels and became interested in the question "of whether it was the first feminist movement in Europe." She has spent the last three decades visiting beguinages, maintaining her website and newsletter, writing a book and adapting it into a short documentary, and making all of her research available in multiple languages.

Though it was fairly easy to find the texts of the most famous beguine mystics, I understood that they were famous *because* their texts had survived. We would never know the names of most, because their legacy had been destroyed. It was harder to research the beguines than it is more formalized religious movements because their historiography has not been institutionalized and is mostly conducted by contemporary feminist scholars like Silvana.

Partly, this is because female monasticism has been largely ignored by male historians and more so because the beguinal movement was stamped out by men of the Catholic Church, who persistently attempted to brand them heretics. In 1311–12 with the Council of Vienne, they officially succeeded, but even before then, many beguines were tried and executed. Perhaps most famous among these martyrs was Marguerite Porete, who was burned at the stake in 1310 after refusing to recant her book, *The Mirror of Simple Souls,* which described practices of accessing *agape*—divine love.

Despite living in the Middle Ages, when they could be killed for merely existing let alone spreading their ideas in writing, the "gray women," as they were sometimes referred to due to their plain garb, lived more freely than most women have throughout human history. They lived in closer accordance with their own convictions than most people I have known, certainly more than I ever had. I supposed that was why I kept coming back to them, because my whole project of celibacy had less to do with sex than with conviction, and a hunger for a more authentic way of living.

"The beguines were determined to embrace a new life, and wanted to live their faith and evangelical values in a more radical way, while preserving their secular status, without going through a convent or monastery," Silvana explained. "Renouncement of sexuality, not sensuality, pushes love into its universal dimension." I nodded, listening to her. I had read Mechthild and Hadewijch and Porete's accounts of pious Love. Sensual was an understatement. They may never have had sex as I or anyone in their time defined it, but they knew passion.

"When you don't belong to anyone, you belong to everyone," she said. "You feel able to love without limits." Her words reminded me of my therapist's question: *Do you think you've imposed this fear of the conditional on all of your relationships?* For most of my life, I had understood the concept of "love without limits" as a subsumption of the self into the other, the lover. Love that demanded unlimited contortions of the self. As I listened to Silvana, I saw how simplistic this idea was. To contort oneself for love was a form of self-abuse and also a manipulation of the lover. To define Love as such degraded it.

What would a primary relationship that was truly unconditional look like? I wondered. What would a human partnership that required compromise but not contortion look like?

"When you don't belong to anyone you belong to God," Silvana finished, and I was surprised to find myself on the brink of tears. I stared at the corkboard that hung over my desk, which held a rosary that had belonged to my grandmother and a scribbled quote: "Prayer is for the person praying, God is whatever answers."

The line was still for a few seconds, though I heard her breathing, some five thousand miles away. "You are a person who—excuse me, you can correct me," she said tentatively. "I think you are a person who is looking for a deep love. Is that right, Melissa?"

I N A MOMENT of unusual spontaneity, I decided to spend my accumulated airline miles, annual faculty research allowance, and the last two weeks of summer in Europe chasing the ghosts of my celibate ancestors. I would fly to London, wander the city and surroundings, and finish my trip with a few days in Germany's Rhine Valley. The only other time I had done such a thing was at twenty when I bought a ticket to Paris one summer in an attempt to flee my heroin addiction. The trip failed in that regard (it turned out there was heroin in Paris), but I had never regretted it. This trip felt like the inverse of that one. Instead of running to escape something essential—drugs, myself—I had rotated to an opposite meridian of life and felt the imperative to run *in search* of something essential.

I packed haphazardly and booked a short-term rental in the Bloomsbury neighborhood, where my UK publisher was based, in hopes of a tax write-off for the remaining expenses. As I made arrangements, I realized that the end of my celibate term would fall halfway through my trip.

I imagined being celibate in London: booking a table for one and eating dosas with a book in hand, tracing Woolf's footsteps along the River Ouse, wandering in Hyde Park with nowhere else to be. I might have been fantasizing about a box of fine chocolates. Then I imagined the second half of my trip. My sexual availability ticking on like a neon sign, the dizzy sense of possibility. It wasn't out of the question that I might return to Brooklyn with a new girlfriend in tow.

That possibility notwithstanding, I had little interest in reentering the world of intimacy. I felt very happy in *this* world of intimacy. When I thought about reengaging my romantic life, my old anxiety, which had receded almost entirely, rolled in with the speed of an impending storm. I reminded myself that concluding my period of celibacy did not mean I had to act. Hadn't that been one of my goals? That I become able to resist flinging myself into another's orbit at the first opportunity? Well, I would soon have the opportunity to try.

I hadn't heard from Nora in weeks. In the days before my trip, I left studiously cheerful messages, hoping to entice her to return my calls. She did, finally, the morning of my departure. I had just slid into my cab to the airport.

"I'm on the train to campus," she explained in a hushed tone.

My stomach twisted. I had hoped she might end her relationship in the interval between our calls but knew it was a fantasy— she would have told me. The tone of her voice erased any remaining hope in me. She had probably called me from the train because it did not feel safe to do so in the apartment she now shared with her girlfriend.

"I'm totally broke," she told me, "but she's paying for everything."

I forgot to exercise restraint and groaned audibly.

"*I know*," she said. "I know. I feel crazy all the time, but just fix my face when I go to class."

"Oh, Nora," I said. "I'm so sorry."

"If I don't call her back immediately, even when I'm teaching, she berates me and threatens to leave," she explained. "I'm trying to show up for this job but I feel absolutely torn up. As if I'm being clawed every night." This was the most honest that she had been with me in a long time and I felt desperate to keep her on the phone.

Her words reminded me of the first semester I taught at my university, when I was still in the Maelstrom. My phone might have been a clump of nuclear waste that I dutifully carried in my pocket and laid beside my head when I slept, deranging my thoughts more with each passing minute. On teaching days, I would lock the door of my campus office and curl up in the space under my desk meant for my legs. There I would savagely cry, my face contorted, mouth gasping against my knees. Like a new mother pumping breast milk, when I depleted my stores enough to function, I would tidy my clothes, apply eye drops, and go to class or committee meetings.

My neck clenched once more with stress, but I forced myself to take a measured breath before I responded to Nora. I reminded myself that she was not living my past; she was living her present, and it was grandiose for me to think that I knew her next right action. I thought about myself, hunched under that desk, how little a command would have helped me. I considered what would have been a comfort to hear.

"Listen," I said to my friend. "I don't judge you for any of the choices you are making. I know that this is something you need to see through. I just want to say one thing."

"Okay," she replied cautiously.

"The moment you are ready to end this, I mean *the moment,* you call me and I will be outside of that bitch's apartment with a moving truck and a bouquet of flowers."

Nora laughed.

"We don't have to say anything else about it," I reassured her. "But that offer never expires."

When I hung up the phone, my taxi was bumping down the Belt Parkway through Canarsie. We passed Shirley Chisholm State Park, on the other side of which lay Jamaica Bay, and beyond that the Rockaways. I cracked my window and sea smell billowed into the car. My heartbeat jittered from the proximity to those familiar feelings. I closed my eyes and let the wind batter my face. Inside me, a sharp, fall-on-my-knees gratitude that I was free. And sorrow, too, for myself and for my friend, that I had lived that torment, that she was living it. Every day that passed since the Maelstrom ended this gratitude grew, along with amazement that I had withstood two years of it.

Once, about eighteen months into our affair, my ex had begged me to drive from Brooklyn to D.C., where she was attending a conference. Despite being scheduled to teach a class the following afternoon, I got in my car and sped through the night. I arrived at her hotel around midnight. I'd recently begun smoking again, years after having quit, and had smoked on the drive. When I reached for her in the hotel room she pushed me away.

"You stink," she said. The room had two full beds and she banished me to the unused bed. I did not sleep but spent the night crying furious tears. I vibrated with an anger that had been steadily increasing as she exacted these familiar kinds of punishments.

At first light, I splashed my face with cold water and left. I'm sure she expected me to return. That sort of theater, however undergirded by real emotion, was endemic to our relationship. The hellish part, and what allowed us to enact the same tortured scenes with equal passion, was that they felt brand-new every time.

That morning, I did not return. It was the first time that my anger outweighed the thing I called love.

I drove the six hours north and went straight to work. In the campus parking lot, I turned off my phone, something I never did in those days, and slept in my car for two hours before I taught my class. I arrived home that evening delirious with exhaustion. My girlfriend had been calling me all day and, for the first time, I had not answered. Around 8 p.m., I finally picked up. I was shocked to hear her sob into the phone.

"Come back," she begged. In the eighteen months before that night, I had done many equally demented things. A good friend had even broken up with me, citing that, in addition to my now total unreliability, she literally feared for my life—that I would crash my car or have a heart attack from the unrelenting distress.

This time, something had changed. Despite the near-feral urge to go to my lover, I could not surmount the wrongness of such a decision.

"I can't," I told her, and I meant it. I was physically incapable of getting back into my car. Not only because it would draw upon bodily reserves I had long since cashed, but because my body had finally allied with my misplaced survival instinct, the bud of anger in me that opened more every day.

She called and called that night. I alternated between pacing the floor of my small apartment and tearing at my nails with the effort it took to ignore her calls, and sitting on the floor with the phone to my ear, attempting to explain to her that it would be *dangerous* for me to drive, that to love me right now meant to let me sleep. How pitiful it now seems, this naïve effort. But what an effort it was. I had never resisted her demands and she had never sounded so wretched. The tension of my opposing impulses made my legs shake. At one point, my insides liquified and I nearly shat my pants. Still, I did not go to her.

It took six months more before I was strong enough to leave her, but I understood that incident as my turn toward the end. It had been nearly two years since that end, and as my taxi turned in to the airport, my face flushed with salty wind, I knew that my friend had such a volta ahead of her. I wished that I could help her lean into the turn or share the effort of doing so, but I knew I could not. She had her own reasons for choosing such a gauntlet, and an early interruption to its course would not necessarily serve her.

As I wheeled my suitcase through the revolving door of JFK and toward the ticket counters, I marveled at the perversity of calling my Maelstrom an experience of *love*. What sickness of mind enabled me to believe it for so long? The same that ailed our society. The structure of love worship writ large is the same that propelled me. The troubadours had sung to us for centuries, ventriloquized the pop singers we'd grown up listening to. We'd been instructed our whole lives to minimize ourselves and prioritize our appeal to lovers over every other concern. What a coup, to convince us that we were dependent upon that which needed us.

"I'd had it with handing myself over," the French magazine editor Sophie Fontanel wrote in *The Art of Sleeping Alone,* her memoir about the years she spent celibate. "I'd said yes too much." I whispered a quick prayer for that bud of *no* that grew inside my friend, that it would bloom at the right time.

Later, as my flight to London prepared for takeoff, I stared out the oval window beside my seat and felt that pang of loneliness that there was no one to text, no one to tell that I had boarded my flight.

"*Boarded,*" I whispered to myself. As we rose through the cloud cover into the blazing light just above it, I imagined hurtling through that cool mist toward the ground.

I T SEEMED THE MOST UNLIKELY juncture for my old instincts to rear up. But when I saw the woman on the plane, it was as it had always been: I did not think to look away. I did not think of all my new resolutions. I did not think of my inventory, thick with interludes that had begun this way. My body responded like the trained mechanism it was, like any animal prompted by instinct. The rest of the flight to London is time lost. It was hard not to see her as a challenge perfectly designed by some higher power who wanted to test my progress, which, of course, she was. I picked her myself.

After we spotted each other on the train platform and then boarded the same car, the train resumed its progress. It shuddered against the track as it snaked through a village of clapboard houses with tidy roofs and flower boxes under their windows. I attempted to refocus and smoothed the page of my book as if it could also smooth my mind. An impotent gesture that did nothing to slow the thrum of my blood. I stood and walked down the car's aisle toward the bathroom, lightly touching the corner of each seat as I passed.

The woman, with her short tousled hair and stout backpack in the seat beside her, radiated like a cauldron, warming my body as I neared. My fingers brushed the corner of her seat as I passed and the plastic upholstery might have been the warm curve where her shoulder became neck. I saw it in my periphery, sloping out of her shirt's collar. Desire can do so much with so little. Her gaze flicked up at me and a wave crested over the back of my skull, each hair straining in its follicle. My tongue went thick and my nipples hard. In the cramped restroom, after I had slid the heavy door shut and hovered my hips over the metal toilet to urinate, I found that I was wet.

"What the fuck," I whispered as I pulled up my jeans.

In the beginning of my celibacy, I had felt closer to sex. Not just temporally, but corporeally. In the last two months, this had changed. I surveyed people whom I found attractive and the thought of touching them sexually or being touched by them repelled me, not just a bad idea, but a grotesque one. My body had a new integrity. To submit it to sexual acts would defile this integrity, not for moral reasons, but because it would disrupt the privacy I had cultivated with myself. So odd to remember how urgent the masturbation question once seemed. Exposure to my own hand and a stranger's couldn't be more divergent prospects, a difference as great as that between taking a nap and flying a plane.

How ironic that I had momentarily succumbed to what Woolf had called the "abyss of mediocrity" at this particular moment, when I had come to London, in part, to follow the trail of my celibate role models, beginning with Woolf. Less than twenty-four hours earlier, I had sat in my taxi and marveled at my own capacity for self-delusion. I knew that this was further proof of that capacity, that I would regret any action I took, but *oh*, I had forgotten the rush of it. It was easy to underestimate such power in its absence, because it made no sense. It was beyond sense.

Desire writhed in me now, propelling the soft puppet of my body forward. How sweet it felt to submit! I might have hated roller coasters, but I loved this similar swoon inside, felt giddy with it as I returned from the restroom and sank back into my seat. The difference was that now, even amid this fever, a corner of my mind remained lucid and skeptical. I imagined a tiny stenographer in a long wool skirt, perched in the attic of my brain, recording the symptoms of this relapse on her typewriter. While my body ceded its integrity, she held the transcript of the last six months and cleared her throat punctiliously, intent on reminding me why we were here.

The longer I did not act, the louder the stenographer's presence grew, each key's fall echoing in the marble hall of my conscience. I counted the dwindling stops until my station, trained my eye on the posted diagram. In answer to that insistent tattoo, I felt the cool shadow of an old feeling slip through me. Part dread, part release, it was Augustine's "ecstasy of yielding to the forbidden," the sense of an already foregone conclusion. Like Coyote, my eyeballs bulged from my skull and I itched to leave all sense behind.

I glanced back. The woman's face tilted toward the window, outside of which a field and then a small pond glided by, but I saw the flicker of attention to my movement and felt the hum of the invisible cord between us, its subtle electricity, though I sensed that she would not be the one to act.

I knew how to do this. The right question to break the silence, the conversation to follow, the casual invitation to meet up later. I hadn't missed many of these opportunities in the past. Especially when I was younger, I kissed a lot of near-strangers. In more recent years, I'd collected "friends" that sat like simmering pots, maintaining the warm promise of consummation, if ever I got hungry enough. But something was different, intercepting the usual broadcast like the song of another nearby radio station, snippets of a chorus that I began to recognize.

I remembered how it felt to stand before the sensors of a store from which I was about to steal, or to walk swiftly out of a decrepit building in which I had just purchased drugs: my pupils dilated, palms wet, pulse chugging—how fear swept through me. My excitement was a kind of anxiety. I was anxious because I did not want to act upon this flirtation. I wanted to check into my rental in Bloomsbury and eat a nice dinner, alone. I wanted to release myself from that nervous bondage. To yield to *the perfect freedom of* a different *necessity*.

As the train pulled into my station, I rose and clutched the handle of my suitcase, eager to escape temptation. I turned toward the nearest door and saw that the object of my attention had also risen and hoisted her pack onto her shoulders. I was hardly surprised. A single passenger between us, we filed through the open doors and trundled toward the taxi stand.

When the uniformed attendant inquired where everyone in the line was going, I said, "Bloomsbury, please," and the stranger's voice—grainy and American—echoed me: "Bloomsbury, as well." He directed us into the same cab. I almost laughed aloud. Had this been a movie, my attention might have wavered, so difficult would it have been to suspend my disbelief at this turn of events.

Our seats faced one another in the back of the taxi. I felt her gaze on me but did not return it. She had the stained fingers of a smoker and her cologne smelled of cedarwood. If I looked up, the cord between us would tighten and whatever possibility hovered there would become inevitable. I stared at the shopfronts as we bumped over brick roads and slowly drew my breath. When I released it, I closed my eyes and wished for the power to resist this familiar script. I kept my lids closed for a few moments more, listening to the tick of the stenographer's fingers, and she engraved the moment with sober truth.

When I opened my eyes, the wish had been answered. I felt a subtle but unmistakable steadying inside. I did not believe in an interventionist higher power, but prayers worked like this some-times: as if God happened to be passing by the open door of my mind and overheard. As if divine intervention were simply my own ability to change plus the willingness to do so.

I let the cord go slack. I let it go completely and felt my hands loosen in my lap.

I might have removed a set of headphones from my ears; the music stopped and I could hear the murmur of the driver on his phone call, the honk of other cars, and the distant seesaw of a siren. My body felt hollowed out, every sensation rattling inside me, but I was in there—complete and alone, not casting outside myself toward another body. Not a zombie or a Roomba or a heat-seeking missile, just a woman on her way through London. I turned away from the window and met the stranger's waiting gaze.

"So, where are you coming from?" she asked.

"New York," I answered, and almost broke into a grin, because I was free. As our small talk progressed, I heard the whistle of sexual intrigue leaking from the car like a ruptured balloon. She was a musician, of course. Come to London to meet her girlfriend. Our taxi pulled up in front of an apartment building at whose entrance stood a brunette with an expectant face. As the woman who had been the locus of my attention for the last eighteen hours paid the driver, she might as well have been my brother, a blond, a potential new friend who passed me her email on a scrap of paper while suggesting that we get together later that week.

She gathered her pack, exited the car, and walked straight into the arms of the brunette who had been waiting for her. As the taxi pulled away, I crumpled the slip of paper in my hand and dropped it onto the floor.

The buildings we passed were shorter and prettier than those in New York. Every square had a small park at the center, a green emerald set in pavement. As we glided past storefronts and cafés crowded by al fresco tables, I wondered why my old instincts had arisen at this particular juncture. I was *alone* in a way I had never been. How quick I had been to flee this solitude, the loneliness of traversing in a foreign place without someone to tether me, to follow or lead down each unfamiliar street. I discovered that I *was* lonely, but it was okay. The loneliness a mist that wafted through me and which I trusted would pass.

If it's not hard, you're not doing it. Jung, who wrote that "a man who has not passed through the inferno of his passions has never overcome them," would have agreed with the psychotherapist. Perhaps I did now, too. Shaky and exhausted, but clear, I could see that I had some way yet to go.

"There is, for me, no difference between writing a good poem and moving into sunlight against the body of a woman I love," wrote Audre Lorde, and I thought she meant that there could be a single kind of ecstasy, *the erotic* as she called it, wherein the body can share all of its pleasures with the spirit, and all pleasure rises to a spiritual standard. It was not humility but the day's experience that proved I was not there yet. Had I succumbed to temptation, it would not have been an ecstasy of the spirit. I wanted to move into sunlight against another body only when it could embody the same erotic truth that writing did, that my aloneness had. Until I could do so without abandoning myself. If an instinct, it ought to be the kind I cultivated, not that which had been conditioned in me. I wanted to *choose* it.

As the car approached the address of my short-term rental, I decided to prolong my celibacy. Not for any set time, but for as long as I needed. I had not noticed the tension in my body until it released at this decision. Never had I been more ready for a nap than as I paid the driver and lugged my backpack out of the cab in front of the 1930s Art Deco apartment building with peeling blue-painted railings.

As I waited in the lobby for the ancient elevator and then heaved its metal-grated doors open, I noticed a different kind of excitement in me. Beneath my fatigue, the fizzy sense of looking forward to something. Not a cookie or a smoke or a fuck or a flirt, but a sense of possibility that expanded far beyond any finite treat.

I was happy to see myself after those hours spent lost in a story whose ending I no longer cared to know. I was happy to be alone, to be lonely in this strange city with a future unwritten. I had forgotten that I preferred my own company to that of any stranger. Returning to this knowledge was a return to love, like walking straight into the arms of a friend.

THE SUN ROSE so early in London. The flat I'd rented was on the sixth floor, and when the sun crested the horizon of rowhouses to the east and filled the garden below with light, it also glowed my rooms above it, burnished the pigeons who murmured on the ridge of the roof next door as I lay there, happiness silently detonating in me.

I loved Bloomsbury, with its brick sidewalks and elegant squares. My first morning there, I sat reading in that garden, slowly eating a carton of raspberries. I placed one furred cap on my tongue at a time and crushed them against the roof of my mouth, savoring each tart explosion.

St. Andrew's Gardens was a lush little park that belonged to the neighboring church, with tombs unevenly lodged in its grass where tree roots had displaced them. When I looked up from my book, they reminded me of storage trunks bobbing in a green sea after a shipwreck. "Often, we melt into our ecstasies as though they were jams," wrote Violette Leduc in *The Lady and the Little Fox Fur,* "as though we were sinking into syrupy bowls of gooseberries, of raspberries, of bilberries." It wasn't what Leduc had imagined for the heroine of that novella, an impoverished spinster, but it was a kind of ecstasy that followed my near-slip, a giddy relief at having not found myself powerless yet again. I could make choices, could choose something different. I knew that now, because I had done so.

On a rambling stroll that afternoon, I found the plaque devoted to the Bloomsbury Group in Brunswick Square and the one that marks Woolf's apartment outside of the Tavistock Hotel, whose ladies' bathroom stalls were decorated in collages that paid homage to her famous works. I peed there, against a backdrop of *The Waves*.

Though I was in the city for little more than a week, I immediately established the same routine I'd kept in Brooklyn all summer. I woke without an alarm and spent the mornings reading and writing, followed by lunch, then a walk or a run. In the afternoons, I wrote in my journal and made calls to friends. I spent some time reading in the British Library's rare books room, cozily flanked by academics in sweaters who scowled at books propped on foam bolsters. After an early dinner, I read myself to sleep. I ate the same things every day for breakfast and lunch, and treated myself to dinners from the Lebanese, Turkish, and Indian takeaway storefronts—soft eggplant bursting with lemon and garlic, fresh yeasty pita, and creamy dahl. I slid into bed before the sun fully set and read until my eyes crossed with sleep.

I had never noticed how predictable my instincts were and what comfort it was to experience a new place within the frame of these consistent habits. I had always adapted to the routines of my traveling companions; agreeably replacing the familiar with the novel if they preferred it. I had even done this at home. In years past, I would sometimes scan my own apartment, say, while sharing dinner with my current partner, and imagine how differently I'd arrange the room if it were mine alone, what alternate art would adorn my walls, what other meal I'd have cooked.

I had first read *A Room of One's Own* as a teenager, most recently as a text I assigned my undergraduates, and many times in between. Despite the shiv-like clarity of its most important lines, it is a difficult text to be Woolf's most known one, brief but made cumbersome by metaphor and the convoluted voice she adopted to appeal to her intended audience of disapproving men. Its persistence over time is likely due to the persistent relevance of its arguments. "A woman must have money and a room of her own if she is to write fiction," she claimed. "For masterpieces are not single and solitary births; they are the outcome of many years of thinking in common, of thinking by the body of the people, so that the experience of the mass is behind the single voice." The affluent Woolf certainly did not speak for "the body of the people" in her time nor mine, but it was startling how much I related to her assertions about the resources of time, space, and esteem to be an artist, and all the ways women were deprived of these. I knew enough about the history of women's writing to know that a room was not required, though it certainly did help.

My childhood bedroom was a converted attic with a peaked ceiling and a small window that overlooked a pond. In the late afternoons, the setting sun soaked it with golden light and my little room shone like a prism. In it, I devoured every book in our house and then stacks from our public library. I filled notebooks that I still keep in boxes, busy as those preserved from Octavia Butler's childhood with stories, reflections, and lists. That closed door allowed me to cultivate at such a young age the fierce commitment to art that has steered my life.

I dropped out of school before I reached the legal age to do so, at fifteen, because I wanted to write books and did not see my high school classrooms as the most likely place to learn how. To paraphrase Vincent Millay's college lover: There was a ruthlessness about me from the beginning. My work came first. I had an eye on myself and my future. My life's course had been directed by love, yes, but writing was my first love.

I often wondered where I had gotten that arrogance. A room of one's own did not suffice to explain it; many children had their own rooms and did not grow into such fanatics. However riddled with insecurities in other areas, I possessed an innate sense of purpose, a certainty about my life's work. The older I got, the more that girl's determination amazed me, and the more grateful I was to my parents, who had not thwarted it. I wasn't an easy child to raise but my ambitions were always clear.

As an adult, I had often described my dramatic aversion to work whose purpose was unclear to me or whose purpose I did not support. I could write for hours, loved waiting tables (and most other physical labor), would have read myself into starvation, but ask me to type some innocuous correspondence on behalf of someone I did not respect and a desperate defiance flooded my body. Boredom made me want to punch a hole in the wall or lie down and will myself unconscious. I'm sure I qualified as having attention deficit disorder; a cursory perusal of symptoms confirms it. But a diagnosis is nothing more than a list of characteristics, not an autonomous *thing*. These characteristics were my identity. My resistance to boredom or surveillance rose to the level of *allergy*. I had the freedom to imagine other options—leaving high school, moving out to live on my own before the usual age—and I insisted upon them. I no longer think I was uniquely unsuited to deadening work. We are all unsuited to labor as it is expected, conducted, and remunerated in the U.S. The rarer thing was my feeling of entitlement to do work that held meaning for me.

The rarity of such entitlement in femme artists explains why Jenny Offill's concept of the "art monster," which she coined in her 2015 novel *Dept. of Speculation*, almost immediately entered into the lexicon and has since emerged as a title and subject for multiple other books. "My plan was to never get married," Offill's heroine explains. "I was going to be an art monster instead. Women almost never become art monsters because art monsters only concern themselves with art, never mundane things. Nabokov didn't even fold his umbrella. Vera licked his stamps for him."

I was lucky to have been born, and allowed to become, a child art monster. It was the only longitudinal application of my fiendish internal drive that rivaled that of romance. If the Maelstrom had not threatened my ability to make my art, I might still be captive to its momentum. Despite this, in all of my romantic relationships I had found it near impossible to ask for a room of my own, especially in New York, where an extra room in an apartment cost many more dollars per month than I had. So I learned to write in cafés and reconciled the probability that I would always have to contend with someone slamming drawers while I was writing, or otherwise curtailing my focus. This divided consciousness seemed to be my inheritance as a woman. It was hard to find someone who did not see my work as an adversary. I told myself that I was lucky to have been born in a time during which I could *be* an artist in my relationship, the one greedily hoarding hours, perfecting the adjacent art of half listening while I rearranged sentences in my head. If the price of love must be debited from my creative attention, I was lucky to have enough attention to spare.

The jury was still out on love's price, but it turned out that living alone was not only possible, but gorgeous. It was a sumptuous feast of time that I had not seen clearly until now. Even when I had lived alone before, I had always been distracted by love. How different it was to write with a singular focus, free of the performance of attention, to frown with concentration for hours at my own creations, muttering unselfconsciously and uninterrupted. How on earth had I worked before I could work like this? I knew how: I had adapted to my own divided mind.

Woolf had not managed to survive her depression, but she had stayed married while writing an impressive number of books, books that changed conceptions of what a novel could do and be. I would not learn how to survive from her, but I might learn how to make the most of what time I had.

I rode the train to Lewes in East Sussex on a glorious sunny day. The train deposited me at a platform that hovered, a raft in a sea of green. The River Ouse, where Woolf drowned herself at fifty-nine, stretched into the horizon, specks of people and dogs rambling the paths along its banks. I walked twenty minutes or so through the downs and alongside a small country highway, until I reached the village of Rodmell, where the Woolfs had lived out their days together and where Virginia had written many of her novels, among them *Mrs. Dalloway, To the Lighthouse, Orlando,* and *The Waves.*

"There is little ceremony or precision at Monk's House," Virginia observed after she and Leonard first visited the country cottage. "It is an unpretending house." The rooms were too small for her liking and the kitchen was "distinctly bad" and she loved it immediately. They bought it in 1919, when she was thirty-seven, and kept it as a weekend house while they slowly made updates—*Mrs. Dalloway* bought them a bathroom, *Orlando* an oil stove—until it was livable full-time.

I noticed the bold colors first: the saturated green of the large sitting room, with its low ceilings and painted chairs, Virginia's emblazoned with her initials like a superhero's throne. It was a humble house, but tidy, which it had not been when the Woolfs occupied it. Virginia was a slob and Leonard called Monk's House a place of "ramshackle informality," scattered with books, papers, and bowls of pet food. The walls were hung with art, including several portraits of Leonard, Virginia, and their pets, most painted by friends, and, of course, Vanessa Bell.

As I meandered through its rooms, I thought about the Woolfs' daily routine, which was described in the museum catalog. They deviated from it only while on holiday, a few weeks per year. The couple slept separately and arose at 8 a.m. every day. Leonard cooked breakfast and delivered it to Virginia's room. After eating, she read the previous day's work aloud to herself in the bath. They both wrote for the rest of the morning in their individual studios and lunched at midday, after which they read for about an hour before taking a walk or gardening together. Tea was at 4 p.m., and during it they often wrote letters and journaled. After supper, they read in the sitting room or listened to music. It was essentially the schedule I fell into everywhere I went, if not pulled by the magnetic habits of someone else.

It seemed like the most obvious thing in the world, suddenly. I could live alone and by my own instincts and preferences, or I could find someone with compatible habits. How had I never imagined the option of *sharing* the practices that I craved and on which my peace depended? *Sharing a life* always sounded horrible to me. I didn't want to share. I wanted a whole life for myself. But what if I could live *alongside* someone else and not have to haggle over time and energy, sacrificing independence and fulfillment for connection?

When Leonard Woolf proposed to her, the thirty-six-year-old Virginia wrote him a letter that bluntly acknowledged that she was not attracted to him. They were married later that year. Their marriage was virtually sexless, but supportive and often playful. They were intellectual partners, peers, and best friends. They were both obsessed with their work, but she the bigger art monster. Throughout the cycles of her mental and physical ailments, Leonard became her caretaker, much in the tradition of literary wives throughout history.

Woolf was no stranger to the thrall of romantic ecstasy, though, most famously in her relationship with Vita Sackville-West. While it is widely assumed that the two did have sex, it was not Virginia's sexual trysts that left their deepest mark on her. Rather, it was her (mostly asexual, but very romantic) relationships with other women that made meaning in her life. Among these were her indelible bonds with her sisters, Julia, Stella, and especially Vanessa; and her deep and romantic frenemy-ship with Katherine Mansfield. Even her affair with Vita evolved after two years into another deep and lasting friendship.

In her novels, such passionate connections are set in relief to more constrained heterosexual relationships. "Much preferring my own sex, as I do," as she wrote in a letter to a friend. One of the primary differences between romantic friendship and sexual romance was sustainability. While I knew firsthand that friendships could end dramatically, much in the way of sexual romances, they tended to last longer, to change more easily over time. Sexual lovers often strived to supplant other devotions, whereas romantic friends were more inclined to share them. You could grow alongside a friend without the pressure of having to *share* a life and thus feel defined by the other's choices. The differentiation necessary to maintain intimacy through individual change was easier with friends.

Leonard himself had passionate friendships with other men. Like many of his peers, he believed in the "Greek ideal" of friendships. All of his friends at university were allegedly homosexual or bisexual and his best friend likely in love with him, at least for a time. Both of the Woolfs appeared to be bicons, though Virginia's strongest and most abiding passion was always for her work.

My favorite part of Monk's House was Virginia's bedroom. Built in 1929 while she was writing *A Room of One's Own,* her "airy bedroom" was constructed as an extension to the original house and could be accessed only from outside in the garden, a detail that delighted me. Spare but pleasing, it held a modest twin bed, built-in bookshelves, a sink, and a wooden armchair across whose arms she would often lay a board for a makeshift desk.

The little green room resembled studios I had occupied at my favorite artist residency: every need provided for without frills. The room a canvas, its contents a portrait, each day a face drawn by habit. Behind the chair stood a narrow bookcase that held thirty-nine Arden editions of Shakespeare's plays covered in patterned paper that Virginia had applied during a bout of depression and chronic headaches. Bookbinding was a form of self-therapy that she often found effective. She had intended the room to be her writing studio but it didn't feel right, so they eventually had a separate studio converted from a toolshed in the yard, though she still worked in the little room on colder days.

Perhaps I needed someone to tend me like Leonard had Virginia, or Vera did Vladimir. How indulgent, to imagine not having to worry about the little labors of living. Would I want that relationship, though? I had always been attracted to people whose ambitions rivaled mine, who had hungry minds and knew more than me in multiple areas. But if we didn't need to have a sexual connection, perhaps it could work. It sounded exploitative, but was it possible that someone could be fulfilled by the pastime of caretaking as I was by writing? It was difficult to imagine.

Once, when I was a graduate student, I house-sat for a famous writer couple who occupied a gorgeous brownstone in Brooklyn. His office was on the lowest floor and hers on the uppermost. On their walls hung paintings by artists whose names I recognized, and their Rolodex (they still had one in 2005) was a carousel of my idols. My presence in the house during their absence was intended to discourage break-ins and otherwise without responsibility. A housekeeper came every afternoon to tidy up, stock the kitchen, prep dinner, and run the laundry. I was grumpy for years afterward, to have learned of this possibility in life. It was easier to complacently attend to the mundane work of living when I couldn't imagine someone else doing it for me. Easier to tolerate the noise of a domestic partner when I couldn't imagine two floors between us.

I could not seriously entertain the idea of having a partner who did this labor for me, though. I didn't want to simply relocate within compulsory heterosexual gender roles. I wanted to divest from them. I was more interested in Boston marriages and separatism than I was in the Nabokovs' or Mellvilles' domestic arrangements, wherein one partner had done all of the domestic labor while the other made their art.

I had always imagined that it would be disastrous for me to partner with another writer. I was simply too selfish. If we wanted the same things, wouldn't we compete for resources? It struck me that I might have it backwards. If we both wanted time and space, then taking would mean giving to the other. Perhaps another writer, or someone with symmetrical devotions, was the *only* type of person compatible with me.

A T THE END of my London stay, I rode a train to Manchester to see a friend. The Manchester Art Gallery sits at the intersection of Mosely and Princess Streets. Its grand columned entrance, designed in the Greek Ionic style, has been gathering soot from the port city's streets for two hundred years.

It is a public museum that requires no ticket, and I strolled through the massive doorway into the four-storied mansion's lobby where a posted map of each floor's contents indicated my destination. I climbed the smooth stone stairs to the second floor and stepped through a wide entrance into the gallery.

She was directly around the corner, on the opposite side of the wall. I gasped when our eyes met. I had no idea that she was so big! It turns out that Charles Auguste Mengin's portrait of Sappho on the cliffs over the Ionian Sea is more than seven feet tall and five feet wide. When I plan to see paintings that I have observed only online or as reprints, I generally prepare myself for a *Mona Lisa*-type experience. Paintings, like people, are often smaller in life than they feature in my imagination.

Not Sappho. She towers. Everything striking about the reproductions I had seen was exponentially more so in the painting. Her broody, petulant face, the chiaroscuro of her bare chest and shoulders, that sulky posture. In person, it seemed even more incredible that she was meant to be grieving over a man, that she was painted by a man, even. It was so obviously a portrait of a glowering lesbian. Trouble with a capital *T.* Sad, but not passive. She really couldn't be more my type: a beautiful Eeyore.

The familiar spark of attraction that I'd felt on the plane had had nothing to do with that stranger; it was the rumble of my coyote belly, tempted by a familiar object of desire, a tripped wire that set me into predictable motion. What I felt facing Sappho was related, but a purer distillation. There was nothing to be gotten from her, no one to chase. Just the elemental thrill of the sublime. A longing with nowhere to go, nothing to feed, and therefore no end. It just whirled in me and would for as long as I stood there. A Moskstraumen of desire and appreciation: the chemistry of human consciousness confronted with Beauty. I knew I could return in five or ten years' time and feel the same churn.

Maybe Aristotle would have called it catharsis. Maybe the beguines would have called it holy. I didn't need to call it anything but understood that divestment from the chase did not require I sacrifice the pleasure of this feeling. To assign divine desire to an object one could pursue and consume was a kind of theater. The sublime needed no narrative to exist. It could not be possessed. When I projected it onto people, the feeling withered. The real thing did not insist upon completion because it was already complete. It stretched like Sappho's glowering sky in all directions.

I ARRIVED IN BINGEN after dark at the only hotel in town with any vacancy. It was clean but grim with yellowing tiles and a creaky mattress. A fellow traveler's hacking cough echoed through the wall and I wondered what the hell I was doing there, in a depressing room in a remote German town. Happy anticipation had bubbled in me on the flight from London to Frankfurt, but as the searing scent of a freshly lit cigarette seeped into my room, the whole venture suddenly felt like the height of self-indulgence. It reminded me of writing a new book, when the first flush of inspiration waned and I was left trudging toward the new idea, driven by instinct without clarity. Then, like now, a voice inside me screamed that I was wasting my time. In the case of writing, I rarely was. In fact, I had learned to recognize that voice as a harbinger of revelation. That voice spoke for the part of me that clung to old ideas, that feared a changed mind. I reminded myself of this as I drew the nubbed quilt over me.

I woke before dawn the next morning, pulled on a sweater and sneakers, and descended the narrow staircase that led to the hotel lobby. In the near-dark I downed an espresso from the self-serve machine and then quietly exited the unmanned front door. Outside, I tucked my hands in my pockets and followed the empty sidewalk until I found a small park beside the Rhine. There, I sat on a bench whose wooden slats bled their cold into the backs of my thighs.

Hugging my chest for warmth, I watched the sun rise over the valley, illuminating the orchards that ribboned the hill where Eibingen Abbey, the second community founded by Hildegard, sits. Sunlight spilled over the trees and onto the river at their feet, painting the Rhine's water silvery, then gold. As a spectator to this slow, dazzling display, I no longer felt silly for coming. On that bench, I felt my body warm and understood how that exact landscape had inspired Hildegard to build her multivalent understanding of the divine and all the ways it informed human life. I touched the image of her stepping out of her confinement, which I carried in my mind like a talisman.

When the sun was in full blaze, I toured the site of her first abbey, Rupertsberg, on which a newly built museum and study center now sits. I stood in the empty library—soon to be filled—and wandered the grounds, which already boasted a flourishing garden full of seasonal plants described in Hildegard's *Physica*. In the cavernous basement, a local society meets to celebrate the saint and hold retreats.

When my guide departed, I perused the plants, found the mint and lemon balm, also known as *Melissa officinalis,* whose leaves left a citrus perfume on my fingers. I stood for a while on the bluff, beneath which the river wound. Below me, gulls and cormorants pumped their wings and wheeled, scanning the water's rippling surface. I peered down on them, then up at the sky. I was so far from everything I had ever known. I felt infinitesimal and secure, a grain of sand embedded in the great shell of history, a place to which anything I might think or feel was recognizable. An ancient, unshockable, unshakable place, powerful enough to hold still any ravenous thing.

Even as a child I'd had an inherent sense of the interconnected divinity of all life. Humans, with our busy self-consciousnesses, have designed so many models for delineating it. From therapy models to theology to astrology to rocks and crystals not so far from Hildegard's methods, I recognized early on that they all sought to describe and draw from the same source, and were therefore all analogous. Hildegard's writings from over nine hundred years ago are no different. There are maps in them to all of my twenty-first-century beliefs.

I felt it as I gazed down at the Rhine and the wheeling birds: the basic fact that divinity was manifest in everything, including me. I knew that Hildegard had understood it, the place that all religions allude to. I could have converted to any religion, because any religion, any ritual, any practice could provide a route to its worship. In this reality, I was connected to the most ancient lineage, the lineage I never expected: that of all the truly faithful, who live in recognition of the infinite divine. It was a basic truth that human self-consciousness, which distinguishes us from other animals, so often includes an awareness of divine creative power. *The perfect freedom of single necessity.* To walk toward God.

Carl Jung, Hildegard, Augustine, Joan Chittister, Jesus Christ, the beguines, Catherine of Siena, the Shakers, Father Divine, and just about every spiritual figure I have ever read about has said in some terms that "all desire is the desire for God." Even Buddhism's tanhā and the inevitable suffering it wreaks indicates the steerage of human desire toward wrong objects. Its antidote is sometimes called *chanda:* a desire to seek spiritual enlightenment without materialism, to walk toward it.

Religious words were a problem: *good, evil, purity, sin,* and, most of all, *God.* They were insufficient and moreover tainted by the human violences done under their banner. The philosophers fared better, semantically. Jung liked *numenous.* When I wrote in my diary as a teen about my sense of the divine, I represented it with the infinity symbol: ∞. First used by John Wallis in 1655, it refers in mathematics to infinite processes rather than infinite values. Along with its sister symbol, the alchemists' ouroboros—the snake eating its tail—the infinity symbol has been popular with mystics throughout history, as well as artists from Nabokov and Borges to Hilma af Klint.

Buddhism has the mystic knot, Hinduism the serpent Ananta. To younger me, it carried an intellectual connotation, seemed distant enough from Catholicism to be permissible.

I used to have a recurrent conversation with the therapist I saw in my mid-twenties, when I was newly sober, broke, and facing an uncertain future. I often explained to her the sense I felt that there was an ultimate truth underneath my consuming but superficial daily concerns. To acknowledge it, I speculated, would probably mean abandoning my ambitions and volunteering for a life of service. I pictured building huts somewhere muddy and renouncing material belongings, maybe begging for alms like some monks and nuns.

I was a grad student then and had not written anything good yet. I did not understand that a life of service and divinity could be manifested in an infinite number of ways. It did not have to take the shape of some questionable missionary project. A decade later, it seemed clear that all good work was predicated on the same willingness: to align our wills with the will of ∞, a higher power. It was the integration work of therapy, the care and transmission of teaching, the daily kindnesses and presence with friends. It was what Audre Lorde called *the erotic,* and what the Benedictines call a *consecrated life.* It was *agape.* Most potential human actions were empty of moral or spiritual value; they could be enacted in the spirit of the divine or not.

At thirty-five, I already had a sense of what shape that life would take for me, but I hadn't been available to give it my full attention. My devotion to love had competed with my devotion to Love. Coyote had no relationship to ∞; he worshipped only what he imagined would satiate him. He was all tanhā. As I stood over the glinting Rhine, I understood with perfect clarity that this break was not an effort to be a better lover of individuals, but to step toward real Love, toward ∞.

.   .   .

Hildegard was nicknamed Sibyl of the Rhine, and as I left Bingen I thought about those ancient prophetesses, "frenzied women from whose lips the god speaks." She was my Sibyl, too. I wanted to hold on to that feeling of deep knowing I'd felt beside her river, but as I waited for my cab the next morning, I was daunted by the prospect of my return home. Like all worshippers, my faith would have to combine with work and will if I wanted it to persist when the urgent mundanities of my daily life took hold. I would need talismans to hold as concrete reminders.

As my cab navigated the winding road out of town, I drew a small mandala in my notebook and scrawled a line inside it from one of Hildegard's antiphons: *Hodie aperuit nobis clausa porta.*

III

I FINALLY SET the date to read my inventory to my spiritual director. If I was avoiding something, that was it. I had completed it months ago, the spiral notebook swollen with scribbled pages. There would be no surprises. I knew what was in there. I also knew the difference between holding some piece of clarity inside myself and saying it aloud to another person. A confession could have the power of a spell or an incantation that lifted one. Releasing the truth before a witness made it harder to augment or avoid. It made change an imperative. I clung to these last days, savoring the power to postpone whatever those utterances would demand.

In the days before my confession, I went for many long, rambling walks around the city. Autumn had always been my favorite season in New York, and that year was no exception. How reliable were the sweeping emotions of fall, the tonic of sorrow and excitement that swirled in me as the leaves changed. I had lived in the city my whole adult life and every neighborhood was a palimpsest, overlaid with memories: the scummy West Village bars and that restaurant with five-dollar entrées made edible by the sweet carrot dressing they put on everything—all replaced by bank branches and cocktail lounges, the vegan restaurant where I once had a Valentine's Day breakup, the long-standing café in SoHo where I had two first kisses and one memorable sob, and Tompkins Square Park, where I used to cop drugs and once got sick in a public trash can.

On these walks, I also noticed the shift in how I moved through spaces: with fewer interruptions by men. Six months ago, I would have steeled myself for the commentary of passing men on such a walk. But now, they said nothing. A few stares, maybe. What a difference it made to traverse these streets without makeup, in clothes chosen for comfort.

As I hypothesized at the beginning of my celibacy, I had indeed become more of a sneakers person. Though I wore heels most days from ages eighteen to thirty-five, I was aware of misrepresenting myself. I was not someone who wore heels every day except for the fact that I literally wore heels every day. Despite my enthusiasm for high femme style, I had always felt more of a sneakers person on the inside.

Now I was less visible, but more me. That is, I was less visible to men and to women who dress for men and whose eyes are attuned to the aesthetics defined by an internalized male gaze. I, Melissa, was in fact more visible than I had been for years. Some days, when I walked through the city and no man commented on my body with his eyes or his mouth, I felt like a ghost, or a superhero. I felt the way I imagined white men must feel: totally safe. Except that few white men walk around thinking, *Wow, I feel totally safe.*

In the early days of my celibacy when I noticed this lack of sexual visibility for the first time, the pleasure of it prompted a pulse of anxiety. I did not put words to it, but if I had they might have been: *Oh god. If I truly let go of being sexually desirable to men, I will lose the soft power I have enjoyed by participating in the heterosexual economy.* I tried to imagine what I would miss by absenting myself from that economy. Strange men smiling at me? The occasional free soda refill? This appeal had provided me with few of the benefits people assume it does. It had made me vulnerable in many more tangible ways. I suspected that it had hurt my career more than helped it. The one measurable benefit I could dredge up was that it would be harder to talk my way out of speeding tickets. But that was white privilege as much as beauty privilege.

Still, the idea of truly setting down that belief system scared me. I might never shave my legs again. I might not restrict my eating in the small but fascistic ways that I still did every day. I might spend my mornings drawing tarot cards and upon my divine energy. I might end up with more pets than lovers. I might become something unrecognizable and even pitied by heterosexual society. I might stay invisible to men and recognizable to myself for good.

Then, I thought, *Oh.* What a savvy trick, to convince women that we should not want all of this. As Gloria Steinem pointed out: "Any woman who chooses to behave like a full human being should be warned that the armies of the status quo will treat her as something of a dirty joke." Humiliation is painful and distracting, even from the fact that one is otherwise happy.

I had been similarly afraid to let go of drugs and sex work, two pastimes that had defined me for years. In each case, I had known it was time to let them go and I wanted to, but still I felt desperate and sad at the prospect. I could not imagine the unknown future, thus it seemed I might cease to exist without these markers. When I did let them go, there was grief, but also the shocking realization that they had not composed my personality but obscured it. Similar to my romantic obsessions, I had been kneeling before a locked door, peering through its keyhole into a single room. When I finally turned around, the whole world was behind me.

There was nothing new about these thoughts. They were not even new to me. They were thoughts that many feminists, and people who did not call themselves feminists but were interested in justice, had thought for centuries. "A feminist movement," Sara Ahmed writes, "is built from many moments of beginning again." Everything I had ever written was a citation for something some other feminists had written. The nature of feminist work is to keep realizing that we are not free, until we are.

ON THE DESIGNATED Sunday morning, I carried my list across Brooklyn to my spiritual director's apartment, which sat along the southeast corner of Prospect Park. I climbed the familiar stairs, strains of soca music and the scent of bacon seeping out from apartment doors as I passed. My spiritual director greeted me with a hug and we caught up while they brewed some tea.

My spiritual director had two gorgeous dogs, a hound and a pit bull, who barked when I walked into their apartment and eventually settled: one on the couch between us, one in a bed on the floor. The dogs also made me nervous, though I was besotted with them. We sipped from our mugs of tea and traded mundanities until their stare became expectant.

"Okay," I said with a sigh, and pulled my notebook out of my tote bag. I flipped open the cover and cleared my throat. They huffed a little laugh and waved me on, "Go ahead!"

I began reading. They listened with an open notebook in their lap, into which they scribbled an occasional note. The earliest half of my inventory told the same story over and over, with small variations: I stayed too long, one relationship overlapped with the next, I caused more harm by avoiding the truth and soon regretted it. While I read the entry for my Best Ex, I made a sharp pivot from rote recital to Real Feeling. Tears filled my eyes instantly, like a cartoon, and plinked onto my cheeks. My spiritual director passed me a box of tissues with the warm detachment of a therapist. I kept reading and the tears passed.

They interrupted me periodically to ask for clarification. Questions like, "Did you communicate that?" and "What did *you* do?" It soon became clear that I had a habit of offering complex analyses of dynamics and intentions in lieu of simple statements, such as: I lied. I cheated. I misled. I avoided.

The second half of my inventory, which covered the time that followed the Maelstrom, repeated a different story. In this one—which applied to the curator, the Last Man, the twenty-five-year-old, the music producer, and the last woman I kissed—I hurried intimacy with inappropriate or unavailable people while sending mixed messages about my own availability. I told them that I was not interested in anything serious and then texted them all day, like someone falling in love. I ignored my own ambivalence, accelerated the flirtations, and then let the affairs drag on beyond the point when I knew I wanted to end them.

In both sets of narratives, I had sex when I did not want to, failed to set limits, and caused greater wreckage by avoiding or procrastinating actions that I feared would generate others' disappointment.

When I finished reading, the sun had fallen and late-afternoon light burnished the apartment. The dogs snored peacefully, one with her warm head leaned against my thigh.

I looked up at my spiritual director and felt the weight of all I had divulged. It hung like moisture in the air. A wave of embarrassment prompted me to make a little motion with my hands, like, *ta-da!*, which they mercifully ignored.

"I'm going to lay some truth on you," they said, holding my gaze. "It might feel kind of harsh."

I felt a flutter in my diaphragm that was part fear, part excitement.

"You're a user," they said. "You use people."

It struck deep, the way truth always does when I'm ready to hear it. Still, I mustered a half-hearted defense, having just listened to a lifelong inventory of all the ways I had contorted myself for the imagined satisfactions of other people.

"I thought I was a people-*pleaser,*" I said.

"People-pleasing is people-using," they confirmed.

After that I had nothing. Just the sunken relief of the truth.

I walked home slowly from my spiritual director's apartment, which took two hours. I thought about why it was so hard to admit my own faults. Some, fine. It was easy to own that I was easily distracted, haphazard, frivolous, and vain. I could be incredibly self-centered. But that I *used* people? It did feel harsh. It did not accord with my self-image. I had been *used.* I did not want to share a category with the people who had used me. I wanted to shout at my spiritual director, at the people striding past me on the sidewalk, at the impartial trees: *But I have worked so hard to make other people happy!*

I could hear the defeated whine of it, even in my mind. I knew that it had been labor in service of my own comfort. It was not out of love that I sought to please, but an effort to placate others so that I might be released from my own obsession with pleasing, my own intolerance for their disappointment. Codependence, we called it. Ugh, the pain of being ordinarily terrible.

I wandered south along the outside perimeter of Prospect Park. When I passed the zoo, I stopped to peer through the fence at an ambling peacock and inhale the musty animal smells.

The fact that I had used people did not mean that I hadn't also loved them well. It didn't mean that I was a "bad" person except in the sense that I was a person, ever moving closer to or farther from the will of ∞. Every time I had entertained the attention of someone that I was not interested in, I had used them. All the diners in all the restaurants that had ever employed me. My former professor. My partner in the Maelstrom, whom I had worked harder to please than anyone, in the hope of extracting some sense of security from her. Even Carlo, who I'd used not only as a model, but as a mirror to minimize the perils of my own habits.

It was possible to use and be used, or even abused. Victimhood did not preclude harm. Our wounds absolved us of nothing. If I wanted to change, I had to face my similarities to those who had hurt me. To avoid that confrontation would ensure their perpetuation. It would ensure that I continued "merely settling for a shift of characters in the same weary drama." By facing my truer role in my story, I became more myself and less the *comfortable pilgrim*, less likely to enact the same narrative over and over.

I had always shuddered to imagine dating myself, certain that I would not. For the first time, I felt amazed that I had always stopped there. I had never asked myself why, then, anyone else ought to date me, or what this aversion might suggest about my treatment of others. I had known all along that I was loving selfishly. We usually know the truth about ourselves, whether or not we are able to face it. It would be easier if the truth surfaced on its own, but mostly it doesn't. Self-mythologies are self-perpetuating. The truth must be *sought*.

The manner in which I had loved people was a symptom of how I moved through the world and understood my place in it. I had understood one of my life's tasks to be the management of others' perceptions of me. It was my job to attract them and then meet or placate their desires. I had performed this unconscious labor in every realm of social life. I had earned my living that way, my self-esteem, and my physical safety. It defined the silent economy of all my romantic relationships, which insisted that the rest of my life's passions must fit into the space cleared by a lover's satisfaction. My freedom was earned by their contentment. No one in possession of that ruthless part, whose first love was art, could sustain such a dynamic. Eventually, it exhausted me, the relationship collapsed, and I was on to the next. I had not invented it, but I could choose to set it down.

After I arrived home, I pulled my notebook back out of my bag and opened to an empty page. On it, I described the person I wanted to be in my future relationships. In some cases I worked backwards from my inventory, the habits that I wanted to change or reverse. Then I described the ways I would have to change my behavior if I wanted to be that person. When I finished, there was a list of twelve items.

I tore the sheet of paper from my notebook and pinned it to my bulletin board, next to the mandala that I'd drawn with Hildegard's words in it. At the sight of it, I fought an urge to rip it down again. How exposed I felt, my hopes pinned to the wall like that. The paper nearly glowed with plaintive feeling. I winced at the prospect of confronting it every time I walked by my desk or sat down to work. Still, I left it there. I didn't want to forget that feeling. I had once read in a piece of recovery literature that I trusted: "True ambition is not what we thought it was. True ambition is the deep desire to live usefully and walk humbly under the grace of God." It was yet another reiteration of Dillard's thesis. The concept of aligning one's will with the will of ∞. That list was an important reminder of my own true ambition.

Over the days that followed, I flinched a little every time I looked at it. Then I stopped flinching. It became recognizable, part of the visual landscape of my life: white paper, black pen, twelve numbered items. That painful aura burned off those words like a mist under the sun of my attention until they, too, became familiar, uncloaked of secondary meaning. Not admonishments or exposures, but description. A distillation of my changed ideal. A vision.

A week later, I unpinned the list and brought it to my therapy appointment. I told my therapist about my confession, how indignant I'd felt when my spiritual director called me a user, and how quickly I'd seen that they were right. Then I read her my list of ideals. Before the end of it, a great wave of remorse broke over me and suddenly I was sobbing.

"Ugh," I said, fiercely wiping my cheeks. "I'm sorry. I don't know why I'm crying so hard."

"Don't you?" she said, sounding so much like a therapist that I chuckled through the tears.

I did know. It hurt to have hurt people, many of whom I did love, if not always in the ways that counted most. The ability to hurt those I loved had required detachment from the *feeling* of love. Love, in my experience, was fundamentally empathic, characterized not by the false empathy of codependence, which is ultimately self-interested, but by a true feeling of care, a desire to protect, to see the other fulfilled. Years after the incidents I had described in my inventory and secure in my desire to change, I no longer needed to detach from that feeling. Here it was, still in me, having waited all those years.

I thought of the tarot's ten of swords, in which a human figure is pierced by ten blades. One of the more devastating cards in the deck, it signified apocalypse, a bottom or ending beyond which change is possible. Sitting in my therapist's office, I felt like that figure. Inside me, a sealed purse had been punctured. Its contents seeped out, flooding into me, an infusion of love and grief. It was not only the care I felt for my past lovers, but that for my past self, the one I had also betrayed in my fear and my selfishness, whom I had given away so many times.

"What do you want to say to her?" my therapist asked. "The one that you silenced, who wanted to love differently."

"*I'll take it from here,*" I said.

I T HAD BEEN a great summer for music and I had danced more that year than any other of my life. Now, it was early autumn, some days streaked with cold, others still humid and warm. Good dancing didn't get started at clubs until at least 11 p.m., so my teaching schedule inevitably curtailed my nightlife.

Nonetheless, one Saturday Ray convinced me to join her at a dance party at the Brooklyn Museum that started early. I hadn't seen her since my return from London, and in the crush of warm bodies we two-stepped and hovered in lascivious squats, gyrating inches above the wood floor as it pulsed with the weight of a few hundred dancers. However erotic our dance styles, we kept the usual studious distance between our bodies, as if some chaperone might pop by at any moment brandishing a ruler. We made eye contact, smiled, and then looked away.

When the party ended we poured into the night, bodies steaming. It was only midnight, so we bought cheese sandwiches at the bodega and ate them in my car, grunting softly with pleasure and swiping our faces with paper napkins from my glove box as a confetti of shredded lettuce collected in our laps. Sated, we stared through the windshield at passersby as they roved in small groups to the next bar or homeward alone from evening work shifts.

"So," Ray began. I heard something unfamiliar in her voice and turned to look at her.

"Yeah?" I said.

"About this sexual tension between us." She smiled cutely and I saw that she was nervous. The hesitance made her face look younger than ever.

I nodded slowly, less in agreement than as if my head were a metronome. I looked at my hands, which rested on the bottom of the steering wheel.

After a few beats, she continued. "Are we going to do anything about it, or . . . ?"

Only a few more seconds passed, but in that time I shuttled through all of my options. First, I considered denying any tension, but I didn't want to gaslight her, so I nixed it. Next, I considered kissing her, because of course the tension was real and I had indeed thought about it, though more as an idea than an option. To my surprise, I recoiled viscerally from the thought. Not because it wouldn't be pleasurable, but because I was fresh from my intensive study of what lay behind that door and I could already taste the grief of what would be lost if I chose it: probably our friendship, as well as my integrity. I could vividly imagine the shame of violating my celibacy, breaking trust with myself, and disrupting my sweet relationship with Ray. I knew that I must not, that I would not.

As soon as I foreclosed this option, the aperture of my perception widened. I felt Ray's excitement, her nerves, but also a tinny jangle of fear, some part of her that wanted me to shut it down.

"No," I said. "We're not." The confidence of my voice surprised me. How could I be so sure when a moment earlier I had considered kissing her? I was, though. I could never have kissed her, because I loved her, and the best way to love her was to keep my hands on the steering wheel. I also knew that this might not have been the case merely one year ago.

"You're gorgeous," I told her. "You're so fun and smart. And you're twelve years younger than me, so no, I won't, not ever."

Ray nodded.

"I like being your friend," I said. "Let's keep being friends."

"Sounds good," she said. We smiled at each other and didn't look away this time.

In the week that followed, something lifted. I felt it in my body: limbs bendy as birch switches, face flushed and open, pulse fizzing at my wrists. I sprang into each morning and ran through Prospect Park, its trees bright as struck matches, my heart pounding, elated, until I was drenched with sweat and soft-brained. I smiled at everyone, felt delighted by hot showers and dinners of cheese, green apple slices, and pickles. I felt *in love*, as I only ever had toward other people.

The trick of shame is that it only becomes visible once you set it down. I had thought I was yoked to the gravity of lovers when it was my own regret to which I was bound. Since my confession, a curtain had drawn back, the rooms of my life illuminated. I had thought their darkness inherent. I was reminded of Carl Jung's words: "One does not become enlightened by imagining figures of light, but by making the darkness conscious." How many times would I fumble through a dark room before I remembered to open the blinds? I could circle for years, groping the same corners without recognizing them, until I was ready to face it. Avoidance could be the sharpest blade and it could also be mercy, a kind of patience. Then, another room, bright and finite.

In the radiant room of my small apartment with its tall ceilings, I spent a whole weekend reading mysteries, chubby paperbacks that I held in front of my face while I boiled water and sat on the toilet. Oh, the joy of disappearing when there was nothing to run from, lounging in the middle of the day on the couch or the soft new rug, feet propped on a chair or the wall, absolutely gone.

I had been reading myself into a trance since I was five years old and for just as long marveling at the startle back to myself when the trance broke. The startling part was that for a few moments after I put the book down or looked up from its pages, there was no story, just a body in a room, soft rug under my legs, dust motes spinning in the buttery afternoon sunlight. I fell out of one story and drifted for a few vaporous moments before settling back into the story of myself.

That's how it felt to wake up alone. I could be anyone or no one. Just an animal with a past. Identity is a story other people tell us, that we learn to tell ourselves, that is housed inside relationships. It is a comfort to be known, to be anchored by these touchstones, and they can limit us. To live outside of another person's story, the shared story of that relationship, revealed other possibilities, other truths. There was another kind of self that I felt standing on the bank of the Rhine, that I felt during those drifting moments after reading, and while writing.

It reminded me of a poem by the beguine mystic Hadewijch:

> You who want
> knowledge,
> seek the Oneness
> within.
>
> There you
> will find
> the clear mirror
> already waiting.

I liked to imagine the Middle Ages as literacy began to spread across Europe and people experienced this unhinging of self for the first time, free of any human mediator. No man of the church intoning incoherent Latin, or his interpretation, but the evacuation of self into story and that return, the glimpse of a clear mirror, the self revealed as an invention of the shared imagination. No wonder it incited a mass movement of women who abandoned the story of their lives for a different one.

HEARTENED BY THE EFFECT that honesty had on my friendship with Ray, I decided to try and make some other repairs. I finally felt capable of aligning my words with my actions. The last woman I kissed agreed to meet me in a café on the Upper East Side after she got off work. I arrived early and secured a table in the back of the café, which was quiet in the early evening, near closing time. I saw her walk in and as she weaved around tables toward me, I smiled, belying the nerves that clenched my chest. She looked well, dressed in dark jeans, sneakers, and a well-tailored jacket. She had cropped her shoulder-length hair.

I wasn't sure what she remembered about that night in the hotel in Los Angeles. We had shared some awkward text exchanges since, but that was all. Thoughts of her made me clench my face, grimace to banish the uneasy feeling that rose. My inventory had revealed a combination of shame and anger, along with grief at the potential friendship I'd ruined. I was fairly certain that she considered me the bad actor in our little drama, and I understood why. I had invited her to the café in order to apologize, to ratify my own mistakes without mention of hers. Before my inventory, this would have been impossible. My defensiveness had melted when I faced my own culpability. I'd cast myself as the hero too often in my own story. However sympathetic I might find Wile E. Coyote, he still left everything in pieces. I wanted to make amends.

She unzipped her jacket and settled in her chair. We exchanged a few stiff pleasantries until she looked at me expectantly.

"I realize that during our relationship, I harmed you," I said. "I was selfish and didn't want to take responsibility for what I was doing. I sent a lot of mixed signals between what I said and did, and I know it was both confusing and hurtful to you."

Her head bobbed gently as I spoke, like mine had while I listened to Ray, keeping the time of our conversation. I desperately wanted to stare at my hands or my cup as I talked, but kept my gaze on her face.

"I respect you enormously," I said. "I feel terrible that I lost you as a friend."

She was quiet for a few moments. "It *was* confusing," she said. "I was angry with you. That night in the hotel . . ."

I must have betrayed something with my face because she caught herself.

"What?" she said, and in that word I felt the serrated edge of her anger.

"Nothing," I said.

"No, tell me," she insisted.

"Really, there's nothing."

"I was very drunk," she said.

"I know."

"I don't remember it very clearly."

I nodded.

"Will you tell me what you remember?" she asked.

I thought of her repeating, *I just want to make you feel good.* I thought of her standing in front of the door, how I had gently pushed her out of the way. I felt the walls of the dark hotel room close in.

"You didn't want to take no for an answer," I said softly.

Her face contracted, mortified, and I immediately wished I could take it back. *I am fucking this up,* I thought, and desperation rose in me. I thought about saying, *It's not a big deal,* or *It was fine, really,* but those were lies and I could not utter them.

Her face flushed, and she turned away from me toward the window, outside of which pedestrians passed with stiff shopping bags swinging from their arms. I frantically wanted to apologize for embarrassing her. I had not come there to embarrass her, could think of no less intended outcome. But I could not bring myself to apologize for telling her the truth. The seconds before she spoke swelled with every possible response. I braced myself for an outburst, for her to leave, to cry, to laugh, to spit at me. The truth was that we didn't know each other very well.

"I'm sorry I did that," she said, interrupting my frenzied thoughts. It was she who held my gaze, then. I could hardly believe it. I wanted to collapse at her feet with gratitude. She chose not to blame me, but to take responsibility for her own part. She hadn't needed nine months of celibacy and a confession of her life's romantic exploits to do so, either. I saw the strength of her character and felt a pang of sadness. I could have been getting to know her all this time. I also felt a pang of attraction. Integrity is appealing. I knew better, finally. However much I wanted to shower her with grateful kisses, I would not move an inch. I owed her better.

"Thank you," I said.

I was too dialed up inside for the subway, so I flipped my collar toward the evening chill and decided to walk downtown. I'd just crossed Eighty-Sixth Street when my phone rang.

I knew as soon as Nora said my name. It had finally happened. Her voice wobbled as she recounted the story, but she sounded clear, like herself.

A few days earlier she had planned to get drinks with her dissertation adviser. That afternoon a snowstorm swept across the city. The lawyer didn't want Nora to go out in the storm, but Nora, in a rare moment of rebellion, donned her boots and left the apartment.

She stayed out for hours, knowing her girlfriend would be enraged. The snow was blinding when she returned late that evening, a little drunk. As her numb fingers fumbled with the keys, Nora discovered that the lawyer had locked her out of the apartment. She banged on the door and shouted up at the windows but didn't want to wake her neighbors, so she huddled in an all-night diner a few blocks away, calling and calling.

When the lawyer finally let her back into the apartment, an explosive fight erupted. The lawyer said many violent things. She called Nora boring, lazy, and untrustworthy, and then she hit Nora in the face.

Nora woke the next morning and fingered the bruise on her cheek. *Well,* she thought. Nora still did not want to leave, but she recognized the bruise on her face as a threshold that, once crossed, indicated a new realm of possible mistreatment, and of self-abandonment. Before she could second-guess her decision, she booked a short-term rental near campus, packed a bag, and left.

Despite the new clarity in her voice, she sounded ragged and small. She was still fighting inside. She wanted to go back. The tether that tied her to the lawyer tugged and tugged.

"Don't go back," I told her. "Please don't go back."

"I won't," she said.

"I'm here for you," I said. "Whatever you need."

When I hung up the phone, I inhaled deeply and watched the breath emerge from my mouth in a white cloud as I exhaled. I reminded myself that Nora's path was her own. That she had left of her own volition. That whatever followed would be her choice. That she would probably not go back, and if she did, there would be another route through it. I turned my focus back to myself, to the real source of my fear.

After only two months of living together and a failed first attempt at breaking up, I had finally exited the Maelstrom. I was not proud of my method. Early one morning, I wrote my lover a letter. I told her that it was over between us and that I was sorry. I asked her to leave.

She had kept her old place after moving in with me, and I promised that I would mail anything she left behind. Then I drove to work and once there handed off my phone to a friend. I could not afford to offer my lover an opportunity to talk me out of it. I knew I would not be able to resist. For two days and two nights, I stayed elsewhere, sleepless and numb. The friend who put me up remarked afterward that she'd never seen such a breakup before. "It was like a cult extraction," she said. I agreed. Like many who join cults, my worst adversary had been my own mind. I had convinced myself I could not live without her when in fact our relationship was killing me.

As I walked downtown, my gaze combed through the windows of shops. I had been sick with anxiety throughout the ordeal but still unable to fully feel my own fear or grief. I was too accustomed to suppressing my instincts and too afraid of going back to her. Now, I was far enough away, I realized.

The fear I felt for Nora was a fear that belonged to me. My own fear of going back. Of the stranger I had become during those years. As I wove through clusters of tourists and stopped at a curb to wait for a red stoplight, that fear felt fresh, cool as the wind that chilled my face. But it wasn't fresh. It had been stored in my body, waiting for me to let it out, to let it go. I didn't need to fear the Maelstrom anymore. I was never going back.

Trust, whether in another or in oneself, is not a contract. It is not binding and guarantees nothing. It is always conditional. It is a form of faith, something we choose to believe until we can't anymore. I knew the possibility of losing myself remained, if I ever went back to that old way, just like I could choose to pick up a drink or a drug. I knew that the more I hid from myself, the farther away from ∞ I got, the less of a choice it became.

A FEW WEEKS LATER, I rode the train to the Museum of Modern Art to see Nan Goldin's *The Ballad of Sexual Dependency*, a slide show of intimate portraits taken by the New York photographer between 1979 and 1986, accompanied by a soundtrack that included songs by the Velvet Underground, Screamin' Jay Hawkins, and Nina Simone. The show debuted publicly at the 1985 Whitney Biennial, though Goldin first played it for a private audience of its subjects. The photographs feature Goldin and members of her community in intimate settings: lounging on couches, in beds and cars, behind bars. Goldin developed her style while photographing her drag queen friends on the Lower East Side, and over time, as her social milieu grew, her subjects expanded to include a wide array of outsider figures, rich with artists, queers, and addicts. In a *New Yorker* profile published while the MoMA show ran, Hilton Als described the photographs as "noncommercial images that promoted not glamour but lawless bohemianism, or just lawlessness."

Like every artist of a certain age who took photography classes in college, I had been obsessed with the show and was thrilled by the opportunity to finally see it in person. At twenty, I'd studied the photographs, their haunting depictions of a New York scene that I was heartbroken to have missed—the legacy of every young artist who comes to New York. I was especially compelled by the exposure of such private moments in the lives of her subjects. The show includes a disturbing series that captures Goldin covered in bruises after a gruesome beating from her boyfriend, and many that reminded me of the house parties we held in my first apartments in Boston: a bunch of young queers who had made it to the city, immersed in the magical combination of drugs and chosen family finally found, giddy with freedom, so many consequences still offstage. They were images that only a participant in those scenes would have been capable of capturing.

"*The Ballad of Sexual Dependency* is the diary I let people read," Goldin wrote in the book that was published the year after the show debuted. "The diary is my form of control over my life." She described it as "an exploration of my own desires and problems," and it became, as Als wrote, "a benchmark for photographers who believe, as she does, in the narrative of the self, the private and public exhibition we call 'being.'" It had been a benchmark for writers like me, too.

I sat in the dark gallery for a long time as the slideshow ticked by and then started again, those familiar songs filling the room, songs I had listened to while making art and getting high, that were steeped in memories of my late teens and early twenties. I felt close to tears the whole time I sat there. Now ten years older than most of her subjects, I could grasp their vulnerability in ways I hadn't as a younger woman. "For me," Als wrote, "'The Ballad' is poised at the threshold of doom; it's a last dance before AIDS swallowed that world." I, too, felt the tidal wave of tragedy surging just behind them. It was AIDS, but also the predictable agonies of addiction, its terrible ends; the legacies of trauma that were still waiting when the party ended.

Those images also carried the ghostly impressions of my own young self, drug-addled and manic with freedom, ignorant to my own sexual dependencies, teetering on the edge of annihilation. I hadn't been able to protect her from all of those ends, but I had done more than survive.

Critics have often used the diaristic nature of "confessional" writing by women to dismiss and denigrate it. I'd experienced it repeatedly when I'd published my first book. This second book was aesthetically different, more experimental and more ambitious, but no less exposing. I knew that it was the best thing I have ever made and also the most personal. As the publication approached, tendrils of fear crept through my limbs.

Over the previous month, I had apologized to the twenty-five-year-old, to the last woman I kissed, to everyone I could address directly without causing them more harm. To leave some people alone was the best amends. I knew I could not write memoir without upsetting anyone, but I did not want to cause superfluous harm. I wanted to mitigate the hurt as much as I could without compromising the integrity of my work.

From the start of writing my second book, I knew that there could be no trace of retribution in the final draft. I could not publish it until I had found a peace with my experience in the Maelstrom. Though excruciating, it had been instructive to watch Nora and all the ways that she ran toward her own annihilation, insisted upon it. Yes, she had been manipulated, but she was also an adult with her own inscrutable motives and redemptive agendas.

It was so much easier to see this reality from a distance, that it had been the same for me. Prior to the Maelstrom, I had recoiled from dependency in love but spent decades handing my body over as if I had no choice. This polarized relationship to intimacy created fertile conditions for a maelstrom. When one arose, no one had forced me to stay in it for two years. Having done so did not make me a monster. I had been powerless to leave any sooner than I did. "Sex is only one aspect of sexual dependency," Nan Goldin wrote in her book, and I think she meant that we like to seed our redemptions inside of other people, cast them in the dramas of our pasts so that we have something concrete to pursue. But humans are not built for that. Too often they simply reiterate the past, rather than cure us of it.

Seeing Nora through her ordeal had clarified this. All I could give her was love. It was all I could give to my past self, too, the only thing that would prevent me from suffering that way again. This abstinence—not only from sex but from all the pursuits that estranged me from myself and reinforced a dialectical conception of intimacy—was a form of self-love, of redefinition.

What I had looked for in a lover I had found in art, in the creation of that very book. During the final days of writing it, I had felt great swells of sympathy for my former lover. She, too, had been caught in the Maelstrom. Only when I rebuilt the diorama of our undoing could I see that clearly, and in seeing it, I loved her more than I ever had. Still, I knew she would not recognize that love in the artifact. She was likely to see it as an act of violence. I could not prevent that outcome, except to abstain from writing or publishing the book, and in the certainty from which my art emerged, I knew that I must do both. That I was willing to face the consequences. Some kinds of love do not depend upon their recognition.

Even now, I don't begrudge my ex her sense of betrayal. That book was full of my truth but not hers, and in that sense it will always be an incomplete story, an incorrect one. "I am no more the solitary author of this book than I alone invent the fiction of my life," writes Robert Glück. "I am also the reader, oscillating in a nowhere between what I invent and what changes me." To submit ourselves to a single narrative is less precise, more fictional than finding ways of representing experience's multiplicity, the many narratives by which we understand it.

The Maelstrom did not have a single meaning. My understanding of it is a collage of narratives featuring two animals responding to the patterns in which they live, shuttling forward through history, blood, land, and, eventually, art. I had tried to represent that in my book and to some extent failed, as we always do. I have learned to live with that.

Outside, I zipped my coat all the way up. It was truly cold now, early winter. On my walk to the train, I dipped into a bookstore I'd never seen before. I wandered through the labyrinth of shelves, and fell into a familiar route, a kind of scavenger hunt that I set for myself. I always started with the hard-to-find ones first, because nonfiction is scattered by category all over a bookstore. I found James Baldwin, Adrienne Rich, a volume of Woolf's diaries, and a new edition of some Audre Lorde essays, which I pulled from the shelf. I closed my eyes and flipped the book's pages, then interrupted their flutter with my finger. This little game of bibliomancy I'd been playing since I was a child. I ran my finger down the page and stopped, then opened my eyes. Recognizing the words, I laughed. The results of this divination weren't always perfect, but sometimes they were.

I headed to fiction. Here, I looked for the books that raised me: *Written on the Body, Sula, Cat's Eye, Rubyfruit Jungle, Kindred,* and *Bastard Out of Carolina.* When I found one, I pressed the tip of my index finger against its spine, like the tiniest hug. *Hello, old friend.*

I remembered going to our public library after school one day when I was fourteen and reading Dorothy Allison's *Bastard Out of Carolina* straight through. To read a whole book in a single sitting, something I did a lot as a young person, is like being dipped in someone else's consciousness. I looked up at the end to find that night had fallen without my noticing; I had been too enraptured by the story of Bone, the young narrator. The library's overhead lighting tinted everything the yellow of chicken broth. As I stared at the silhouettes of trees outside the library window, I burst into tears, grief flooding through me.

The stories I chose to escape into became portals that delivered me into their world, but they also delivered the world into me. It wasn't always grief that poured through. Farther along the alphabetized shelves, I found Jack London's 1906 novel, *White Fang*, which I had read at nine or ten years old. It contains a scene in which a man huddles by a fire in the wilds of the Yukon Territory, surrounded by hungry wolves. As he feeds the fire, exhausted by fear and lack of sleep, the encroaching wolves murmur in the shadows and the man stares down at his hands, suddenly "interested in the cunning mechanism of his fingers." He falls into a kind of reverie, as "By the light of the fire he crooked his fingers slowly and repeatedly, now one at a time, now all together . . . and he grew suddenly fond of this subtle flesh of his that worked so beautifully and smoothly and delicately."

For the rest of my childhood I recalled this scene almost daily. I still think of it often. I understood exactly the man's wonder at his body's "cunning mechanism." I, too, marveled at my own *subtle flesh* that *worked so beautifully*. Solitude was the whetstone against which this consciousness sharpened most pleasurably. I had thought of the *cunning mechanism* of my body so many times over my celibacy, as if seeing myself for the first time.

I returned the London to the shelf and wandered to my final stop: the poetry section. There, I found Rilke, Plath, and Olds, but not Sexton. I pressed their spines and then perused the new releases. I picked up one whose title caught my eye: *Bestiary*. I had always been infatuated with those medieval compendiums of beasts both mythical and real, loved that one encyclopedia could contain both. I purchased the book. In the café adjacent to the bookstore I bought a coffee and sat at a table by a steam-fogged window. I opened the book to its dedication and didn't look up until I reached the last page.

It was a sublime experience, like seeing Sappho for the first time. The way the poet used images struck me as deeply familiar. "I have never known a field as wild / as your heart," she wrote in one poem. In another, "I am a witness / to the sea and the sun, to your body / lashed to the mast." The recognition I felt was not that of seeing a famous actor on the streets of New York, as one often does, but more like glimpsing my own reflection in a window before realizing it was me. When I closed the book, I felt with utter certainty that the mind behind those poems shared something uncommon with my own. Her book had lit my lamp, illuminated that shared place from which we drew our art. I felt suddenly excited about the book I had written, ready to let it go.

A fundamental part of the consecrated life, as described by mystics and nuns, is *lectio divina,* the study of holy scriptures. The process comprises practices of reading, meditation, prayer, and contemplation of "divine reading." In my study over the past year, I had recognized the corollary to it in my own life.

Reading is not always a holy act, of course. Like all spiritual practices, one has to work to feel close to the divinity in a text. I had to keep my heart turned on, the same way I had to keep my brain turned on when reading critically. Sometimes, however, the divine rose straight up to meet me, as in *Bestiary.* Sometimes, as Woolf wrote in *To the Lighthouse,* "there curled up off the floor of the mind, rose from the lake of one's being, a mist, a bride to meet her lover." It reminded me that art had always opened my channel to the divine, been what held it open. I felt so moved that I jotted a short fan letter to the author and sent it from my phone.

I walked the rest of the way to the subway, my scarf wound tightly around my neck. The sky was overcast but bright. I heard the crisp percussion of shoes on the sidewalk and the cry of car horns and noticed that the melancholy of a week ago, before my confession, was gone. I passed a newsstand and scanned the headlines. They were as bad as ever. It was my perspective that had changed. There was no more injustice today than there had been in the Middle Ages, and still those women found ways to manifest a consecrated life. Still they made art and celebrated and forged radical paths of independence and interdependence. Their faith had made it possible. I had faith, too.

I thought about Agnes Martin, Octavia Butler, the beguines, Hildegard, May Sarton, and Nan Goldin. There was plenty of hideous shit in their lifetimes and they turned, again and again, to that most reliable higher power: art. I had faith in that practice, in the great shell of history that held us all, in the work of listening through divine reading, of speaking back into that vastness through art. It was the divine that would hold my hungry parts, that had enough love to quiet them. This felt like a weight-bearing fact, something to lean into when my other resolves weakened. It would steady me.

I cradled that faithful feeling between my palms like a birthday candle. When I got home, I wrote the words my finger had found in the bookstore and tacked that scrap of paper over my desk: "I want to live the rest of my life, however long or short, with as much sweetness as I can decently manage, loving all the people I love, and doing as much as I can of the work I still have to do. I am going to write fire until it comes out of my ears, my eyes, my noseholes—everywhere. Until it's every breath I breathe. I'm going to go out like a fucking meteor!"

T HE POET WROTE BACK to me almost immediately. I
responded, and then we had a correspondence. It was helpful, as I moved through my anxieties toward the new book's
release. It turned out that she had read my first book, as well as some
of my essays. *I can't imagine being that vulnerable in prose,* she wrote
in one email. Reading it, I chuckled. Everything I had ever written
felt vulnerable, sure, but as I explained to the poet, I had been able to
tell myself it was a private exercise, because it was. I postponed the
potential that other eyes might see it, which created the privacy that
made the writing possible.

My second book was different. It had been harder to postpone
the pressure of those other eyes, especially those of my ex-lover.
In the first iteration of the book, I tried to write a version of my story
that protected her and would protect me from her anger. That version was a lie. Readers who had witnessed the events therein told
me so, and I knew they were right. Though I wrote the truer version
of the book with more love for my ex and myself, it was impossible
to avoid indicting us both.

Whatever happens, I reminded myself, it wouldn't be harder
than living it had been.

.   .   .

In early December, I caught a train from Grand Central to Connecticut. Nora had rented a small apartment in a complex near the train station, a river, and a Ruby Tuesday. Trees surrounded the small development, and I could hear the flow of traffic from one direction and that of water from the other. Walter had been retrieved from exile and was clearly at home in the new place, his big body roosting in a commandeered cardboard box freckled with claw-punctures.

Nora was bereft. Her creamy complexion gone sallow, her rosette mouth downturned. I could tell that it took all of her energy to make the gestures of hospitality, to hoist her mouth into a smile. Still, she took me to a very nice restaurant where I gorged on fresh-made pita and small plates of glistening labneh and hummus.

"I know I can't go back, that she is poison, but it doesn't stop everything in me from craving her," she said in a low voice. Every time she spoke about the lawyer, her eyes filled.

"Oh, sweetheart." I reached across the table and squeezed her hand. "I promise this will pass." I knew the dark room of such grief and also the rare tincture of common experience. I tried to infuse her with my knowing, beam my surety into her through my eyes and my fingers that enclosed hers. "I know that feeling," I told her.

After I left the Maelstrom, I craved it, too. I had reached my end and still I longed for my former lover just as I had once longed for heroin, with a desire that blotted out the certainty of what would follow, how temporary the relief. For those two years she had been my *pharmakon,* the Greek term for a substance that could be either poison or cure. She had been both, and, like all the substances I had ever relied upon, I sweated her out. After four days—the exact same number of days it had taken me to pass through the most acute stage of heroin withdrawal—my sweat dried and my vision cleared. I was still sick, morose for weeks after that, in the stage Nora now occupied. The nature of such grief, and all grief, is that it speaks in superlatives: you will always feel this way, you will never feel that way again. The ringing credibility of that voice passes, too, if one only waits long enough without relapse.

I got her to laugh a few times, speaking in hyperboles. "I think I'm going to stay celibate forever," I said, and realized that I sort of meant it. My imagination stuttered to visualize the conditions under which I would be willing to imperil what I now had. "At least, if I ever date again, it won't be monogamously, and I will never cohabitate again. It will have to be like Sontag and Annie Leibovitz: adjacent apartments, adjacent lives."

Nora looked at me like I was transmitting a broadcast from Mars, but her smile was genuine.

"Even the phrases we use to describe it make my skin crawl," I went on. " 'Share a life'? 'Be as one'? 'Better half'?" I grimaced. "I've never wanted *one* of anything. I've already got my own better half and I'd like to keep both halves."

I convinced her to eat at the Ruby Tuesday with me before I left, because I loved all salad bars and because I wanted to leave her with some positive associations to the new surroundings. As we chewed our shredded lettuce and croutons, I stared at my brilliant friend, her sad and lovely face, and felt certain that she would recover from this. This was a gauntlet she would never have to walk again. I was so grateful she'd survived it and to count her among my chosen family.

I had been laughing when I said it, but days after I returned from Connecticut, I still wondered whether I'd ever want to be coupled again. I drove to and from work in New Jersey, trying to imagine a relationship that would not compromise my freedom. On Saturday, I woke in the still of early morning, before the sun spilled over the buildings across the street, and made a pot of coffee. I sat at my desk, opened a notebook, picked up a favorite green pen, and tried to think through it in writing.

When I imagined living with another person or people, my whole body revolted, as if I had imagined being buried alive. I had lived alone for two years before my celibacy began, but I was not alone. I was always inviting someone else in who ate up all the light in my small apartment. I enjoyed my own company more than that of anyone I had ever dated.

In *The Art of Sleeping Alone,* when a former lover makes a final attempt to woo Sophie Fontanel back, he takes in her "new, affable face" and glowing demeanor and asks if she has fallen in love with another man.

"What's his name?" another friend asks her.

"As soon as you find yourself," she replies, "others start trying to guess who the new person is."

"I know who it was," she writes. "The one for whom I was leaving everything: the girl I'd been years ago."

I knew now, too. I had given her away so many times. She had never felt more safe than in these months we'd spent alone. I knew that it would be easier to stay here. Still, when I tested the decision in my mind, it sat uneasily. I couldn't quite believe in it.

Mostly what I had gleaned that year was clarity, which is not the same thing as being changed. Change happens in action, in true effort to live with conviction, in facing and surmounting obstacles to that task. I might not be able do any more of this work alone. But if I moved back into relationships, opened myself to that possibility, I wanted to hold on to myself. It's so much easier to make a person one's higher power. Easier to pursue redemption in them than to look inward. I was afraid that I would betray her again, that girl who was both the agent and the victim of my romantic cycle.

The essential pain of the Maelstrom, the lever that modulated it, was my lover's withdrawal. When I displeased her or she got scared, she would withdraw love, affection, affirmation, approval, attention, sex. It disabled me completely. That response drew from the deep lessons of women's history, the ancient double bind that simultaneously charges us with the care of others and insists upon our own dependence. If we are not useful to the other, to men, if we are not desired and seen as having a purpose that serves them, it tells us, then we will be outcast or die.

Jacques Derrida, in his writing about the word *pharmakon,* draws a connection between it and the word *pharmakeus,* which means sorcerer or magician. While in the Maelstrom, I sometimes saw my lover as a kind of magician, because I could not make sense of what was happening to me. I was unrecognizable to myself. It is impossible, now, to communicate the degree to which I was transformed in that relationship. It is unbelievable, except by those who saw me through it and those who have lived through similar. I went into the box a woman and came out a rabbit.

When I wrote that book, I saw how wrong I was. Road Runner isn't a magician. The only magic of such devastation is that which exists inside Coyote, the spell or curse that sends him back again and again, no matter how many identical cliffs he meets. My lover was no *pharmakeus,* but rather *pharmakos:* a scapegoat.

If I wanted to stay myself in love, I had to feed Coyote something better than a lover. If I wanted to be responsible to my beliefs over my ingrained patterns, I had to relinquish that old set of beliefs, the one I did not write or choose but which had continued to guide my decisions. They constrained everything from my relationship to my body and to pleasure, to the shoes I wore, what food I ate, and how I spent my time. All of them could be distilled to some version of that ultimatum, which I wrote out by hand on a piece of paper:

> *If I am not wanted, I will die.*
> *If I am not wanted, I do not deserve to live.*
> *If I am not loved, I do not exist.*

By this measure, my survival depended upon the task of appealing to others. It took priority above all else.

The words on that page looked super dramatic, even to me. I had been taught to think this about my feminist thoughts. I had been encouraged to doubt them. I had been encouraged to believe that they were not the deep lessons of women's history, the inherited thoughts of my ancestors for whom they were literally true. I had been encouraged to think instead that these ideas were risible and retrograde. They were nothing more than evidence of my own dramatic nature. They were *hysterical.* They were an individual character flaw that happened to be ascribed only to women. "Suppressing the knowledge produced by any oppressed group makes it easier for dominant groups to rule because the seeming absence of dissent suggests that subordinate groups willingly collaborate in their own victimization," writes Patricia Hill Collins, echoing the conclusion drawn by justice activists across history.

As a millennial woman who had been raised on the tenets of second wave feminism and then learned to critique their flaws, I had made jokes about consciousness raising. But that was an accurate description of what I had been doing. I had been trying to raise my own consciousness in an area of life that I had lived unconsciously. I had made choices in love based on how I "felt," and sometimes a feeling is simply the twitch of an inherited belief, the belief that my worth was contingent on my lovability. I needed to replace those tendencies with what Sara Ahmed calls "feminist tendencies."

I had struggled so often that year with the perception—mine and others'—that my mission was ridiculous. *Three months off of dating and sex? Six months? A year? Give me a break.* I still had moments of doubt, but I knew it wasn't ridiculous. "The power of a free mind consists of trusting your own mind to ask the questions that need to be asked and your own capacity to figure out the strategies you need to get those questions answered," writes Collins. Living against the grain of one's society is grueling work, plagued by doubt. We are designed to seek social approval. But those doubts did not spring from my own inner knowledge; they came from other people. Divestment had revealed how sensitive I was to the influence of others. It hadn't mattered that I liked my own strong, short legs; I had still worn heels for decades to disguise them. When I spent time with friends who denigrated their own bodies, my own shame dilated. I felt shocked when I reflected on all the empty consent I'd given, the unwanted sex I'd had with partners and near-strangers, but then I remembered the endless stream of jokes we are all exposed to in which women having unwanted sex is the punch line. What was more normal than women having unwanted sex?

My resistance, however small—be it three months of celibacy, a pair of sneakers, the ability to tolerate a partner's disappointment or to interrupt sex I wasn't enjoying—undermined that influence. Every act of resistance restored my own will. I needed to hold on to that. My past partners were not responsible. It was my dependence upon managing them, upon the belief that I must. For the dependent person, a single day of independence is radical. For the addict, a single day is the only unit of freedom. Before my celibate period, I had not gone a day in twenty years without entertaining the ways I did or should or would or could appeal to other people and conform to their desires. My attempt to replace dependence with independence and interdependence, to share my questions and answers with the women who came before and after me, was the radical basis of all feminisms. It was the basis of all freedoms. It was my inheritance.

Abstinence felt safe because in it I could securely hold on to the knowledge that my worth was not contingent on my lovability. That I was already loved by forces greater than any single human.

Well, it was the test that made it *faith*.

I stared out my apartment window, now aglow with morning light. The bare branches of the maple tree outside shuddered as a breeze swept through. I took a deep breath and held that dug-up belief in the light, like a swollen tick: *My worth is contingent on my lovability*. I underlined it on the page. It had been feeding off of me and I needed to burn it to ash.

The next morning, I rode the Q train out to Coney Island. I stood on the beach and watched the winter waves roll in, jagged points that formed and dissolved. The ocean was the first infinity I had ever loved, older god than art or love. I knelt before it, my knees in the cool sand, and dug a shallow hole with my cold fingers. When the breeze settled, I pulled the list out of my pocket. I said a prayer and flicked the lighter a few times before it lit the page's corner. The flame swelled and I dropped the paper into the hole, shielding it with my hands. In seconds, it was ash. I ended my promise to stay celibate and made a new promise, to remain faithful to what I had found.

D O YOU STILL get crushes?" I asked my mother. We were in the middle of one of our long rambling conversations while I packed for the big writers' conference, which was in Washington, D.C., this year.

"Not really," she said. "Maybe briefly, but they don't last. A crush is a fantasy, a projection, right? Once I get to know someone, it dissolves. The amount I have to know someone in order to dispel the fantasy has just gotten shorter over time. At this point, I might simultaneously notice an attraction to someone and recognize the very thing in them that would drive me crazy if we were together."

"That makes sense," I said. That year, seeing the mechanism of projection in myself or someone else was often enough to turn me off completely.

"People are just people," my mother went on. "Every relationship is work and I can't pretend that it won't be anymore. I'm happy with the person and the work I've chosen."

I taught my last class before the conference, which would segue into spring break, with the vigor of someone who knew she wouldn't be back to work for two weeks. The ongoing truth was that I had had more consistent energy for my students than ever before in my teaching career, as I also did for my friends, my family, and my work.

Without the funnel of romantic obsession siphoning off large quantities of energy, it is distributed more generously and evenly among all my relationships. The patterns of my energy and time spent reflected my heart's investments more accurately than ever.

I talked with my students that evening about a favorite Jamaica Kincaid essay. I attempted, through detailed appreciation for the skill and intention behind the work, to infuse them with my love for it, for her subtle, furious sentences. As our discussion unfolded, I felt a great rush of love for the people who sat around the seminar table. Though I had known this feeling for all of my time teaching, it had arisen more frequently this year. I beamed at them with gratitude for their effort, their willingness to remain open to that which they did not yet understand, to step *toward* it, even—such a tremendous challenge for humans.

I was "an animal with a past," and spoke to them from my individual experience replete with all its privileges and biases, but there was also a *we* among us, among artists, among writers, and in that sense, the first-person point of view from which I spoke was sometimes a lyric *I*. This was part of what I wanted to teach them. How we animals with our distinct pasts can speak not *for* each other but *to* each other in the language of art. In art, we can access a collective intelligence, share the burden of our histories, seek our unnamed inheritances, and invite each other inside that great shell, big enough to hold all of us.

After class, I scurried to my car across the starkly lit parking lot, the frozen pavement contracted under my heels. I sat in the driver's seat while the engine warmed, weary but happy, charged up in the way only teaching made me, and huffed breath on my fingers. Teaching, as Edward Hirsch wrote of lyric poetry, really could be "a highly concentrated and passionate form of communication between strangers."

Sixteen hours later, I sat on an airplane once again. It was midmorning and the rain had paused, but the sky was dark. In anticipation, I imagined the moment when the plane would rise above the cloud cover into the blazing light above. I felt jittery with excitement. It had been almost one year since the last time I attended the conference, since the scene with the last woman I kissed in the hotel room in Los Angeles, since I resolved to do something truly different. *Nothing changes if nothing changes.* So much had changed since then.

A few days earlier, Ray had come by for lunch.

"Happy end of celibacy!" she sang upon entering my apartment. We both laughed as we hugged. How easy our dynamic felt now that the question of sexual tension had been answered. Rather, it had always been easy, but it now felt secure. I had never been able to relax into a space until I knew exactly where its boundaries lay, and Ray was the same.

As she readied to leave an hour later, I opened my computer and logged into my email. Bulky in her winter coat, she leaned down and wrapped her arm around my shoulders for a quick parting hug. In doing so, she glimpsed the email draft I'd just opened, which was addressed to the author of *Bestiary.*

"Ah, corresponding with a poet, I see," she said, and waggled her eyebrows suggestively.

"It's not like that!" I retorted with play indignance, and, I thought, sincerity. Then a wave of heat sifted up my entire body, as if someone held a magnet over my head, coaxing all my blood upward until the top of my skull tingled and dampened with sweat.

My friend observed this progression, or at least the flush of my confused face, and grinned at me. "What is it like, then?" she asked.

When she was gone, I asked myself if I had been flirting with the poet. The answer was no, but it didn't preclude the possibility. She was queer and, I knew from her emails, in the process of getting divorced. Not an ideal prospect, but not an out-of-bounds one. I thought about it while I packed, while I spoke to my mother, while I cleaned my apartment, and while I did the laundry at the laundromat, listening to the rhythmic thump of the machines with a book in my hands. At home, I put the clean laundry away, wheeled my packed suitcase against the wall, ate a quesadilla, washed my dish, and opened my email again. I deleted the email I had drafted to her.

Are you going to the conference? I typed instead. *If so, would you like to get lunch with me?* She responded immediately to say that she was going to the conference, and, yes, she would like to have lunch with me.

I couldn't pinpoint what was different about our messages that evening. Maybe there was nothing that could be pointed to except the feeling inside me. I had made a choice and saw the altering power of my intention. After I closed my computer, I stared at the list tacked over the desk.

I didn't think about her over the first day of the conference, which was a flurry of friends and panels. By the second day, my hotel room was littered with shoes, discarded clothes, and half-empty coffee cups. I was as messy away from my home as I was tidy in it. I wandered the conference center and the surrounding neighborhood, hugging friends from far-flung places and sharing spontaneous meals. I savored the freedom to do what I pleased, no need to run it by anyone. I slept in the middle of the enormous hotel bed, bolstered by long white pillows, wearing an eye mask and earplugs. In the evening, I skipped the hotel bar swarmed by writers and ordered takeout to eat in bed while watching the giant television.

The poet and I had planned to meet for lunch at midday after I finished a signing in the conference book fair. When the time of our meeting arrived, I was still seated behind a long table, flanked by stacks of books. A small line waited patiently, mostly young women clutching their own copies. In every direction, crowds of writers wound around the cavernous space, perusing tables covered in books, pamphlets, magazines, pencils, and bookmarks emblazoned with university logos.

She approached quietly as I scribbled my name on a title page. When I looked up, there she was. I felt stunned by her face, so beautiful and inexplicably familiar, her smile that was part-frown, how it already felt known to me.

Over the eight years since this meeting, she and I have had an ongoing conversation about sexual magnetism—what it is, who has it—and at one point, I argued that magnetism is not just an attracting power, passively held by some and not others, like a light bulb that never turns off. Magnetism is *control* over one's attracting power, access to the switch that turns on the light, and directs it toward specific others. Even when one has that access, not every instance of attraction is engineered by such magnetism. All of this to say that I flipped no switch to accelerate the chemistry of our first meeting; it simply was, a radiant current that illuminated the distance between us and promised to close it.

It wasn't the first time I'd experienced chemistry, of course. I had cultivated enough self-awareness over the previous year to question my first impulse, which urged me toward her. As we walked to a nearby café, I was acutely aware of her shape in my periphery and the distance between our swinging hands. I turned my attention outward, expanded it to include the budding trees that lined the sidewalk and the stream of people that rushed toward us. I waved hello to passing acquaintances and so did she. I wiggled my fingers and noted the cool tip of my nose, a slight pinch in my left shoe, the smell of French fries wafting from somewhere nearby. I looked up at the bright gray sky and felt my pupils tighten. I was here, in my body, in the city of Washington, D.C., walking down the sidewalk beside a tall stranger. Choices all the way.

Six years later

G HENT IS A CITY of canals and bridges studded with bursts
of flowers. The Gothic architecture rises against the sky like
elaborate sandcastles. The bells of Saint Bavo's Cathedral
tolled for a long time as I navigated the cobbled streets and morning
commuters whizzed by me on bicycles.

Our-Lady Ter Hooyen, known as "the little beguinage," was built
in 1234, funded by two Flemish countesses, but what stands today
was mostly constructed five or six hundred years later. A classic
"court beguinage," it is enclosed by a high white wall and has only
one gated entrance. Inside the walls of the little beguinage is an elegant courtyard framed by lime and beech trees. The beguine hous-
ing faces this courtyard, the apartment protected by another white
brick wall that connects each small green doorway, some adorned
with tributes to saints. The buildings themselves are red brick with
white accents. Bicycles leaned against the inner wall, and through
the windows I spotted drying racks and neatly stacked dishes, a
bowl of fruit.

Harder to describe is the feel of the place. I arrived in early morning, at exactly the right moment for the rising sun to spill its light
down the cobbled walkways, through tree branches whose shadows
it cast dramatically along the white wall. The beguinage is located

in a residential neighborhood, some distance from the bustle of Ghent's center. That day it was deserted and quiet but for the rustle of drying leaves. I sat on a bench and savored my aloneness, imagined how much more precious it would have been eight hundred years ago in exactly that location.

In *The Wisdom of the Beguines,* Sister Laura Swan depicts the common practice of beguines' vitae: autobiographical stories (usually recorded by their confessors) in which the narrative and its moral takes primacy. She describes them as "stories of women's search for a genuine self, seeking to put into language the process of discovering that self, and inviting others to join her in that search." Reading her words, I was startled to find such a perfect description of a memoirist's work. It reminded me of standing under the trees in that courtyard, how I expected to feel a stranger and instead found myself at home.

Nora had found her way home, too. After I returned from Belgium, we had a long catch-up by phone, in which we both reflected on all that had changed in the six years since my celibacy. She had spent many of those years celibate herself.

"I felt forced into it for a long time," she explained. "A terrible lonely solitude. But that has shifted. Now, it feels a little bit like a superpower." She laughed and I could hear the clink of dishes as she moved around her kitchen. "I've just really learned how to take care of myself."

I marveled at how radically our paths had diverged over time, while still bearing such parallels. What a privilege it was to grow alongside someone across the years. Our celibacies were the result of opposite instincts in us and over time had yielded similar gifts. A part of me envied her years of solitude, the wisdom they'd imbued her with. I was at the foot of my next great hill: marriage, and feeling the novice again.

Her perspective on those years with the lawyer had evolved, too. "After I went on antidepressants and got a new therapist," she told me, "I realized that I'd been depressed for twenty years. That led to rethinking my own behavior, my own neediness in that relationship."

I nodded as I listened. "I totally relate to that. It's a relief to feel less like a victim in hindsight, isn't it?"

"Totally. I've started to see my dependence on her approval and love as not just a result of her being abusive to me, but also my having an inability to fully care for myself in a dynamic with someone else."

"Damn," I said. I exhaled slowly, thinking of all the ways I was still learning how to do that.

"Yeah, right?"

I flew to Seattle that autumn and drove to the nearby St. Placid Priory, where the community of Benedictine nuns to which Sister Laura has belonged for thirty-four years live. I stayed in a small room with two narrow beds, a sink, a window that overlooked the wet leaves of a rhododendron outside. *Viriditas,* I thought, closing the door behind me. On the outside of that door hung a plaque that read: *Hildegard.* Other doors in the hallway read: *Mechthild, Hadewijch, Marguerite,* and *Benedicta.*

On the desk sat a binder that contained a summary of Hildegard's life. I lay in the narrow bed and read it, comforted by the familiar contours of her story, my reliable wonder at her determination to lead a life so unlike the one offered to her. Making a way outside of the known is the only path to freedom from it.

I had come here because holy places helped to locate the holy in me. I cracked open the window of my little room, so that I could smell the wet ground, the fecund greenery, and heard a lone bird's call. I read once that birds "write" their songs. Over time, audio recordings show them drafting a sequence of notes over a period of days, practicing and revising the song, muttering it even in sleep.

In order to lead the life that called me, I had to find aloneness in the company of the one I loved. I thought it would be impossible, but it was not. Nor was it easy. My task was to cultivate and protect that space in me without pushing her away. It was easier to be alone, easier to blame her for the pressure inside of me, the instinct to collapse and reshape myself in the imagined image of her desires. I knew that this nuanced integrity depended upon my relationship to ∞.

Shortly after the poet and I met, and years before we married, I had that line of Dillard's tattooed on my back: *yielding at every moment to the perfect freedom of single necessity.* I wanted that faith and the agency it implied to become habit. I had hoped that some-day I would be done working for it. But like any other kind of devo-tion, faith requires tending and attention. Simone Weil famously wrote that "attention is the sincerest form of prayer . . . We have to try to cure our faults by attention and not by will." My best form of attention is writing. It is the place where I perform that work of crea-tion, of transformation, of worship. As Hildegard wrote in her vita: "I was afflicted until I named the place where I am now."

So, here I sat. Over the desk a window of green leaves, on it a blank page. My ancestors were there, too, a chorus of chosen teach-ers: desert mothers, saints, scoundrels, warriors, furies, and artists— their stories spooling back through centuries. The ones who took on the work of freedom, who understand it as synonymous with love. Audre, Sara, Sappho, Adrienne, Virginia, Nan, May, Colette, Agnes, Etty, Margery, Ann, Vincent, Patricia, Roxanne, Octavia. To begin can be the hardest part. I closed my eyes and said a little prayer for help.

Begin here, they said. *It is raining.*

Acknowledgments

My terrific editor, Vanessa Haughton, and everyone at Knopf, including Jordan Pavlin, Melissa Yoon, Jordan Rodman, Anna Noone, Emily Murphy, Marisa Nakasone, Hilary DiLoreto, and Kelly Blair.

My agent, Ethan Bassoff, for all the years of his acumen, good counsel, and humor. Everyone at WME, including Elizabeth DeNoma, Alex Levenberg, and Anna Deroy.

Helena Gonda and everyone at Canongate.

David Ross and everyone at Penguin Canada.

Kimberly Burns and Sarah Jean Grimm for their enthusiasm and advocacy.

Sister Laura Swan, Silvana Panciera, and Graham Keen for their generous insights and inspiration.

Louisa Hall, Leslie Jamison, Lydi Conklin, Kaveh Akbar, Jill Jarvis, and May Conley for their invaluable feedback and friendship.

Caitlin Delohery, Emily Anderson, Hallie Goodman, Tisa Bryant, Tara Bynum, Sarah Minor, Paige Lewis, Inara Verzemnieks, Margo Steines, David Adjmi, Dean Bakopoulos, Jordan Kisner, Helen Macdonald, Jeremy Atherton Lin, Mary Karr, Shanté Paradigm Smalls, Forsyth Harmon, Joy Priest, Kianna Eberle, Kara McMullen, Alexander Chee, Hossannah Asuncion, Syreeta McFadden, Jo Ann Beard, Paul Lisicky, John D'Agata, Vijay Seshadri, and my many other beloveds, fellows, teachers, and friends for insight, laughter, and letters along the way.

Cathryn Klusmeier for citational support.

All the people who appear in these pages, whose identifying characteristics I have mostly changed to protect their privacy: I'm sorry I couldn't include all of it, especially the best parts.

The John Simon Guggenheim Memorial Foundation, the National Endowment for the Arts, the British Library, Black Mountain Institute, the Bogliasco Foundation, and the University of Iowa for time and resources that helped me to write this book.

My colleagues in the English department, the Nonfiction Writing Program, and elsewhere at the University of Iowa, for their support and collaboration.

The publications in which early versions of these pages first appeared, and the editors who solicited them: Cornelia Channing at *The New York Times*; Zoë Bossiere and Erica Trabold, editors of *The Lyric Essay as Resistance*; Eliza Smith and Haley Swanson, editors of *Sex and the Single Woman*; Natalie Eve Garrett, editor of *The Lonely Stories*.

Donika Kelly, my love, for too much to mention here. How lucky I am to have found you. Thank God we didn't meet until I was ready.

Appendix

1. Going slow. Not committing before I get to know someone. Refraining from accelerating intimacy before I know someone, or know if I'm available/interested. Being honest with myself about what I see in other people.
2. Not becoming/acting interested just because the other person is and that feels good.
3. Not introducing partners to all my family and friends until I really get to know them.
4. Refraining from lying, cheating, seduction, intriguing outside of a relationship once I'm in one.
5. Continuing to nurture all the parts of my life that are precious even when I am in a relationship: my friendships, family, sobriety, physical health, professional life, my job, and creative work.
6. Maintaining healthy differentiation in a relationship: time alone, time with others, and intentional time together.
7. Leaving relationships as soon as I know I don't want to be in them. Maintaining clear boundaries after I've broken up with someone. Refraining from looking for or enacting any new relationship while I am still in or ending one. Truly letting people go after the relationship ends.
8. Being faithful to my deepest wisdom at all times. Refraining from intriguing with people I know I'm not interested in. Never

having sex when I don't want to. Never expressing romance, intimacy, or sexual expression that I don't feel.

9. Acting with integrity, honesty, and respect for myself and others. Letting go of the high and power trip of sexual charisma. Letting my partner into my reality, giving them agency in the relationship by sharing all the information I have.

10. Treating my partner as I wish to be treated in a relationship. Not trying to change or manipulate them, or their feelings for me.

11. Treating sex as an expression and form of intimacy, not a shortcut to or substitution for other kinds of intimacy.

12. Staying away from triangles, married or otherwise entangled people. No long-distance relationships. No mess in professional forums.

Notes

20   Though celibate and unmarried: The term *celibacy* is basically synonymous with *unmarried* to beguines; what I call celibacy they would call *chastity*.

26   trauma that produces 'humans': Blasing, Mutlu Konuk. *Lyric Poetry: The Pain and Pleasure of Words*. Princeton University Press, 2007.

52   "They do not mistake the lover for their own pleasure": Olds, Sharon. "Sex without Love." *The Iowa Review*, vol. 12, no. 2–3, Apr. 1981, p. 264.

69   a sex and love addict: As distinct from a "sex addict." There are different recovery communities for each.

70   god of heterosexual fetishism: Apparently, I think of sex and love addiction as kind of a straight thing, which I know isn't true. I would wager lesbians are at the bottom of the list of those most likely to be sex addicts, and near the top of the list of love addicts, demographically speaking.

70   something called "rain checks": In the 1880s, "rain checks" were issued to ticket holders if a baseball game was rained out. It entitled them to future admission for the postponed game.

73   "the animal within the animal": Centuries later, Sigmund Freud developed the theory of the unconscious mind—the mind within the mind—which he similarly characterized as a sort of wild animal. He also wrote, with the physician Josef Breuer, an entire book about hysteria, *Studies in Hysteria*, published in 1895.

74   and still does: While writing these chapters, I was continually frustrated by the deficit of synonyms for "masturbation," which is such an ungainly word and occurred so many times, but all of the alternatives were either phallocentric or gross, and most were both. Some alternative options that I solicited from friends: she-bop, winnowing, polishing the pearl, fracking, rubbing one out (originally intended for those with penises but clearly applies more aptly to clitoral masturbation), flicking the bean, clicking the mouse, petting the squirrel, andy tooling, Jilling off, spackling, and diddling the skittle. I personally came

up with "the Circle Game," although it may be too specific to my own masturbatory motions plus my affinity for Joni Mitchell. Eve Kosofsky Sedgwick's
"isometric exercise" is also a favorite.

78   "... no desire capable of taking it away": Haynes, April R. *Riotous Flesh: Women,
Physiology, and the Solitary Vice in Nineteenth-Century America.* The University of
Chicago Press, 2015.

89   the imperative of infidelity: I actually think my default constitution is exactly
oriented to be capable of protracted affairs: I am adept at compartmentalizing,
have a compulsive nature and poor impulse control, and am powerfully swayed
by the hormonal pull of attraction. I had, however, been sober at this point for
more than a decade and the work of that time and since has been that of culti-
vating a consciousness and a set of instincts counter to my given disposition.

90   in addition to adultery: A New Hampshire court denied a woman divorce in
1836, despite the fact that her husband had locked her in a cellar and beaten her
with a horse whip while spewing insults, because she had a "high bold, masculine spirit" that had rendered her unwifely. The court decided that it was up to
her to improve herself and thus her marriage.

96   "No writing, no books;—inconceivable.": Lee, Hermione. *Virginia Woolf.* Vintage, 1997.

100   exceptional for its occurrence in the open sea: The Moskstraumen also appears
in Jules Verne's *Twenty Thousand Leagues Under the Sea,* and is mentioned by
Melville's Captain Ahab in *Moby-Dick.*

107   "... whom the roots of passion shoot deeper than in me": Milford, Nancy. *Savage Beauty: The Life of Edna St. Vincent Millay.* Random House, 2004.

109   "The Anactoria Poem": Sappho. *If Not, Winter: Fragments of Sappho.* Translated
by Anne Carson. Alfred A. Knopf, 2002.

111   "I was a real alcoholic": Josipovici, Gabriel. "Risking an Opinion," in *The Times
Literary Supplement,* no. 4536, March 9 & 15, 1990, p. 248.

118   the parallels pleased me: Pythagoras wouldn't eat legumes because he thought
them the "first child of the earth." The fava bean in particular, he and his aco-
lytes believed to be a supernatural symbol of death. According to Pliny, he even
believed them capable of carrying the souls of the dead (a fact mocked by Hor-
ace, who called fava beans "Pythagoras' children," and other Greeks, who ate
them frequently). Though he became something of a laughingstock for his vegetarian diet (known more as a Pythagorean diet then, and in some places until
the nineteenth century) and his related belief in metempsychosis (the theory
of transmigration of souls), he inspired the likes of Seneca, Ovid, and Plutarch,
the last of whom wrote quite a bit about his ethical reasons for not eating meat.

127   *empty consent:* I explain this term in detail in *Girlhood.* Bloomsbury, 2021.

146   "... the earth becomes fruitful through moisture": Fox, Matthew. *Illuminations
of Hildegard von Bingen.* Simon & Schuster, 2002.

160   "a human religion in which another person is believed in": Tennov, Dorothy.
Love and Limerence: The Experience of Being in Love. Scarborough House, 1999.

176   so evocative of bodily experiences I *had* had: "Martha finally flung herself onto my shore, and through violent sobs kissed me, as if drenched in my juices as she had become, eyes glued shut, stringy-haired, fever-cheeked, parched and gasping for water and air, she'd been born out of *me* in those hours, bodied forth by titantic orgasm, and now she was helplessly, utterly mine for the rest of all time."

181   ". . . from them as much as possible": W., Bill. *Alcoholics Anonymous: The Story of How Many Thousands of Men and Women Have Recovered from Alcoholism.* Alcoholics Anonymous World Services, 2002.

182   ". . . like a hail of hot stones": Choi, Susan. *My Education: A Novel.* Penguin, 2013.

204   but writing was my first love: From Hermione Lee's biography: "there was a ruthlessness about Vincent . . . her work came first . . . She always thought Vincent had an eye on herself, her future . . . She felt it was her first love, and perhaps her only one: her poetry."

217   ". . . frenzied women from whose lips the god speaks": Burkert, Walter. *Greek Religion.* 1st ed. Wiley, 2013.

217   *Hodie aperuit nobis clausa porta:* "Today a closed portal has been opened."

223   They were not even new to me: When I was a young teenager, I read the classic Victorian novella *The Yellow Wallpaper,* and became infatuated with its author, Charlotte Perkins Gilman, who was a great champion of women's sartorial liberation and was known for sewing generous pockets onto all of her clothes. It was many more years before I learned of Gilman's repellent "nativist" ideas, which would today label her a white nationalist.

228   a list of twelve items: See Appendix.

233   already waiting: "You Who Want . . ." translated by Jane Hirshfield.

246   "I'm going to go out like a fucking meteor!": Lorde, Audre. *A Burst of Light: And Other Essays.* Courier Dover Publications, 2017.

Works Cited and Consulted

Ahmed, Sara. *Living a Feminist Life*. Duke University Press, 2017.

Als, Hilton. "Nan Goldin's 'The Ballad of Sexual Dependency.'" *The New Yorker*, 27 June 2016, https://www.newyorker.com/magazine/2016/07/04/nan-goldins -the-ballad-of-sexual-dependency.

d'Avigdor, Leon, director. *Agnes Martin: Between the Lines*. Leon d'Avigdor Films, 2002.

Augustine, Saint. *The Confessions*. Oxford Paperbacks, 2008.

Barthes, Roland. *A Lover's Discourse: Fragments*. Macmillan, 1978.

The Bible: Authorized King James Version. Edited by Robert Carroll and Stephen Prickett. Oxford University Press, 2008.

Blasing, Mutlu Konuk. *Lyric Poetry: The Pain and Pleasure of Words*. Princeton University Press, 2007.

Boehringer, Sandra. "Female Homoeroticism." *A Companion to Greek and Roman Sexualities*, edited by Thomas K. Hubbard. Wiley-Blackwell, 2013.

Brown, Helen Gurley. *Sex and the Single Girl: The Unmarried Woman's Guide to Men*. Open Road Media, 2012.

Campion, Nardi Reeder. *Mother Ann Lee: Morning Star of the Shakers*. University Press of New England, 1990.

Capellanus, Andreas. *The Art of Courtly Love*. Columbia University Press, 1990.

Cell 16. *No More Fun and Games: A Journal of Female Liberation*, vol. 1, no. 2, 1968. Women's Liberation Movement Print Culture.

Chertoff, Emily. "Eulogy for a Sex Radical: Shulamith Firestone's Forgotten Feminism." *The Atlantic*, 31 Aug. 2012. https://www.theatlantic.com/politics/archive /2012/08/eulogy-for-a-sex-radical-shulamith-firestones-forgotten-feminism /261834/

Chittister, Joan. *The Monastery of the Heart: An Invitation to a Meaningful Life*. BlueBridge, 2012.

Choi, Susan. *My Education: A Novel*. Penguin, 2013.

Works Cited and Consulted

Colette. *Chéri* and *The End of Chéri*. W. W. Norton & Company, 2022.

Collins, Patricia Hill. *Black Feminist Thought: Knowledge, Consciousness, and the Politics of Empowerment*. Routledge, 2002.

Collins, Patricia Hill. *On Intellectual Activism*. Temple University Press, 2013.

De Munk Victor, and Robert L. Moore. "Love and Limerence with Chinese Characteristics." *Romantic Love and Sexual Behavior: Perspectives from the Social Sciences*. Praeger, Westport, 1998.

Derrida, Jacques. "Plato's Pharmacy," *Dissemination*. University of Chicago Press, 2021.

Dickinson, Emily. *The Master Letters of Emily Dickinson*. University of Massachusetts Press, 1986.

Dillard, Annie. *Teaching a Stone to Talk: Expeditions and Encounters*. HarperCollins, 2009.

Dunbar-Ortiz, Roxanne. *Outlaw Woman: A Memoir of the War Years, 1960–1975, Revised Edition*. University of Oklahoma Press, 2014.

Duras, Marguerite. *The Lover*. Pantheon, 2011.

Eco, Umberto. *On Beauty*. Harvill Secker, 2004.

Ekman, Paul. "Universal Facial Expressions of Emotion." *California Mental Health Research Digest*, vol. 8, no. 4, 1970, pp. 151–58.

Father's Kingdom. Directed by Lenny Feinberg, 2017.

Firestone, Shulamith. *The Dialectic of Sex: The Case for Feminist Revolution*. Farrar, Straus and Giroux, 2003.

Fontanel, Sophie. *The Art of Sleeping Alone: Why One French Woman Suddenly Gave Up Sex*. Simon & Schuster, 2014.

Foucault, Michel. *The History of Sexuality, Volume 1: An Introduction*. Translated by Robert Hurley. Pantheon Books, 1978.

Fox, Matthew. *Illuminations of Hildegard of Bingen*. Simon & Schuster, 2002.

Fox, Matthew. *Hildegard of Bingen: A Saint for Our Times*. Namaste Publishing, 2012.

Francis, Richard. *Ann the Word: The Story of Ann Lee, Female Messiah, Mother of the Shakers, the Woman Clothed with the Sun*. Skyhorse Publishing Inc., 2013.

Fudgé, Thomas A. *Medieval Religion and Its Anxieties: History and Mystery in the Other Middle Ages*. Palgrave Macmillan, 2016.

Gaillardetz, Richard R. "Sexual Vulnerability and a Spirituality of Suffering: Explorations in the Writing of Etty Hillesum." *Pacifica: Australasian Theological Studies*, vol. 22, no. 1, Feb. 2009, pp. 75–89, doi:10.1177/1030570x0902200105.

Gilman, Sander L. et al. *Hysteria Beyond Freud*. University of California Press, 2022.

Glück, Robert. *Margery Kempe*. New York Review of Books Classics, 2020.

Goldin, Nan. *The Ballad of Sexual Dependency*. Aperture, 1986.

Hadewijch. "You Who Want." *Women in Praise of the Sacred*. Translated by Jane Hirshfield, HarperCollins, 1994.

Hadewijch. *The Complete Works*. Paulist Press, 1980.

Hayes, Nicky. *Foundations of Psychology*. 3rd edition, Thomson Learning, 2000.

Haynes, April R. *Riotous Flesh: Women, Physiology, and the Solitary Vice in Nineteenth-Century America*. The University of Chicago Press, 2015.

Heidegger, Martin. *Being and Time*. HarperCollins, 2008.

Hildegard of Bingen. *Selected Writings*. Penguin UK, 2005.

Hildegard of Bingen. *Hildegard of Bingen: Scivias (Classics of Western Spirituality)*. Paulist Press, 1990.

Hirsch, Edward. "In the Beginning Is the Relation." *Poetry Foundation*, 12 Jan. 2006, https://www.poetryfoundation.org/articles/68414/in-the-beginning-is-the -relation.

Hitchcock, Alfred, director. *Vertigo*. Paramount Pictures, 1958.

hooks, bell. *Communion: The Female Search for Love*. HarperCollins, 2021.

hooks, bell. *All About Love: New Visions*. HarperCollins, 2018.

Jung, Carl G. *Memories, Dreams, Reflections*. Vintage, 2011.

Kant, Immanuel et al. *The Critique of Judgement*. Clarendon, 1982.

Kelly, Donika. *Bestiary*. Graywolf Press, 2016.

Knight, Etheridge. "Feeling Fucked Up." *Poetry Foundation*, 1 Jan. 1986, https://www .poetryfoundation.org/poems/48752/feeling-fucked-up.

Korducki, Kelli María. *Hard to Do: The Surprising, Feminist History of Breaking Up*. Coach House Books, 2018.

Leduc, Violette. *The Lady and the Little Fox Fur*. Peter Owen, 1967.

Lee, Hermione. *Virginia Woolf*. Vintage, 1997.

Lieberman, Hallie. *Buzz: The Stimulating History of the Sex Toy*. Pegasus Books, 2019.

London, Jack. *White Fang*. The Macmillan Company, 1906.

Lorde, Audre. "Uses of the Erotic: The Erotic as Power." *Sister Outsider: Essays and Speeches*. Penguin, 1984.

Lorde, Audre. *A Burst of Light: And Other Essays*. Courier Dover Publications, 2017.

Maddocks, Fiona. *Hildegard of Bingen: The Woman of Her Age*. Faber & Faber, 2013.

Maines, Rachel P. *The Technology of Orgasm "Hysteria," the Vibrator, and Women's Sexual Satisfaction*. The Johns Hopkins University Press, 1999.

Mairs, Nancy. "On Not Liking Sex," *Plaintext*. University of Arizona Press, 1992.

Margery, Kempe. *The Book of Margery Kempe*. Penguin UK, 1985.

Masset, Claire. *Virginia Woolf at Monk's House*. National Trust, 2022.

Mengin, Charles Auguste. *Sappho*. 1877.

Milford, Nancy. *Savage Beauty: The Life of Edna St. Vincent Millay*. Random House, 2004.

Millay, Edna St. Vincent. *Collected Poems*. Harper Perennial, 2011.

Offill, Jenny. *Dept. of Speculation*. Vintage, 2014.

Olds, Sharon. "Sex without Love." *The Iowa Review*, vol. 12, no. 2–3, Apr. 1981, p. 264.

Once a Fury. Directed by Jacqueline Rhodes, 2020.

Panciera, Silvana. *The Beguines*. Published by the author, 2014.

Panciera, Silvana. Interview. Conducted by Melissa Febos over Zoom, 4 Aug. 2022.

Poe, Edgar Allan. "A Descent into the Maelstrom." 1841.

Porete, Marguerite. *The Mirror of Simple Souls*. Paulist Press, 1993.

Princenthal, Nancy. *Agnes Martin: Her Life and Art*. Thames & Hudson, 2015.

Powell, Jim. "The Anactoria Poem." *The Poetry of Sappho*. Oxford University Press, 2007.

Rich, Adrienne. *On Lies, Secrets, and Silence: Selected Prose 1966–1978*. W. W. Norton & Company, 1995.

Works Cited and Consulted

Sackville-West, Vita. *Saint Joan of Arc.* Vintage Classic, 2018.

Sappho. *If Not, Winter: Fragments of Sappho.* Translated by Anne Carson. Alfred A. Knopf, 2002.

Sarton, May. *Journal of a Solitude.* W. W. Norton & Company, 1992.

Sharratt, Mary. *Illuminations: A Novel of Hildegard von Bingen.* Houghton Mifflin Harcourt, 2012.

Sontag, Susan. *Notes on Camp.* Penguin UK, 2018.

Sontag, Susan. *Reborn: Journals and Notebooks, 1947–1963.* Macmillan, 2009.

Starr, Mirabai. *Showings of Julian of Norwich: A New Translation.* Hampton Roads Publishing, 2013.

Svoboda, Elizabeth. "In Search of Etty Hillesum." *Longreads,* 30 Apr. 2020, https:// longreads.com/2020/04/30/in-search-of-etty-hillesum/.

Swan, Laura. *The Wisdom of the Beguines: The Forgotten Story of a Medieval Women's Movement.* BlueBridge, 2016.

Swan, Laura. *The Forgotten Desert Mothers: Sayings, Lives, and Stories of Early Christian Women.* 2nd edition, Paulist Press, 2022.

Swan, Sister Laura. Interview. Conducted by Melissa Febos over telephone, 2 Oct. 2022.

Swan, Sister Laura. Interview. Conducted by Melissa Febos, St. Placid Priory, WA, 17 Jan. 2023.

Taylor, Keeanga-Yamahtta, ed. *How We Get Free: Black Feminism and the Combahee River Collective.* Haymarket Books, 2017.

Tennov, Dorothy. *Love and Limerence: The Experience of Being in Love.* Scarborough House, 1999.

Traister, Rebecca. *All the Single Ladies: Unmarried Women and the Rise of an Independent Nation.* Simon & Schuster, 2016.

The Unruly Mystic: Saint Hildegard of Bingen. Directed by Michael M. Conti. Michael Conti Productions, 2014.

Vera, created by Ann Cleeves. Silverprint Pictures, 2011–2024.

Van Doren, Carl. *Many Minds: Critical Essays on American Writers.* Greenwood, 1975.

W., Bill. *Alcoholics Anonymous: The Story of How Many Thousands of Men and Women Have Recovered from Alcoholism.* Alcoholics Anonymous World Services, 2002.

Ward, Jane. *The Tragedy of Heterosexuality.* NYU Press, 2020.

Waters, John. *Hairspray, Female Trouble, and Multiple Maniacs: Three More Screenplays.* Running Press Adult, 2005.

Watts, Jill. *God, Harlem U.S.A.: The Father Divine Story.* University of California Press, 1992.

Weil, Simone. *Gravity and Grace.* Routledge, 2002.

White, April. *The Divorce Colony: How Women Revolutionized Marriage and Found Freedom on the American Frontier.* Hachette Books, 2022.

Woolf, Virginia. *A Room of One's Own.* Macmillan Collector's Library, 2017.

Woolf, Virginia. *To the Lighthouse.* Harcourt Brace Jovanovich, 1989.

A NOTE ABOUT THE AUTHOR

MELISSA FEBOS is the national bestselling author of four previous books: *Whip Smart, Abandon Me, Girlhood*—which won the National Book Critics Circle Award in Criticism—and *Body Work: The Radical Power of Personal Narrative.* She has been awarded prizes and fellowships from the Guggenheim Foundation, Lambda Literary, the National Endowment for the Arts, the British Library, the Black Mountain Institute, the Bogliasco Foundation, MacDowell, the American Library in Paris, and others. Her work has appeared in *The Paris Review, The New Yorker, The New York Times Magazine, The Best American Essays, Vogue, The Sewanee Review, The New York Review of Books,* and elsewhere. Febos is a Professor at the University of Iowa and lives in Iowa City with her wife, the poet Donika Kelly.

A NOTE ABOUT THE TYPE

This book was set in Arno. Named after the Florentine river which runs through the heart of the Italian Renaissance, Arno draws on the warmth and readability of early humanist typefaces of the fifteenth and sixteenth centuries. While inspired by the past, Arno is distinctly contemporary in both appearance and function. Designed by Adobe Principal Designer Robert Slimbach, Arno is a meticulously crafted face in the tradition of early Venetian and Aldine book typefaces. Embodying themes Slimbach has explored in typefaces such as Minion and Brioso, Arno represents a distillation of his design ideals and a refinement of his craft.

Typeset by Scribe
Philadelphia, Pennsylvania

Designed by Marisa Nakasone